A SENS
DU

A SENSE OF
DUTY

My Father, My American Journey

QUANG X. PHAM

4/8/06
For Jacqui —
I can't wait
to read about Ft. Chaffee, my
Ellis Island.
Best,
Quang

BALLANTINE BOOKS NEW YORK

Published in the United States by Ballantine Books, an imprint of The Random House Publishing Group, a division of Random House, Inc., New York.

Ballantine and colophon are trademarks of Random House, Inc.

LIBRARY OF CONGRESS CATALOGING-IN-PUBLICATION DATA
Quang X. Pham.
   A sense of duty : my father, my American journey / by Quang X. Pham.—1st ed.
      p.   cm.
   ISBN 0-89141-873-3
   1. Quang X. Pham.   2. Vietnamese Conflict, 1961–1975—Personal narratives, Vietnamese.   3. Pham, Van Haa d. 2000.   4. Vietnamese Americans—Biography. 5. Refugees—United States—Biography.   I. Title.
   E184.V53Q36 2005
   959.704'3'092—dc22   2004063383

Printed in the United States of America

Ballantine Books website address: www.ballantinebooks.com

987654321

First Edition

Text design by rlf design

For my mother, Nguyễn Thị Niệm,
and my father, Phạm Văn Hòa

CONTENTS

AUTHOR'S NOTE

Out of respect, the names of elderly Vietnamese appear in this book in the Vietnamese language format, with the family name listed first. My father's name appears as Pham Van Hoa while mine is written as Quang X. Pham. With several exceptions, I have also chosen not to include accent marks.

Most of the spelling of geographical locations (cities, provinces) is in the form of the American English language usage of the time. Danang, Saigon, and Vietnam are three words in the Vietnamese language format.

I am grateful for the following works which I consulted during my research on the Vietnamese Air Force, the signing of the Paris Peace Accords, the fall of Saigon, and the reeducation camps: *No Peace, No Honor: Nixon, Kissinger and the Betrayal in Vietnam,* Larry Berman (The Free Press, 2001); *U.S. Marines in Vietnam: The Bitter End 1973–1975,* George R. Dunham and David A. Quinlan (Headquarters, U.S. Marine Corps, 1990); *Reeducation in Postwar Vietnam: Personal Postscripts to Peace,* Edward P. Meltzner (Texas A&M University Press, 2001); *A Gift of Barbed Wire: America's Allies Abandoned in South Vietnam,* Robert S. McKelvey (University of Washington Press, 2002); *Flying Dragons, The South Vietnamese Air Force,* Robert C. Mikesh (Schiffer, 2005); *The A-1 Skyraider in Vietnam: The Spad's Last War,* Wayne Mutza (Schiffer, 2004); *Their War: Perspectives of the South Vietnamese in American Literature and in Their Own Words,* Julie Pham (a paper, 2000); *A Better War: The Unexamined Victories and Final Tragedy of America's Last Years in Vietnam,* Lewis Sorley (Harcourt & Brace, 1999).

I have changed the names of several people in the book to protect their privacy. To my knowledge and memory, everything else is true.

ACKNOWLEDGMENTS

This book has been in the works for a decade. My father left behind writings of his experience in the Vietnamese Air Force (VNAF) and his years in the prison camps. Part of the writing is his; his legacy became my destiny. My mother walked me through our family's history amid our country's struggles. Her never-ending role as a teacher remained with me throughout my adult life. It was extremely painful for her to recall our final days in Vietnam and our initial years in the United States. Her sacrifice for our family is symbolic of the strong-willed Vietnamese woman, resilient like a bamboo in the wind.

I could not have completed the book without the love and support of my wife, Shannon. Forgoing normalcy for months, she would attest that it is no fun being the wife of a first-time hack. Mike Tharp or "Uncle Buck," a true friend, a Vietnam veteran and longtime journalist, has been with me the entire journey. He helped me "walk the walk."

My sisters Thi, Uyen, and Thu have been supportive of me, especially during my overseas deployments, and have put up with me over the years. Their love for my parents is no less than mine. Even though I don't see my relatives often (in this country and all over the world), they are on my mind. My Aunt Nhang is the glue that holds all of us together. She nurtured my father through his years in captivity and forwarded our letters to him.

Without my father's taped interview provided by my friend Bernie Edelman, another Vietnam veteran, it would have been difficult to summarize my father's feelings on the war. Bernie also introduced me to my agent, Flip Brophy, president of Sterling Lord Literistic. She took me on as a client even though I was an amateur and at times, annoying. Cia Glover, Flip's assistant, always responded with a smile. Ron Doering, my editor and Nancy Miller, editor in chief of Ballantine Books, saw possibilities in the manuscript beyond my original intent.

I greatly value the friendships I made with the boys of Oxnard, California, namely Mark Adams, John Gadd, Bill McGuire, and James Stewart. They helped me with my transition to this nation, making it much easier. Ed Christian and I attended UCLA and flight school together and we shared some fun times on the road.

My father's VNAF colleagues, students, and senior officers have been extremely helpful. I would like to thank Ho Dang Tri, Ly Ngoc An, Pham Gia Bao, Nguyen Qui Chan, Pham Long Suu, Pham Quang Diem, Pham Quang Khiem, Tran Ba Hoi, and Vo Kim Long. No one spent more time with me than Nguyen Cau, who not only served with my father during his entire twenty-one-year career, but also nearly a decade in six reeducation/prison camps. Joe Saueressig, a former U.S. Air Force adviser to the VNAF's 514th Fighter Squadron, mailed me photographs and my father's Presidential Unit Citation.

Two U.S. Marines turned authors gave me their precious time and invaluable advice. I thank former secretary of the Navy James Webb for his comments on my book proposal. David Morris, who penned *Storm on the Horizon,* lent me his ears.

Marvin Wolf, co-author of *Buddha's Child,* spent hours with me on the phone about the publishing world. Thank you for your help.

I am most proud of my Marine Corps affiliation. To the Marines I had the privilege of serving alongside, thank you for your friendship and support: Mike Brennan, Guy Close, Doug Hamlin, Mark Henderson, Bob Hermes, Dave Giannetta, Phil Grathwol, Joe Heneghan, Rick Jarlowe, Clark Taylor, Tom Reid, and Tom Rollins, my commanding officer of Marine Medium Helicopter Squadron 161. Thanks to the following general officers for their encouragement and their friendship over the years: Paul Fratarangelo, Kevin Kuklok, Francis Quinlan, and Mike Wholley. I personally know of no one who has donated more money to Marine Corps and other charities than Donald Bren. Giving back to society is an admirable example of being *semper fidelis.*

To Col. John Braddon, U.S. Marine Corps (Retired), thank you for rescuing my father on April 27, 1964, in Do Xa, Republic of Vietnam. Otherwise, life for the Pham family might have turned out quite differently.

Finally, I realize the painful truth that I may never set foot in my birthplace again. For my brother An, this book is about our father and his honorable service. Former officers and soldiers of South Vietnam are not "traitors" and "American puppets." They were simply doing their duty for their country. The war is over, but telling the truth has not been easy. I can forgive but I can never forget.

A portion of the proceeds from the book will be donated to community and veteran nonprofit organizations, including the Marine Corps Scholarship Foundation.

A SENSE OF
DUTY

FOR FATHER, FOR COUNTRY

I WAS BORN A VIETNAMESE IN AN OLD FRENCH HOSPITAL SIX months before President Lyndon B. Johnson ordered thousands of U.S. Marines into my country. That tiny scimitar-shaped peninsula in Southeast Asia still considers me a citizen (for military conscription purposes only) even though I escaped three decades ago. Ask me where my hometown is on a map and I can still show you. But it now bears the name Ho Chi Minh City. Saigon is gone—but then again, it isn't. I can't tell people why that happened without choking up. John F. Kennedy said, "Victory has 100 fathers and defeat is an orphan." As a half-orphan of that war, I chose to find out on my own. Vietnam will remain a part of me for as long as I live, as will my love for *nuôc Mỹ,* Vietnamese for the United States, and now *my* country.

When I turned twenty I became an American by choice. Actually I was already a by-product, derived from a failed U.S.-backed regime fighting to keep the "dominoes" from falling in Asia. I could have kept my green card and maintained a legal-resident status. (Out of principle a few Vietnamese who remain bitter toward the United States still refuse to become naturalized.) But I knew I had to be a citizen in order to join the military as an officer. My childhood dream was to become a pilot like my father. Unknowingly, the pursuit of that dream would enable me to pay back the rewards of my precious new citizenship and to seek the truth about my father's service in a long-ago war. Or as he once wrote, "It was either simple coincidence or you may call it destiny. You're in the same Marine unit that I flew support for and was rescued by in the early days of the war."

It was no coincidence.

This book is not a personal condemnation of six U.S. presidents, the U.S. Congress, arrogant Pentagon leaders from the supposed "greatest generation," or hippie antiwar protestors for their roles in the multisided quagmire known as "Vietnam." Nor will it patronize a press corps that, in my opinion, ultimately took sides while covering Southeast Asia, later claiming credit for swaying the American public that helped prevent the early deaths of many more.

Neither will these pages vindicate former leaders of South Vietnam for losing their country in such a rapid, public, and humiliating way. Certainly this book will not honor the victorious Communists, long on military tactics but short on domestic reforms and human rights. Hell-bent on punishing the losers, they have wasted nearly three decades after victory over the mightiest nation on the earth. Their insistence on ideological purity over the well-being of their people has kept Vietnam years behind emerging Asian countries.

This is simply a story about a refugee boy who grew up without his father and became confused by an enduring nostalgia for Vietnam. Buoyed by a calling inscribed just before his birth, he bought into the American Dream, despite prejudice and other obstacles. Yet he would find an unexpected reconciliation through his father, the man he sought to honor but who expected no such payback.

In 1975, a week before North Vietnamese forces overran Saigon, my mother, my three sisters, and I fled Vietnam. Our country was falling apart; our hopes for freedom in our own nation were dashed. Unbeknownst to us, we would join the ranks of the thousands of families of the prisoners of war (POWs).

Images of desperate refugees scaling the U.S. Embassy fence, clinging to the skids of helicopters, and jamming leaky fishing boats have been seared into our consciousness. Some Americans celebrated our loss, while a handful gave their all to evacuate as many South Vietnamese as they could.

My mother raised the four of us in California by herself. When we landed in the United States, she was thirty-nine, spoke no English, and had never traveled abroad. We spoke French, but I thank God, and Buddha, that we didn't go to Paris to live with my aunt, because there I wouldn't have been able to realize my dreams.

As it turned out, our worst fear at the time we left had come to pass. My father was incarcerated after the war: he was sentenced to more than twelve years in prison camps—after he was told by his communist captors to report for thirty days. After listening (or pretending) to communist indoctrination (the euphemism was "reeducation") for a few months, he spent the remaining years in hard-labor prison camps facing beriberi, dysentery, malaria, starvation, beatings, and death. He and those of his generation thought the United States would stand by them forever. He had served in the military during his country's twenty-one years of post–World War II existence—his entire adulthood. But once he arrived on these shores he never received a welcome home, veteran's benefits, or a pension.

Despite all that, our family did survive the war, while many others didn't. (Approximately 3 million Vietnamese from both sides died in the war.) For the fortunate refugees who escaped, this country gave us a new life filled with opportunities as no other could have. For the prisoners and for those stranded South Vietnamese, the war was supposed to be over but the peace did not come for years.

When I was in the Marine Corps I shuddered at the thought of dying for my country; I wanted to make the enemy die for his. In a way, my native country died for me so that my generation could be spared more fighting, more killing. I am still not sure if it had to happen that way, but I can't rewrite history. Millions suffered in the aftermath, while I and others like me merely "struggled" here. There can be no comparison of our fates, and so our family, minus my father, had taken the less painful route.

When my father died in 2000, his old comrades showed up in force to honor him, as did some of my Marine friends. The afternoon I gave his eulogy was the hardest day of my life: I had lost my father a second time. Swaying behind the lectern at the funeral home, I stared at the standing-room-only crowd of mostly older South Vietnamese veterans long removed from the horrors of combat. The men who had served with my father in squadrons and in the prison camps were there: Bao, Hoi, Thanh, Tien, Tri, Xuong, among many more. They had draped a large yellow flag with the three bright-red horizontal stripes over his coffin. I had to eulogize him in English. I had neglected my native tongue far too long to be able to speak eloquently of his life and legacy in Vietnamese.

After the formal funeral service ended, one person after another came up and told me tales about my father. As I stood next to his casket opened for final viewing, a lifetime of memories were shared with me; some were clear, others hazy. My father's colleagues remembered him as a young, suave fighter pilot and a hothead, eager to show off by briefing his missions in English for the American advisers, and ready to fight anyone, anywhere, anytime. Then he changed. Toward the end of the war he became quiet and nervous in the cockpit, always twitching and touching the flight controls, exhibiting signs of war-weariness.

Yet my father's greatest trait, his sense of humor, his love for teasing and jokes, stayed with him until the end. Not even the Communists could break his spirit. In 1992, just months after he landed in the United States, he penned an open letter to his (South) Vietnamese Air Force (VNAF) buddies where he poked fun at General Rau Kem or "Stiff Mustache," their lavender scarf-donning former air force commander, Nguyen Cao Ky. If asked why he didn't leave before Saigon fell, he'd say . . . "I got stuck. If the lamp posts could walk, they would have gotten out of Vietnam too. Stop asking stupid questions." He also wrote, "I noticed many air force friends have changed their Vietnamese names to Anthony, Steven, William . . . they must be working for Americans, so changing their names for easier pronunciation made sense. If my name was 'Phuoc,' I wouldn't change it because it already has an English equivalent."

I don't think my family fully understood the military tradition of honoring its dead. Nor do they realize the sacrifice my father made during the war and the price he paid for losing our country. But if we don't know ourselves, how could we expect anyone else to understand?

My father was put to rest with full military honors from a country that no longer existed. The honor guard, in ersatz uniforms (long-sleeved blue shirts and trousers), neatly folded the flag of the former Republic of Vietnam into a triangle. The veterans began humming the familiar hymn of what was once the world's fourth-largest air force: *Ôi phi công danh tiếng, muôn đời. O pilot famous for life.* Tears streaked down my cheeks. I hadn't heard the tune since I was a little boy living on Tan Son Nhut Air Base in Saigon. The senior man in attendance presented that flag to me and quietly saluted with his wrinkled hand and bent elbow. He mumbled in Vietnamese: "On behalf of a grateful nation for your father's service, please accept this flag. . . ."

There was no longer such a nation, but by then I knew what he meant.

What did my father do to deserve such honor? Why did these veterans bother with the ceremony? After all, his country had lost the war as its leaders —its so-called best and brightest—scrambled out of Saigon in the first wave, some along with women and children. That was after the fifty-five-day rout in the spring of 1975 when its army of 1 million quickly disintegrated. Blame the United States? That was readily done, and many South Vietnamese still do. Wounds lingered for decades in this country as well. Abandonment of an ally? After more than two decades, $150 billion in aid, and 58,235 U.S. dead, how much more could it have given? Public support for Iraq plummeted after only one year and one thousand dead. How long could the war have been prosecuted? Why didn't my father leave like the rest of us when he could have flown out or boarded any other plane?

I almost didn't get to meet my father at all. I came into this world just after the U.S. Congress had passed the Tonkin Gulf Resolution in August 1964. That triggered massive air strikes against North Vietnam for putative gunboat attacks on the USS *Maddox* and *Turner Joy*. Shortly afterward a reluctant United States dragged itself into full-scale war in Vietnam. Congress, with only two dissenting votes in the Senate, overwhelmingly gave President Lyndon B. Johnson carte blanche.

On April 27, 1964, my father, then 2d Lt. Pham Van Hoa (pronounced "hwa") of the VNAF, was shot down flying in support of the largest heliborne assault up to that point flown by U.S. advisers in their secret war. Rescued and rededicated to his profession, he would fight the good fight in the skies over South Vietnam for another decade before his luck, like that of so many of his countrymen, would eventually run out. For more than twelve grueling years, and indeed for the rest of his life, my father would pay dearly for being on the losing side. His North Vietnamese captors called him unpatriotic, traitor, blood-debtor, American puppet, pirate pilot, and cheap mercenary. They forced him to write numerous confessions denouncing his affiliation with the Saigon government. (His former allies and their journalistic chroniclers, safely home in the United States, portrayed the South Vietnamese as corrupt, incompetent, shadowy figures who had not been worth backing.)

Somebody had to bear the blame for all the death and destruction. Besides the dead, somebody else needed to pay the price for losing. Someone had to accept responsibility.

South Vietnam did have its share of cowards, draft dodgers, and deserters. There were dishonest, incompetent, weak men in the Republic of Vietnam armed forces. From what I've been told at firsthand by a former CIA agent, as well as historians and veterans, they held the highest ranks of leadership. But it was the field-grade officers (my father's group) and those below who bore the brunt of the fighting. For the most part, the latter did their best, given the circumstances, and those who managed to survive kept fighting year after year.

There was no end until the end.

No military is ever perfect. The U.S. military itself faced desertion, drug, morale, and racial problems in Vietnam during its final years in the country and for a decade after its withdrawal. The few U.S. veterans, mostly military advisers who actually flew, fought, ate, and slept alongside the South Vietnamese, spoke respectfully of them. Some of the advisers (who still felt the same years later) became four-star generals like H. Norman Schwarzkopf and Anthony Zinni, both eventually heading the U.S. Central Command. Others included military author Lewis Sorley and Earl Woods (the father of Tiger Woods).

No one was more emphatic than retired U.S. Army Gen. Barry McCaffrey. "In no way denigrating the Americans, but the best assault troops I ever saw in my life [in three conflicts] were the Vietnamese Airborne soldiers. Hands down, the best air support I ever saw in combat, bar none, were Vietnamese [Air Force] A-1 Skyraiders. We cheered when we got them."

Hollywood made one-sided movies, often dismissing Army of the Republic of Vietnam (ARVN) soldiers and mocking them as troops who ran away from skirmishes. In *Apocalypse Now,* the arrogant Colonel Kilgore visits a dying Viet Cong guerrilla with a group of U.S. soldiers and an ARVN soldier. Kilgore knocks the ARVN soldier to the side and yells, "Get out of here before I kick your fucking ass." In *Full Metal Jacket,* several U.S. Marines fighting in Hue City exchange their thoughts on the South Vietnamese. "I'm not real keen on some of these fellers who are supposedly on our side. I keep meeting them coming the other way. We keep getting killed for all these people and they don't even appreciate it. If you ask me, we shooting the wrong gooks." Later in the movie, an ARVN officer is a pimp, offering young Vietnamese prostitutes to the Marines taking a break from combat.

What was I to think of my father's colleagues who had escaped and were preparing to retire by the time he got to this country. Several even considered him stupid for not leaving when he could.

As I grew up in the United States, I almost believed what I had heard and what I had read, but I never stopped loving my father. I didn't know what he had done to deserve more than twelve years in captivity. Did he commit atrocities? After all, the longest a U.S. POW was held in Vietnam (Jim Thompson) was nine years. I couldn't figure out how my father had survived such suffering. I didn't think he could adjust to a peacetime United States after I became aware of the post-traumatic stress disorder (PTSD) that U.S. veterans were undergoing. (In World War I it was "shell shock"; in World War II it was "battle fatigue." In Korea, "operation exhaustion" was the expression.)

By 1987, when my father was still in captivity, I had evolved from one of the "first to flee" to becoming one of the "first to fight." After I graduated from the University of California, Los Angeles (UCLA), and became a U.S. Marine 2d lieutenant in training, I sat through hours of eye-glazingly long lectures in Quantico, Virginia, about history and warfare. Unavoidably, the subject of Vietnam would come up in a "law of war" class sandwiched between strategy and tactics courses. The infamous picture of a South Vietnamese general executing a Viet Cong twenty years earlier triggered lively discussions about morality and rules of engagement. We were given no further explanations. No history. No context. A still photograph that arguably helped turned the tide against the war and South Vietnam had not lost its power.

I was handed a reading list approved by the commandant of the Marine Corps. The Corps wanted its rank and file to be intellectual warriors, while we lieutenants only cared about leading troops and earning medals (and getting laid). Depending on rank, each Marine was supposed to read a certain number of books per year from a list put out by Marine Corps Headquarters. I hardly knew anyone back then who read any of those books except for James Webb's *Fields of Fire* and Philip Caputo's *A Rumor of War*—one a memoir, and the other a novel. Both were bestsellers (and with very different perspectives) penned by combat Marine lieutenants in Vietnam. Also on the list were Sun Tzu's *The Art of War,* Stephen Ambrose's *Band of Brothers,* and *How We Won the War* by North Vietnam's Gen. Vo Nguyen Giap. I remember flipping through the first few pages of Giap's thin book before wanting to punch something or somebody. Instead, I took off on a long run alone, on paved roads surrounding the woods and buildings named for dead Marines, sick at heart while recalling that last night in Saigon. Even my beloved Corps had bought into communist propaganda.

Now I am forty, about my father's age when South Vietnam was defeated, and I think I understand. I am living a comfortable life, mostly because my father had gotten us out of Vietnam when he did and because of the Americans who helped us along the way. My journey through the marines introduced me to U.S. veterans who had bravely fought for my cause, despite growing opposition back home. On my personal odyssey I've discovered many heroic acts, including ones that touched our family deeply. Of course I knew little of all of this until recent years. I needed time. I was too busy trying to prove my patriotism. For most Vietnamese and other immigrants, getting an education, paying taxes, obeying the law, and owning a home—the American Dream—were enough for us, the "model minority."

For me, however, there was an unfinished mission. Every U.S. conflict since Vietnam has been compared with it, rightly and wrongly. There's a Vietnam generation that is still fighting the war, exchanging barbs all the way to the voting booth in every national election.

As I entered that debate, something was still missing. What happened after the war? Who really won and who really lost? Have we learned anything? Even the Vietnamese elders in the United States had been silent. What should they tell the younger generation about the war and their roles in it? Reeducation camps remain a taboo topic, especially in modern Vietnam, its government making no mention of them. Tourists can't visit the former prison camps, and the Communists vehemently deny their existence.

Maybe my father's postwar predicament has distorted my understanding of Vietnam.

For the first few years after his capture, I thought my father was dead. Perhaps from grief, or anger, I couldn't conjure any positive attitudes toward the South Vietnamese. It was easier to blame them the same way we are now pointing fingers at the Iraqis for not holding their own against the insurgents. I could not summon enough strength to deal with my own emotions until my father came back into my life. All too soon, before my personal *shantih* could be achieved, he left again.

More than two years after his death, I finally got an opportunity to honor my father in public. The ceremony was in front of a new war memorial, with a full band and military helicopter flyover (courtesy of my Marine buddies on a "training" mission), the way this nation honors its own veterans. (The Westminster Vietnam War Memorial's dedication took place soon after U.S. troops had "liberated" Baghdad in April 2003. Ironically, it had also been three decades since Henry Kissinger signed the Paris Peace Accords that sent American boys home and thus catalyzed what would be a slow, sure death for South Vietnam.)

The memorial was not The Wall in Washington, D.C. It was a smaller memorial in California, where two 11-foot bronze statues of a GI and a slightly shorter resolute South Vietnamese soldier stand side by side with their M-16s, facing a flaming urn, and with two flagpoles behind the soldiers.

They stand together in Westminster, designated an all-American city but now popularly known as Little Saigon, much to the dismay of longtime white residents. Once a decaying suburb in the middle of conservative Orange County, it had evolved into the bustling, explosive de facto capital of Vietnam War refugees. Its *pho*-like flavor of pre-1975 Saigon politics is slipping away slowly as a new generation comes of age.

If truth was the first casualty of the Vietnam War, then this memorial should serve to announce one of its honest legacies. The statues' thousand-yard stares peer out to the west, where the Pacific Ocean connects North America and Vietnam, where the present meets the past with its anger, guilt, and shame. Westminster is also where 15,000 disgruntled refugees marched against a Vietnamese American video store owner who flew the communist flag and displayed a picture of Ho Chi Minh in public. This is where aging men spend their days sipping French coffee, smoking cigarettes, and talking about what might have been. Here the cultural and generational gaps sometimes seem to be widening rather than narrowing. Here, finally, is where my father felt most at ease in this country, playing tennis, shuffling mah-jongg tiles, or eating noodles with his former military comrades.

After the ceremonial fly-by and a series of speeches by veterans, a Vietnamese singer wearing camouflage-pattern pants took center stage. As she bellowed the anthem of the former Republic of Vietnam, the yellow flag with its three red stripes ascended slowly in the background:

Này công dân ôi! Quốc gia đến ngày giải phóng.

O People! The country nears its freedom day.

Ten thousand attendees rose to their feet, nearly all in tears, including me, even though I couldn't recite more than the first verse. Next "The Star Spangled Banner" was sung as Old Glory rose in a slight breeze. I knew every line.

I had come to Westminster to honor my father, the same way I had paid my tribute to the Americans at The Wall in Washington, D.C. The first time I visited the Vietnam Veterans Memorial was in 1986. It was difficult to stand before the names of those who gave their lives to fight for my freedom. They were not even from my country. Why didn't they go to Canada? Why didn't they question their orders? Where would I be now if they hadn't fought the Communists?

On the other hand, I knew that Americans were not the only ones who fought the Communists in Vietnam. Nearly 245,000 South Vietnamese died in defense of their country, about four for every U.S. forces death. Another 65,000* political victims were executed, while thousands more perished in the reeducation camps from disease, exhaustion, malnutrition, or suicide. I saw all the marked graves—those not bulldozed by the Communists after their victory—on the outskirts of Saigon when I returned there a decade ago.

I remember as a boy visiting my father's squadron and shaking hands with the other pilots all wearing green flight suits, pistols on their hips.

The first Americans I ever met were the advisers in his unit.

In the final years of the war my father would leave the house before dawn, sometimes arriving home in time for dinner. His job was to dump ordnance on Viet Cong (VC) positions, drop flares at night, and ferry troops and supplies. I used to think that was probably why the Communists kept him in captivity for so long after the war: a day for each VC he killed.

I wish my father were still alive. He died just eight brief years after leaving Vietnam. For all that—and despite the fact that he sometimes felt betrayed by the United States—he wouldn't have missed the memorial's dedication ceremony for anything. He fought alongside the Americans in Vietnam and was proud to have done so.

He didn't die in combat. I used to wish he had so I could have been rid of the burden of explaining what happened to him. In the United States, there is more recognition for dying than for surviving a war unless you are a POW celebrity like Jessica Lynch. No one questions the dead about commitment, duty, or sacrifice. My father accomplished a much more difficult challenge by surviving years of captivity, only to become a *nobody,* a cipher, in this country.

That's what happens when you lose a war and your country. The winners take away your family, your freedom, your people, and your flag. They tried to erase my father's mind, to destroy his dignity, to "enlighten" him about communism. But they could not take away his soul.

There is no memorial yet for my war, the Persian Gulf War that supposedly "kicked the Vietnam syndrome" in 1991 (or so President George H. W. Bush said to Congress). But Westminster's Vietnam War memorial is an es-

*In 1985, University of California at Berkeley researchers Jacqueline Desbarats and Karl D. Jackson published their research among Vietnamese refugees in the *Wall Street Journal.*

sential piece of our history. It honors my father and those fallen fighters who answered the call of duty during a time of turmoil for both countries.

He never looked back and no longer will I. It took thirty years, but my questions have been answered. The United States provided my family a second chance to live in freedom and peace and to get to know each other again; it did not forget about my father and his fellow detainees. And for that we are indebted. This is our story.

Top left: *Hoa at aircraft mechanic school, Rochefort, France, 1955. (Author's Collection)*
Top right: *VNAF Aviation Cadets Hoa and An at the Statue of Liberty, Christmas 1957. (Courtesy of Ly Ngoc An)*
Bottom: *Hoa as a student pilot in a B-25, Reese Air Force Base, Texas, 1958. (Author's Collection)*

FIRST FLIGHT

W HEN I WAS SIX I TOOK MY FIRST AIRPLANE RIDE. MY entire immediate family came along, as well as an older cousin. We were so excited we kept talking about the excursion for days in advance, and I could hardly sleep the night before. A white mosquito net covered my small body and blurred my half-asleep vision. Waking and turning, I tried to count the different cricket sounds through the night; their cadence rang in unison like a kinetic, unseen symphony. In the distance, faint explosions occasionally interrupted the cricket chirping but didn't silence them. Just like the people in my neighborhood, the insects were used to war. On most nights I would sleep right through the detonations. On this night I wished I knew what the crickets were saying.

I wasn't alone. My mother lay nearby, and my sisters slept in the same room; that's the way it was in our country. Families lived together and slept together. Our grandparents had lived with us until they passed away in 1969, within a year of each other. But little did we know that one day the Vietnamese diaspora would sprinkle us all over the world; we would all have our own houses.

Summer vacation had begun and we were heading for the low mountains of Da Lat, some 200 miles north of Saigon, to cool off for the day. When I was growing up, we hardly ever had any family vacations, so this would be a rare treat.

Because the countryside was dangerous, especially at night, for us air travel was safer—and we knew the pilot. That day the rain came and went, washing away the red clay on the pothole-filled dirt road leading to the airport. At the airport we moved among airplanes worth millions of dollars, yet we only had to step outside the gate to see a country mired in poverty. Our driver had dropped us off near an old, yellow half-cylindrical aluminum hangar from which we watched dozens of planes taxiing for takeoff and landing. We weren't at the civilian passenger terminal. We stood on the military side of Tan Son Nhut Airport, one of the busiest in the world in 1970.

We boarded a World War II–era C-47, the military version of the DC-3, a reliable, twin-engine transport. On its fuselage was the South Vietnamese national insignia, a white star on a blue disk surrounded by an outer red ring, with red and yellow sidebars. A national vertical yellow flag with three red horizontal stripes was painted on its rudder. The other passengers included families of military men, some in uniform. After a quick safety briefing by a crew member, we sat quietly on the red canvas seats usually reserved for airborne troops.

As the plane lumbered down the runway and took to the air, I looked out the window while gripping my mother's hand. She was also holding my older sister Thi, who sat on her other side. I could barely make out smoggy Saigon receding beneath the wings. Soon green rice fields and grass-roofed villages appeared. We were flying low enough to see tiny farmers and their water buffaloes dragging wooden plows. Growing up in the city, I had only seen buffaloes and fields in newspaper photographs.

After about fifteen minutes, the pilot in the left seat motioned to me to come into the cockpit. I unbuckled my belt and stumbled up the aisle, nearly tripping over the rollers on the floor. He picked me up and placed me on his lap. I could smell his signature Aqua Velva after-shave lotion and sweat. I hesitated to touch the controls even as he assured me that it was all right to steer the plane. He smiled to the copilot as I cautiously reached out and slightly pushed on the steering column.

There in front of me was our beautiful country. Tall, sharp mountains guarded deep green valleys, and the brown Mekong River wound sinuously through its delta to the sea. Large thunderclouds were scattered throughout the skies, ready to strike lightning and dump rain on those below. The plane was buffeted by the stormy air. The hazy countryside appeared so peaceful. But unbeknownst to me at that age was that our people, of the north and south, had been at war for almost two decades, the two sides supported by opposing superpowers. They had to choose sides or, unfortunately for many, face the wrath of all.

The pilot was my father. He had become one of the most experienced pilots in the VNAF. He pulled out a cigarette and turned his head to the left to blow the smoke out the small, sliding cockpit window. He hoisted me up by the waist so I could see over the nose of the aircraft. It was dizzying to be staring straight down at the ground as it moved underneath us.

We landed and spent the day in Da Lat. The return trip took nearly two hours, but I could hardly wait for us to land so I could go brag to my friends. I was hooked on flying that day. It would take another twenty years before I would become like my father, soaring over the plains of Texas, serving *my* country as a military aviator.

Top left: *My parents on their wedding day, Saigon, 1963. (Author's Collection)*
Top right: *With my mother and my older sister Thi, Saigon, 1966. (Author's Collection)*
Bottom left: *The only picture of all four kids with their father in Vietnam. Tan Son Nhut Air Base, Saigon, 1972. (Author's Collection)*
Bottom left: *Mama's boy at age one and his mother Nguyen Thi Niem, Saigon, 1965. (Author's Collection)*

CHAPTER 2

THE SHAMEFUL END

Today, America can regain the sense of pride that existed before Vietnam.
But it cannot be achieved by re-fighting a war that is finished as far as
America is concerned. These events, tragic as they are, portend neither the
end of the world nor of America's leadership in the world.

—President Gerald Ford, Tulane University, April 23, 1975

THE SECOND TIME I BOARDED AN AIRPLANE, FIVE YEARS later, was sheer terror for me.

As President Ford commented on the events unfolding in Vietnam, the rowdy crowd at Tulane University roared and gave him a standing ovation. They were cheering the impending loss of my homeland, even though most of them—like their predecessors of the 1960s—would never feel the lasting impact of the Vietnam War. The military draft had ended and U.S. troops and POWs had come home two years earlier. So why were they celebrating our misery?

President Ford must have known the end was near. Two weeks earlier, Congress had denied his request for $722 million in aid to South Vietnam. American support finally came to an end as the North Vietnamese sped toward Saigon with eighteen combat divisions backed by tanks for the "final offensive." Their actions were in clear violation of the 1973 Paris Peace Accords, even though everyone knew at the time of signing that the accords were a joke. Except for Henry Kissinger, who eventually took home the Nobel Peace Prize, while his corecipient, North Vietnamese counterpart, Le Duc Tho, rightfully declined. The United States withdrew its remaining troops, and its 591 POWs were rightly released, but there would be no peace or honor to follow.

Images of the impending slaughter began airing in early March 1975. Long-ingrained photographs of barefoot rice farmers toting AK-47s had morphed into professional soldiers in green pith helmets armed to the teeth. They roared through the South Vietnamese central cities the way the U.S. Marines stormed Kuwait City sixteen years later, then Baghdad a dozen years after that.

Halfway around the world my family, along with the several thousand fortunate South Vietnamese who would live to tell about it, watched the unfolding of those tragic events. For us it was the worst of times. It seemed like the end of the world to me, even though I was only ten years old. That night remains as clear to me today as it was then. Every once in a while something triggers that haunting memory, and I am struck immobile.

On a recent Christmas vacation, my wife and I flew to Vermont to visit her family. Her father, Jim, and her sister Amy's husband, Bill, greeted us in the terminal. They were dressed in full snow garb, while we Californians strolled off the plane in skimpy jeans and thin turtlenecks. Snow had fallen, and it was freezing cold as we drove north through Connecticut and Massachusetts, with temperatures dipping into the teens. Steady flakes struck the windshield of Bill's SUV as visibility diminished to less than a quarter-mile.

I was riding in the back, barely able to make out road signs through the fog and snow. Jim put on a holiday CD, prepping us for the Christmas eve feast ahead: Nat King Cole sang, and then Bing Crosby did "White Christmas." My body went numb and my vision blurred. Flashes of Saigon came to life, and its night landscape filled my memory. I could hear the sound of helicopters approaching overhead.

"Daddy, can you skip that?" Shannon promptly asked Jim. She probably felt me squirming next to her, sliding across the leather seat like a car fishtailing across an icy road, uncontrollably and unpredictably. She understood. She had seen me react like this before when we were watching Vietnam documentaries on the History Channel.

To this day I cannot listen to "White Christmas." It is not because it's a terrible song. Indeed, it is still recognized as one of America's most favorite tunes. Written by Irving Berlin for a movie Crosby made with Fred Astaire called "Holiday Inn" in 1942, Crosby sang it often, especially during his visits with GIs during World War II, bringing many to tears, yearning for home.

But in Vietnam that week, his song signaled the end.

Some sicko must have thought of using such a sweet song as a warning. A simple, "Let's get the fuck out of here," over Armed Forces Radio, would have worked as well. Instead the announcer broadcast "It's 105 degrees and the temperature is rising," then played Crosby's hit to warn the remaining Americans in Saigon to head to the U.S. Embassy for the evacuation.

That was on April 29, 1975, the day before the end. The ARVN's ragtag 18th Division, the last unit standing before Saigon, was decimated at Xuan Loc despite putting up a valiant fight. A few VNAF pilots managed to get airborne and put up a heroic but futile final battle against the enemy.

I can't seem to get the night I left Saigon out of my mind. I still wonder what President Ford was thinking when he gave that speech acknowledging our impending loss. Could he have known how tragic this disaster really was to those of us who were there? Why were the Marines already waiting off the coast? Was there a secret negotiation for the evacuation, the way Kissinger had bypassed the South Vietnamese government at the 1973 Paris Peace Conference?

At the end of March 1975, the mood in Saigon became somber after Hue City fell so quickly to the NVA. This time, the Marines weren't there to fight door to door as they did during the 1968 Tet offensive. Danang was swollen by then with 2 million refugees, all scrambling south for safety along single-lane Route 7B while getting pounded by merciless North Vietnamese Army (NVA) artillery. Nearly 40,000 innocents died in the "convoy of tears," even though victory was within reach of the Communists. (This slaughter has gone almost unmentioned in the thousands of books about the war.) The NVA must have wanted to send a final signal to Saigon and Washington. Fleeing South Vietnamese were so afraid of the Communists that some hung desperately onto the landing gear of the last passenger jet plane leaving Danang and were crushed in its wheel wells. North Vietnam had committed its army to unrestricted killing to end the war, and the United States did nothing to stop this.

My Saigon elementary school classes had been canceled for two weeks, since the attack on the Presidential Palace on April 8. On that day, I nearly became a war casualty. It was my closest brush with death in Vietnam, having hunkered down in our family bunker many times.

I was attending my last class as a student in Saigon, where I had been learning to speak decent French after four long, tongue-twisting years. Final exams. Yes, even fifth-graders had to take them. I had cruised through the first test by 9 a.m. I took a short break and stared out the large window to the left of the classroom. Large trees hid the barbed-wire fence on top of the gates surrounding the Presidential Palace across the street. But I knew that the fence and the armed guards were there, having seen the palace many times on my way home from school. It was the equivalent of attending a public school on Pennsylvania Avenue, right across from the White House.

As I gazed out the schoolroom window, I savored dreams of a long summer, fishing in the bomb craters carved by VC artillery and B-52 Arc Light strikes. No more Mr. Bui and his disciplinary slaps; no more Mademoiselle Juneau and her Gallic bickering: *merci beaucoup* and *au revoir*. I was daydreaming when my teacher handed me the second exam.

Ka-boom.

My ears rang as if someone had lit a firecracker inside my head. The concussion of the first bomb sucked the air from my tiny lungs while I struggled to hold on to my chair, gasping to catch a breath. A wall of air pushed me to the ground. The entire classroom, focused and silent a minute before, now looked like an insane asylum, with screaming kids scurrying every which way to get under desks. Even Mr. Bui crawled on his knees in front of the class, seeking shelter. I remained under my desk, having experienced numerous VC attacks on Saigon before, although none ever this close.

Ka-Boom.

The second explosion convinced me to stay put. Bracing myself against my chair, I heard the shriek of a diving jet fighter overhead. The shock wave shook the room viciously and sent books and notes flying everywhere. I thought it was all over. Peeking out from under my desk, I saw red antiaircraft fire fly skyward and heard a staccato of automatic weapons. These last rounds must have come from a guard post on the palace's grounds shortly after the second bomb struck. I wondered if anyone from my school had died. Two of my sisters were also in class that morning; my mother was here too, but she was teaching in a classroom on the other side of the school.

The deadly roars of the jet soon faded. There were no more explosions, just chaos inside my classroom. I was still in shock and scared, like the rest of my classmates. Many I would never see again. The ever-firm Mr. Bui remained under his desk. He looked awkward and funny to me, and probably to the other kids, too, and we all laughed, even under the morning's terrible spell of fear. Classes were canceled by noon, and we were all sent home. A curfew took effect shortly after.

My mother and sisters were all unhurt. We began to recover from the shock of being under attack. A few days later my father announced what had happened. The pilot who had bombed the Presidential Palace had been in the VNAF, one of our own. I was devastated; those pilots were my only heroes.

The true price of attending school next to the president's residence came to light that day. I suppose my experience was not an anomaly. In the modern world coup d'états and assassination attempts on presidents in their homes are not uncommon, and South Vietnam's turbulent history included a few.

For the Vietnamese the war was a part of our life whether we liked it, whether we had supported it, or whether the United States, China, or the Soviet Union had had enough. Civilians living in a war zone were subject to its horrors, much as the Israelis, Palestinians, Afghanis, Iraqis, and Kosovars were in subsequent years. Governments called the shots and soldiers carried out the orders. As an adult, I would puzzle over why some Americans had thought the war in Vietnam was a mistake when Ho Chi Minh and his supporters had tried to unite our countries at any cost. (If South Korea was worth defending for fifty years, why wasn't South Vietnam? Kuwait was worth liberating, so oil must be worth more than rice and rubber. Time will tell if the war in Iraq will be able to absorb more American blood.)

After the rogue jet attack panic began to spread like blood from a fatal wound. Fear was something we could touch and smell in our neighborhood, especially when soldiers and tanks crowded the streets in front of our house. The atmosphere at the base housing at Tan Son Nhut Air Base was thick with rumors and jet fuel fumes. Most children remained indoors, and families were glued to radios listening to the BBC for the latest update on the imminent invasion by North Vietnam. Our neighbors were gone; I didn't know when they had left and I never found out.

Tuesday, April 22, 1975, dissolved into a dark and sticky Saigon night. Under pressure from U.S. Ambassador Graham Martin, President Nguyen Van Thieu had resigned the day before. This had ignited widespread terror in Saigon and those with money and connections began to leave. Our family had the latter, but only by luck.

A cousin of my father, who had worked at the U.S. Embassy, told him to get us out of Saigon as soon as the evacuation began; thus we were among the very first to flee. My father came home from the airfield at about 11 p.m. My mother had been asleep for about two hours when my father, driving wildly, brought his Lambretta scooter to a screeching halt in our driveway.

My mother tried to get my sisters and me out of bed all at once. Lights were out, darkness surrounded us, but I knew exactly where my belongings were. Since we had gone through so many attacks on previous nights, the drill was set. Well prepared for war, we followed our instincts at the sound of an explosion, a shrieking air raid siren, or my mother's voice in the middle of the night. The sound of the Lambretta engine outside punctuated the silence; our dog, Milou, began to bark mournfully. Before I could even begin to fathom what was happening, he sensed our imminent departure. My mother hurried back and forth between the drawers and the suitcases on her bed, stuffing them at random. Her long silhouette was cast against the back wall, a precursor of her lasting impact on my life, replacing my father's role. She held a kerosene lamp in one hand and packed the luggage with the other. The room was barely lit as the tiny flame flickered and then slowly disappeared. I stumbled to the living room and reached for the light switch.

"Turn the damn lights off!" screamed my father. By now my mother had gone outside with my sisters. Standing alone in the dark bedroom, I wondered why we were packing our belongings and hurrying to go somewhere. I thought this was another attack and that we should be running toward our bomb shelter down the hallway from our bedroom. Not this time, though. I then realized that everyone was waiting for me. I grabbed my jacket and slipped on my sneakers. I took my favorite toy, a steel model A-37 Dragonfly, and ran to the porch. My sisters all had half-asleep, blank stares on their faces, but Thu, my two-year-old baby sister, was crying loudly.

"Where are we going, Mother?"

"I don't know yet, but we have to leave now. We'll be all right, sweetheart." My mother sounded nervous, yet she never would have guessed our fate that night, let alone envisioned bringing up her children in a strange land beginning only a week later.

My father wore his usual green flight suit and black boots. He was very quiet. He mustered a few words to get all of us on his scooter. Milou, our skinny, dirty-white poodle, stared at all of us. He looked sad. He was the only dog we'd had that had not been stolen at Tan Son Nhut. I sat in back, holding on to my mother for dear life, as we took up every inch on that worn leather seat.

My father kicked the overloaded scooter into gear with all six of us aboard, and we started weaving toward the dirt alley. I looked back at our house and wondered if I would ever see it again. The sandbags above our homemade bomb shelter seemed to be sliding off the roof; the shadows of the trees in the front yard shifted with the wind; the fragrance from our green mango tree floated in the air. Our house. Our home. I got one last look before the scooter sped away. Milou ran after us, but we couldn't take him along. We lost him in a dust cloud kicked up by the scooter. We abandoned him, the same way the United States left South Vietnam, like a dog that just didn't fit into its plans.

We sped across the base through a slight breeze. Most of the lights were out for security. In the distance flares and tracers lit the skies; artillery shells exploded sporadically, reminding us of the danger closing in. It was an unusually frenzied morning. Until I saw *The Great Santini* years later, I never thought of myself as a military brat. That morning in 1975 was like the fictional Colonel "Bull" Meachum hurrying his family out of bed to move to another base. Except we weren't singing "Battle Hymn of the Republic" or the "Marine Corps Hymn." The military called it a "permanent change of station" (PCS) move. But our move could have been abbreviated PCC, for "permanent change of country." No movers came, and there were no packers, no moving trucks, no farewell parties, and no goodbyes to our neighbors. It was simply an escape in the middle of the night.

As we lurched through Tan Son Nhut, I looked for familiar signposts and tried to catch last glimpses of my receding childhood. It had been filled with joy amid the fear of death. We had moved onto the base in 1972 from a Saigon suburb, and I had enjoyed that move more than my sisters did. The fires of my childhood dreams that set me on the path of becoming a pilot were stoked daily as I watched VNAF aircraft returning from missions. I would go to the squadron with my father and fantasize about *Twelve O'Clock High,* a popular World War II series shown on Armed Forces Television. The hangar, the post exchange (PX), the movie theater, the ruined tanks on the playground, the old warplanes—all had been my favorite hangouts. From the back of the scooter, and trying not to slide off the seat, I saw the tall grass waving in the wind, the place that had once made a perfect hideout from enemies during a chase game with my friends next door.

We finally reached the darkened airport gym. A bus was parked in the front lot, its oil-smelling diesel engine idling. My father stopped the scooter and walked over to a group of men standing at the rear of the bus. I could not hear the conversation, but I sensed the importance of the moment from the look on my mother's face as she stood there, quietly holding my youngest sister. He walked back and whispered a few words into my mother's ear.

"OK. It's time to go, kids. I'll see you later." My father then reached into his pocket and pulled out several strange green bills. He handed the money to my mother and picked up two bags of clothes and his attaché case containing his military records and family photographs. I had my belongings in his green helmet bag, standard issue for military aviators everywhere. He winked at me and rubbed my head. We boarded the hot and crowded bus without him. I managed to get to a window and inhaled a breath of fresh air. I looked out into the darkness and found my father's face. He stood there waving and, as we pulled away, disappeared into the darkness.

The bus moved slowly. I was sure the driver couldn't see the road because his lights, and all the lights on base, were off that night. Then we stopped. Minutes went by. An hour passed. I began to suffer from extreme claustrophobia in the steamy, packed-sardine atmosphere of the bus. (Years later, I would have a panic attack in pilot survival training during a simulated imprisonment, a throwback to this moment.) I had lost sight of my mother and sisters. They were somewhere on the bus but no longer right next to me. But I saw my father again briefly, this time talking to some Americans also in flight suits. How could I have known it would take seventeen years before I would again see his face?

Finally, the bus doors swung open and everyone quickly piled out. It was still dark as I stumbled off the bus, searching for my mother and sisters. I found them, staggering along two families in front of me. I didn't know where I was on the tarmac until I felt the hot air from the propellers of a large camouflage-painted aircraft. From the profile, I knew it was a C-130 Hercules like the one my father flew. But it was not from the VNAF. Its fuselage had faint U.S. Air Force (USAF) insignia. Its ramp was down and two USAF crewmen tried to control the crowd rushing the aircraft. I smelled the familiar odor of aviation fuel as the Hercules' four turbine engines idled, ready for an immediate takeoff.

I held my mother's hand as we sat on the steel floor of the plane, layered with tracks and rollers used to load cargo. The canvas seats were rolled up on the sides of the cabin. No seats, no meals, no stewardesses. The only lighting came from several red and green lights in the cargo bay. There must have been over 200 people on an aircraft that ordinarily carries half that number. Improbably, the reasonable thought occurred to me as we waited that Vietnamese people are smaller than Americans, so more of us could fit on this airplane. In front of the crowd sitting on the floor was some sort of dark canvas tarp. I could not figure out what it was, though it took up room where several rows of people could have been.

The ramp screeched up and the engine noise of the plane quieted for a few minutes as the pilot began to taxi. The two crewmen struggled through the crowd to their takeoff seats near the two open windows, one on each side of the aircraft. I held on tightly to the floor railings to keep from bouncing every time the aircraft rolled over a bump on the tarmac.

The pilot made what seemed like a sharp turn followed by an immediate acceleration, signaling the takeoff roll. The Hercules roared down the runway. My butt felt every jolt until we were airborne. It seemed to take forever before the landing gear was raised. I would later learn that a long takeoff roll meant we were dangerously heavy. Looking out the dirty Plexiglas bubble window that night, I saw nothing but a faint orange glow bruising a dark sky. I could not catch a last glimpse of Saigon's bright lights, the lights of my hometown.

The crewman on the left stood up and took a large pistol from beneath his seat. A flare gun. He looked downward from the window, perhaps searching for a surface-to-air missile. "What a way to go," I sighed to myself; getting shot down on my way out of Vietnam wasn't exactly my childhood dream of flying. (Several VNAF aircraft would eventually be shot down on the penultimate day of the war by NVA troops firing shoulder-held SA-7s. But ours wouldn't be one of them.)

I wondered what it would feel like to get hit by a missile and tumble out of the sky from our altitude. (No parachutes.) But why would they shoot at us civilians, I wondered naively. Why was flying over Saigon considered dangerous territory? How come we had left at such an odd time? Why didn't my father come with us? The exhausting evening caught up with me and I slowly slid down the cold metal wall and slept.

I woke up to a bright blue sky shining through the window above me. I rubbed my eyes and glanced at my mother and sisters, who were all still asleep and looked drained. Most of the passengers were still sleeping on the floor of the plane. The two crewmen were sitting at their seats, facing the crowd, but without their flare pistols in hand.

In the light I didn't recognize any faces. Strangers. Who were these people? I thought we knew everyone who lived in my neighborhood. I looked toward the front of the crowd for that strange-looking tarp. But it was gone. Instead, there were more people than I remembered being there only a few hours earlier. To my shock and surprise, I recognized several men in the new group. They had served with my father in the VNAF, but they were not wearing their uniforms now. Dressed in civilian clothes and crouched on the floor, the men appeared to be in disguise. Major Binh and Colonel Trung were there. My stare caught the attention of Major Binh, father of my school-mate Tuan. I waved hello to him, but he didn't acknowledge it. Tuan also turned away quickly. I knew that both had seen me. Why were these men on the aircraft with us? How come my father hadn't joined us?

A horrifying thought flashed through my mind. *My father has been left behind!* I woke my mother and told her of my fears. She started crying; the plane's engines drowned out her sobs. I began to cry. Then my mother spotted another familiar face in the crowd and she whispered something to Thi. I didn't recognize the woman until my mother reminded me. Miss Mai was a well-known entertainer in Saigon; now dressed in dowdy clothes and hardly resembling a TV star, she sat huddled two rows behind us. Mai managed a fake smile, as though glad to be recognized by a fan.

The plane nosed over and banked sharply as gravity pulled me against my mother. We were descending, and the engine noise lessened for a moment. Where were we landing? The gears stuttered down noisily and the crewmen signaled the restless crowd to hang on to each other. Two hundred people shifted forward and then backward, as the Hercules touched down and reversed its propellers to slow down. I smelled tire rubber burning. It was a rough landing. I saw swaying palm trees passing the plane as we came to a temporary halt before making a turn off the runway.

The engines idled and the rear ramp was lowered to reveal two military police cars. The men were Asian and they wore khaki uniforms, but I still could not figure out where we were. We hadn't flown to Hanoi, I hoped. The crewman on the ramp motioned us to stand up as he pointed to the rear of the aircraft. My legs were numb after being cramped for hours on the steel rollers. My empty stomach growled for anything to eat. Where were we? Where was my father? Was he meeting us here? What was going to happen to us? Was the war over? My ten-year-old mind had questions that would multiply over the years and preoccupy my adult life.

My father could have easily gotten on that aircraft or flown one like it to the Philippines or Singapore. Others had done just that, but they were among the minority of servicemen who fled early, as I would learn decades later. Eventually over 125,000 South Vietnamese, or less than 1 percent of the entire population, would fearfully depart Saigon over the ensuing week. President Thieu allegedly took millions in gold with him to Taiwan, Britain, and then the United States. Yet he lived modestly until his death in 2001 (unlike many former leaders of the Vietnam era and their excuses, he died in silence).

Former premier Nguyen Cao Ky (by then a private citizen) vowed to fight to the death—but then flew his helicopter with a three-star general to a U.S. Navy ship off the coast. Who was left behind to fight the charging Communists? Where were our mighty American friends? Who remained to lead a desperate nation? I could only wonder.

The Marine Corps would later teach me much about duty and honor. But I already learned about both from my father the night I left Saigon.

Packed like sardines. Evacuation flight to freedom, C-141 to Guam, April 1975. (Courtesy of United States Marine Corps)

CHAPTER 3

GONE AGAIN

*I told myself I'd probably leave at the last minute. But I couldn't leave too
early. As an officer, you have your pride, your duty. You can't change the
past. [Looking at his son in uniform] Besides, if I had left, maybe he
wouldn't have turned out the way he did.*

—My father commenting in a *U.S. News & World Report* article written shortly
after his arrival in the United States in 1992

I PLACED MY FATHER'S WORN, DARK VINYL ATTACHÉ CASE ON
the top of my desk, and opened it. It contained his personal documents,
including those I took with me the night we left Saigon. I spun its two
rusting three-number locks to "000" with my thumbs, sliding them outward
then flipping the lid open. At first, I wondered if he had used a certain combination to lock the case, perhaps his old squadron designation, or his prisoner number, or the number of years he had lost in captivity. Then I realized
that honoring such dates would have presented too many possibilities, and at
his age would have been impossible to recall.

Now I know how wrong I had been about him all along.

A man who witnessed war most of his life, what would my father have remembered most? Was he ready to refight the Vietnam War and win back
our homeland? Was he haunted by all the death and destruction, the kind

that troubled many U.S. servicemen? Would he remember the faces of those Americans who trained him, fought with him, and evacuated his family to safety? What would he say to them now after all this time?

Maybe he simply wanted to forget all those bad times.

I kept hoping and wondering all those years, first waiting for him to appear among the crowds evacuated to the Guam and Arkansas refugee camps where we were flown after Saigon fell, then for the few letters that finally came. I finally gave up. I needed to get on with my own life, to walk out from his shadow once and for all. By becoming a *real* American through the U.S. Marine Corps, I would perhaps shed the last threads of bitterness and resentment whenever the word "Vietnam" was mentioned.

But that didn't happen, because the Marines have not forgotten about Vietnam either.

Just look at the 2004 presidential campaign. Only the Communists seem to be able to put the war behind them. Echoes of Vietnam resonate again as Americans are being tested as to their commitment to a war in another faraway land. The prism of Iraq forces us again to examine the same old questions: Who won? Who really lost in Vietnam? Or, as one prominent *Washington Post* columnist put it, "Who cares?"

I fucking care.

The full impact of war usually takes time to unfurl. It may take years, even decades. That, at least, was the case for me. I believe my father felt the same way.

Now that my father is gone again, I realize I had joined the Marines for him and for South Vietnam, as much as I did for any sense of patriotism to America. I wanted to relieve him of a loser's guilt, a husband's regret, a father's remorse. Most of all, I wanted him to know that he stood for respectability—for duty, honor, and country—and that he taught me those lessons early on. I don't know if I succeeded. My father used to stare at me when I was in uniform, perhaps reminding him of the U.S. Marine who had prevented him from leaving Saigon aboard one of the departing helicopters.

I had hoped that people would come to see my father in a different light—not to feel sorry for him but to appreciate him as the American public has come to acknowledge the sacrifice made by U.S. Vietnam veterans. Giving them their due. No longer blaming them for the quagmire.

Nobody ever welcomed my father home, in Vietnam or in the United States; nobody ever thanked him for serving or acknowledged his suffering.

Not even me, and I knew better. I thought I had more time. I had wanted one more promotion, had to make one more business trip, get one more bonus check before I made time to tell him how much I appreciated all he went through for us.

The attaché case holds most of his important documents, many needed as proof for senior citizen discounts in his new country. He needed all the help he could get at his age. Despite serving his country for two decades, not even counting the twelve-year imprisonment and hard labor, he had no pension. Nor could he rely on U.S. Veterans' Administration (VA) hospitals to treat him the way they finally accepted Filipino veterans.*

My father had lost a war *and* his country, and along with this all benefits (assuming the South Vietnamese government would have provided any). Yet he never once complained to me. Perhaps he thought his American Marine son would make snide remarks to him, the way the U.S. advisers did in the war.

When I was growing up in this country, I hated him for not coming along with us the night we left Vietnam. I loathed him for not being there when my mother bounced from job to job while learning English. My sisters and I hid in fear under the covers at night, locked inside a small, rundown apartment in a shoddy part of town, not knowing what to say or whom to call when someone knocked on our door at night.

I detested him whenever we stood in line at the grocery store, food stamps in hand, clutching several Twinkies while being scolded by the clerk as if we children on welfare were not allowed to enjoy such treats.

I could not stand the hundreds of times I was asked where he was. Almost everyone assumed he had abandoned us (most of the kids in my neighborhood came from single-parent families) or they thought he had died in the war. I often resorted to the latter, mumbling the easier answer.

We hardly interacted at all with the Vietnamese families who were still intact after the evacuation. None of his VNAF buddies wanted to deal with a single mom and four small kids. All of them had their own obstacles to overcome here. When we were scattered from Saigon, every man, woman, and child was for him or herself. The Vietnam tragedy began to resemble one of

---

*In 2003, President George W. Bush signed into law an act enabling World War II Filipino veterans living in the United States to receive VA medical care. Some Filipino veterans had been waiting for nearly sixty years since the U.S. victory over Japan.

those giant anthills in the Ia Drang Valley, their inhabitants running aimlessly in every direction without a leader. When we fled every family was on its own.

Yet I can remember the times I was questioned about whether the "so-called" reeducation camps really even existed. A U.S. Vietnam veteran mockingly asked if reeducation had been "just classroom lectures" or "retraining." I wonder why few of my father's peers, formerly detained, talked to their children or wives about what they endured in Vietnam. It must have been easier to gather at coffee shops in Little Saigon, to be with friends who survived the war, to reminisce about pre-1975 life, than to face their Americanized families. Once my father and I were united, I stopped wondering, waiting for him to open up, to let out that primal scream about losing his fellow soldiers, all respect, the war, his country, and another twelve years of his life. But he never did. He would never say anything bad about his new land, even in private.

Surely the years apart from his family must have been difficult for my father to forgive. He couldn't even pretend to make up for lost time with his children, especially as an old man in a strange land. And perhaps I didn't try hard enough, nor did my sisters or my mother. I guess I was hoping he would call me up one day and we would go fishing and he would tell me all about his life, from his birth and through the war, and he would reveal his true feelings about this country.

I watched *Coming Home, The Deer Hunter, Platoon, We Were Soldiers,* all of it, hoping to get a glimpse of what my father went through. I should have spent time with him. Rather than reading all those Vietnam War books and memoirs by American veterans and journalists, I should have asked him about his new life and its difficulties. The stories portrayed in the movies and books usually ended by the U.S. withdrawal in 1973. Only a few even attempted to capture the painful evacuation of Saigon.

In newsreels at the time, the U.S. Embassy resembled a wasp's nest with insect-like choppers repeatedly taking away desperate humans clinging to the helicopter skids. Many watched their freedom slip away from behind armed Marines and chain-link fences.

I caught a tiny glimpse of my past while watching *Miss Saigon,* only to be disappointed again with another love tale between a GI and a Vietnamese bar girl.

I still seethe when I think of the day I lost my country of birth. I also wanted to know why South Vietnam wasn't able to defend itself. After all, Vietnamization* had been announced in 1969, a full six years before the end.

But seeing those movies and reading those books did help me understand what Americans went through, for it was not *their* war or *their* country that they were fighting for. I wanted to know why some Americans served, while others avoided military service during that era. To many who opposed U.S. involvement South Vietnam was not worthy of America's sacrifice. To some, not even now, when history clearly shows that the Communists' atrocities had begun as early as the late 1940s. Even Jane Fonda has apologized. In his memoir *My Losing Season,* novelist Pat Conroy wished he had served as a Marine in Vietnam and protested the war "after he had done his duty." Why do presidential candidates still have to justify decisions made in their youth nearly four decades ago?

Perhaps Vietnam still haunts because Americans cannot stand losing, and America has never accepted losers in any of its wars, except those who came from my country. We refugees remind them of loss every time they see us.

The politicians were blamed first. Richard Nixon held the U.S. Congress responsible. The U.S. military was once blamed, but that perception has changed over time. To this day, Gen. William Westmoreland still faults the press for undoing his war efforts. Finally, it has become much easier just to point the finger at the South Vietnamese, for those once in charge are now either too old to refute the accusation or they are dead; their children are too busy with daily life, dealing with their own generational and adjustment issues. Who else is left to blame?

FOX News pundit Bill O'Reilly compared the Iraqis with the South Vietnamese during an interview with President George W. Bush on September 27, 2004.

o'REILLY: The South Vietnamese didn't fight for their freedom, which is why they don't have it today.

BUSH: Yes.

o'REILLY: Do you think the Iraqis are going to fight for their freedom?

BUSH: Absolutely.

---

*Vietnamization referred to the process of turning the war back to the South Vietnamese military as U.S. troops withdrew. In 1965 the United States had taken over conduct of the war.

To me, the most hurtful comment came from retired U.S. Army Col. David Hackworth, the nation's most decorated soldier in Korea and Vietnam, in a 2002 interview with *Proceedings.*

> We failed to understand that we couldn't rely on the Afghan supporting force, which was a basic lesson out of Vietnam. We never trusted the South Vietnamese on an operation. If it were an anvil-and-hammer operation, we'd never put the South Vietnamese as the hammer or the anvil, because they wouldn't be there for the job.

> The United States will end up blaming the Iraqis, too. (General John Abizaid, chief of U.S. Central Command, has repeatedly stated that "Iraqis must depend less on the U.S. military, even if that means a bigger risk of violence in coming months. After all, it's their country, it's their future.")

At least in Vietnam, the United States was *asked* to come help. We will never know what would eventually have happened to Vietnam had this country stayed out of Southeast Asia. General Douglas MacArthur's principle, "Always avoid a land war in Asia," was violated and another intervention was embarked upon.

My father's briefcase had been sitting at the bottom of the closet collecting dust and waiting for time to heal my lingering sense of loss. I had put it away to forget, to stop tormenting myself for wasting the short time that I had him back, to help me to move on with my life. Yet there remained an occasional urge for me to riffle through it since he'd left us.

I actually believed my father would escape another brush with early death. For most of his life, he seemed invincible, in war and in captivity and in poverty. Maybe he ran out of lives.

The lock on the briefcase no longer worked; there were no more secrets to hide. The rusty clasps swung open like a coffin door unlocking, inviting me back to his past, to a stack of loose papers, layered on top of weathered brown, unclasped manila folders. Old letters with dry ink like scrimshaw across the onion paper dating back decades. Some were written to him, others were in his hand. I quickly perused several addressees; many letters came from one address in Ho Chi Minh City. I was tempted to try to find details of his life away from my mother, my sisters, and me. I wanted to know because, now that he was gone again, I was ready.

But I hesitated. I felt his stoic gaze on me. A blown-up wood-framed photo of my father as a handsome lieutenant dressed in VNAF service blues stands atop my bookshelf. He is in America but he is not smiling. He was here to learn how to fly while his family was back in a war zone. Next to his portrait lies the neatly folded Republic of Vietnam (RVN) flag given to me at his funeral. I recall being a schoolboy in Saigon, beaming with pride, standing tall with my classmates, singing "Quốc Ca," the national anthem, watching that flag run up the wooden pole before classes began. The words called for citizens to rise up, to prepare for the liberation; it had been written in 1945, when the French were still seeking to reclaim an empire in Indochina. It is still played, and sung tearfully, at Vietnamese expatriate gatherings worldwide. We have not forgotten. RVN flags still flutter at official state and local functions, much to the dismay of the present Consulate General of Vietnam in San Francisco.

An open box with incense sticks ready to be lit stands near the flag. A chevron-shaped pair of silver pilot's wings rests next to an empty bowl reserved for food and fruit offerings to Confucian gods.

I tried to read through the private letters, the ones written to him by the "other" woman and the mother of his second son and my half-brother An, but I could not do it. A dead man deserves his privacy. I put the letters back in the envelope where they remain.

I looked through the stack of loose papers. A résumé simply listed his job history as a teacher's aide and aircraft mechanic—no mention of his pilot career. Two blue passports, one granted by the Socialist Republic of Vietnam, the other from the United States, stuck to each other like two squares of rice paper. Near the bottom of the attaché case was a crumpled document with the words "Camp Nam Ha" at the top left. It stated his 1987 release date from captivity (for the alleged "crimes" of fighting against the people and for "befriending America, the Enemy").

Some of his paperwork winded me; the emotional power of paper and words was too raw for me to absorb. The first time I saw the internment documents I couldn't believe he had kept them. Why would someone want to hold on to those memories of suffering, those "reminders of failures," as he called them.

Several times I asked him what he did in the war. He kept his counsel, but in the notes I found years later, he had repeatedly scribbled: "Why do you want to know what I did in the war? Who wants to know?" He reached out to me from the grave, reasserting his right to silence.

I found several versions, both handwritten and typed, of a single letter like
the one below.

Dear Son,

   *You must know how much it means to me when you decided to give me a
chapter in your book. It will be written by a former South Vietnamese Air
Force pilot in D- English. If it doesn't matter to you what I did was a failure,
then I will tell you some stories of the past. All I've been doing is to get along
with all of you. Things have changed. No one can estimate to what extent. I
was a coward. For you guys see me become a loser, my old combat friends will
see me with another eye.*

   *All I can tell you now that it was fear and shame of what I thought. I was
just lucky that I didn't have my picture posted on the wooden frame displayed
along with the other officers in the Airborne Division, Marines at the roundup
point in front of Ben Thanh Market after April 1975.*

   *This is the only chance to tell about the old days of what I felt, thought, re-
membered of what I went through to you or anyone else who wishes to know
of the past in the Vietnam War. Another reason, either simple coincidence or
you may call it destiny, is you're in the same Marine unit that I used to fly
support for and was rescued by in the early days of the U.S. involvement in
Vietnam.*

   *What the hell did I fight in the war for? Was it for a better living? Nah, it
wasn't. My monthly wage was half of those who drove a Lambretta tricycle in
downtown Saigon. An American will spend that amount in Vietnamese pi-
asters in one night at the Continental Palace Hotel on drinks and girls. It was
still better than the troops and families defending an outpost with steamed rice
and fish sauce.*

   *It was not a war between North and South Vietnam. It was part of the
Cold War. It must not be forgotten that a war had been going on for 21 years
in a very small country at that time with no name on the world map.*

   *What I did in the war was a failure, don't you think? Who wants to know
about us? No one wants to hear about the Vietnam War no more. Everything
involved is degrading . . . the Communist leader slamming his shoes on the
desk at the UN meeting, colonels repairing bicycles in the streets, lieutenant
colonels selling sweet black bean soup.*

   *I am sorry I had taken offense. There is no more sense of getting angry
now. Twenty years have gone by.*

Dear Son, that is quite a big question you gave me. Who cares? Give the old man a break!
—*Pham Van Hoa, 1995*

I sorted through the rest of the remaining loose papers, finally fingering a thick vellum certificate, worn out along its folds with broken gold borders lining the formal calligraphy. None of my U.S. Marine awards even come close to resembling this one, I thought. I immediately noticed the signature of President Nguyen Van Thieu at the bottom right. Even though I have not had any formal education in my native language for years, I could still decipher and appreciate the significance of the award.

"Bao Quoc Huan Chuong. National Order of Vietnam, Fifth Class, awarded on January 28, 1968, to First Lieutenant Pham Van Hoa."*

Two audiocassettes mailed to me by my Vietnam veteran friend and journalist Bernie Edelman rest at the bottom of the briefcase. I played the first one and leaned back on my chair. My father's voice came to life as if he were in the room, sharing his life the way I had always hoped. Maybe this was his way of opening up, able to communicate with a stranger, a veteran like Bernie, even though their paths had never crossed in Vietnam.

I had to hit the stop button twice.

On the tape, my father paused and his voice cracked noticeably, answering the questions posed by Bernie for a book on the Vietnam War. I had to clench my teeth and kept swallowing.

"The U.S. Marines [later] had their own Cobra gunships," my father's voice intoned. "They didn't trust us, the South Vietnamese fighters. But we still went on an operation called Do Xa. D.O.X.A. We were on airborne alert. The helicopters didn't have enough firepower, so they requested support from us. I went in and got hit, and I crashed."

Through my years of studying Marine Corps and Vietnam War history, I had never even heard of Do Xa.

I immediately powered up the computer and Googled "Do Xa." Several search results popped up. I clicked on the one headlined, "Do Xa Troop Insert by the Purple Foxes," and scrolled through pictures of Marines and their relic choppers. A narrative of the assault on Do Xa crowded the web pages, recalling a battle scene from 1964. I continued reading until I came across

---

*The National Order was South Vietnam's highest military decoration.

two pictures of a downed A-1 Skyraider fighter-bomber. A chill went up my spine as I stared in disbelief. The memories of the stench of oily smoke and the thwop-thwop of my Sea Knight helicopter rotors over Kuwait forced themselves into the present, and I transported myself back forty years. I went back to a time when my father flew in another war, supporting the U.S. troopers and the ARVN.

CHAPTER 4

FIGHTER PILOT

A FLIGHT OF FOUR PROPELLER-DRIVEN T-28S CIRCLED OVER-
head before landing on Danang's asphalt runway.
Four young VNAF pilots proudly stepped out of their aircraft,
the core of the newly formed 2d Fighter Squadron (2d FS). They sported
cowboy hats; their flight suits had the new squadron patch emblazoned with
a growling tiger centered on a white five-pointed star. (The squadron's call
sign was Phi Ho or Flying Tigers.) Each had a .38-caliber pistol on his hip.
Flight leader Tuong had dark suntanned skin; his call sign was Tuong "Muc"
or "Inky." Si was one of the tallest pilots in the VNAF, whose call sign was Si
"Co" or "Stork." Round-faced Long was slightly heavy, Long "Heo" or
"Piggy." Then there was my father, Hoa "Diên" or "Crazy." (While in flight
school in the United States in the late 1950s, my father earned his call sign
due to his penchant for brawling.)

For the next fifteen days, the flight would be providing quick-response
close air support* for the northern region of South Vietnam, I Corps.

By order of Air Support Operation Center 1 (ASOC 1), arriving VNAF
pilots had to report to a U.S. intelligence officer immediately after landing. A
USAF first lieutenant, the "IO," was in his comfortable and cool air-
conditioned office. My father had a difficult time understanding why his detachment had to dictate a postflight intelligence report, especially to a U.S.
officer not in his chain of command.

"Five structures destroyed, five damaged, casualties unknown. Ordnance

---

*In late 1961, USAF advisers (known as "co van") arrived in South Vietnam. A detachment called
Farm Gate helped stand up the 2d FS at Nha Trang. U.S. pilots also flew combat missions, in viola-
tion of the 1954 Geneva Accords that had divided Vietnam into two countries.

expended—two cluster bombs, two 100-pound bombs." The IO was never pleased with that simple a report. He often asked with a doubtful and mocking attitude, "How do you know that's ten total?"

"That's what we estimated before we left the area," my father promptly replied, shifting under the weight of the parachute, life raft, clipboard with maps, gunbelt, helmet, and survival gear that all pilots had to wear. "We know how to count from 1 to 100 in Vietnamese, French, and English!"

"How can you be sure of your postflight reports?" the IO asked. It was clear he didn't believe the pilots. It was beyond his comprehension that they could really bomb their own country and people. It wasn't a problem so much of language but of trust. Neither the IO nor my father knew that the numbers were being sent back to the Pentagon for U.S. Secretary of Defense Robert McNamara. His "whiz kids" would crunch the data into pie charts and statistics that may have made sense at the Ford Motor Company but not in Vietnam.

Officially, the VNAF pilots were permitted to use the U.S. facilities while deployed at the air base, but their first time in the mess hall was not pleasant.

"Who let the Vietn'ese guys in here?"

My father immediately stopped and put down his food tray. He couldn't tell who yelled out the insult. The USAF airmen all stared at him and the other Vietnamese pilots. He tried to keep his cool, his voice under control. By now he was used to this condescending attitude; it reminded him of his days in the United States when he had trained there.

Since the T-28, an old trainer, had an empty seat in the back, my father offered the IO (not a pilot) a chance to see the real war up close. Taking unauthorized passengers on combat missions had been forbidden by the squadron commander, but my father wanted this officer to have something to talk about back home before the end of his tour. The IO came to the flight line the next morning, dressed in sharply starched fatigues and clutching his camera. He wore a gunbelt and survival equipment. After a complete briefing of safety and bailout procedures they took off. The officer was thrilled to see the beautiful countryside, something he may not have seen before. Then he got airsick and threw up all over the backseat. The flight quickly came to an end. It remains unclear whether what the IO observed on that flight was ever incorporated into a Pentagon briefing.

Most of the 2d FS missions revolved around close air support for the ARVN and prestrike sorties for U.S. Marine Corps helicopters ferrying ARVN troops. Circling overhead, the helicopters would quickly spiral down to insert the troops before the VC could flee. Along with the 1st FS, the VNAF fighters would strike suspected VC outposts in coordination with an airborne forward air controller (FAC).

American involvement, even at this early stage, meant that Vietnamese pilots had to adopt to the fighting style of their new allies. The lessons learned from the French in their 1945–1954 fight against the Viet Minh had no place in the new paradigm.

For the ARVN, that meant depending on fire support (especially air power), heliborne operations, and a bottomless supply chain. The "American" way of fighting had proved its successes on the battlefields of World War II, and in Korea. Yet the application of firepower would prove not to work in Southeast Asia. Regardless, for South Vietnam, accepting U.S. military and economic aid meant that was the "only" way.

It was also in the interest of Vietnamese officers to "please" their U.S. advisers. As former Premier Ky later observed in his memoir *Buddha's Child,* "When advisers went home, they usually received the highest decoration, a medal that only their Vietnamese counterpart was in a position to recommend. Such decorations were important to careers, so many American advisers promoted their own interests by reporting that an ARVN general was terrific and ran a crack unit."

At the battalion and squadron levels, relations between U.S. advisers and their South Vietnamese counterparts proved to be less self-serving. But at a high level, this two-way denial would keep the military status quo as well as work to increase South Vietnam's dependence on the United States (until the fall of Saigon).

In January 1963 there was a skirmish south of Saigon at the village of Ap Bac, resulting in the shooting down of several U.S. Army helicopters. U.S. advisers were highly critical of their ARVN counterparts for ignoring the recommendation to attack to relieve a besieged unit. That failure led to the death of a U.S. Army captain.

At about the same time, my parents, after years of an off-and-on relationship, finally married. My father (when not flying missions) was a frequent and debonair fixture of Saigon nightlife and could not have been more different from my mother. A quiet college graduate, she preferred teaching during the day and reading books at night. There would be no honeymoon, since my father immediately returned to his squadron and my mother promptly moved in with her new in-laws. (They didn't charge her rent.)

In an attempt to confuse the VC, the VNAF renamed the 1st FS as the

514th and the 2d FS became the 516th. The older T-28s, showing their age, began shedding their wings during bombing runs. They had been designed as trainers, not built for the stresses of routine bombing and strafing, so the decision was made to convert the 516th FS to Skyraiders as well as to move the squadron north to Danang. Fortunately for my father, he picked a number from a hat and was transferred to the 514th FS in Bien Hoa, where he would be closer to my mother and my sister living in Saigon.

In 1960, the U.S. Navy delivered the first of thirty single-seat, AD-6 Skyraiders (also known as A-1H, "ADs," "Able Dogs," and "Spads") to replace the aging F-8s of the 1st FS. Six VNAF students, all experienced F-8 pilots, were sent to the U.S. Naval Air Station at Corpus Christi, Texas, to undergo transition training. The Skyraider was the only tactical fixed-wing aircraft used by U.S. forces and those of South Vietnam simultaneously during the war. At that time, U.S. Navy pilots were still flying the Skyraiders off aircraft carriers. The U.S. Marines had traded in their Skyraiders for jets a few years after the Korean conflict.

The Skyraider carried 8,000 pounds of ordnance, more than the four-engine B-17 of World War II fame. It had four 20mm cannons on its wings. Powered by a 2,700-horsepower engine and a 14-foot, 4-bladed propeller, the aircraft cruised at 320 knots. Long viewed as the finest close air–support aircraft ever built, the lumbering Skyraider would become the airplane most closely identified with the VNAF: with over 350 delivered between 1960 and 1972, South Vietnam's young air force had finally upgraded its offensive capabilities to meet the increasingly deadly VC. The VNAF pilots nicknamed the Skyraider *Trau Dien* or "Crazy Water Buffalo," an appropriate airplane for my father, "Crazy" Hoa.

Soon after my father joined the 514th, a party was thrown at the Bien Hoa officers' club for USAF Maj. J. Stalling, who would soon be going back to the States after completing his one year advisory tour. American and Vietnamese pilots celebrated together with vast quantities of "7th Fleet" booze (89 proof American whiskey) and, brought in at the last minute, "shoum shoum," the local white-rice brandy. Everyone had a good time.

As the camaraderie between USAF and VNAF pilots steadily improved not all cultural gaps could be bridged. Two of the chief complaints against the VNAF pilots were that they flew too little at night and slacked off during the siesta between noon and 3 p.m. The fact that many VNAF pilots could go home at night to their families didn't help matters.

But some understood. A USAF colonel commented in a 1965 *Aviation*

Week & Space Technology article: "I don't blame them for taking their siestas and holidays. We come here for a year, and then we go home. For these guys, there is no end in sight; not even the prospect of an R&R (rest & relaxation) leave in Hong Kong."

Another adviser empathized, "They [the VNAF] take their siestas all right, but, fortunately for us, so do the VC."

Late one afternoon, on his third day in-country, USAF Capt. Clark James arrived at the 514th FS wearing a natty tan class B 505 uniform with short sleeves. He fit the popular image of a West Point graduate—short cropped hair, close shave, heavily starched shirt, and mirror-shiny shoes. No one in the squadron recognized James, since he hadn't attended the going-away party for his predecessor.

As the tropical sun sank below the *nipa* palms and the heat let up, my father and another 2d lieutenant, Tien, stepped outside the operations room. They constituted one of two standby ground-alert crews for the afternoon in case a mission was laid on. They watched as ground maintenance personnel loaded bombs onto the Skyraiders down the flight line. As James strolled up full of confidence, they both knew right away that he was Major Stalling's replacement. They also could tell James was a very young U.S. officer.

After a formal salute nobody relaxed. James, the new adviser, seemed to be bothered by what he saw.

"Do you think there are no more VC?" he asked.

My father and Tien looked at each other in disbelief. My father knew right away that the new adviser was ready for action, eager to get involved, and his arrogance would be tested soon enough (pilots usually waited a few days after arriving to adjust to jet lag). Just before dark a new flight schedule was published for the next day. My father walked down to the squadron operations officer's office to personally bring the good news.

"Sir, Captain James should get his familiarization flight first thing tomorrow."

In Saigon, meanwhile, President Ngo Dinh Diem's popularity had declined. The Binh Xuyen, Cao Dai, and Hoa Hoa religious sects opposed his favoritism toward Catholics, and so chaos erupted. In protest, a Buddhist monk doused himself with gasoline and immolated himself. Malcom Browne, an Associated Press (AP) reporter, captured the shocking image later seen worldwide. In November 1963, President Diem and his brother Nhu were murdered in a coup widely believed by the Vietnamese to have been backed by President Kennedy. A number of VNAF fighter planes attacked the presidential compound in Saigon in support of the coup. (In February 1962, two Skyraiders had bombed the Presidential Palace in another coup attempt.) Three weeks later, former Marine Corps marksman Lee Harvey Oswald fatally shot Kennedy in Dallas. Both shooters, Oswald and an ARVN major who killed Diem, were murdered soon after their crimes. Later, after Senator Robert F. Kennedy was fatally shot in 1968, talk spread among superstitious South Vietnamese for years about an evil curse on the Kennedys for the murders of Diem and Nhu: two brothers for two brothers, one president for another, the spooky incantation was uttered.

Increase in violence against the government and civilians and subsequent coups in South Vietnam led to President Lyndon B. Johnson's decision to send combat troops less than eighteen months later.

After the 1963 coup, the 514th FS received another adviser, Maj. Richard Howard. At fifty, he was older than the other advisers, who tended to be in their late twenties or early thirties. It was only when U.S. Secretary of Defense McNamara visited Vietnam in March 1964 that the pilots of the 514th realized that Howard was part of the specific precautions put in place to thwart the coup-happy VNAF.*

During a squadron meeting, the Vietnamese commanding officer proudly declared, "Today we get rid of McNamara!" What he meant was that McNamara's visit was coming to an end and that he was leaving Vietnam, but the literal translation sounded as if the VNAF pilots were planning to do "something." Right after the meeting, Howard ran to the phone to make a call and soon after, all aircraft were grounded at Bien Hoa for two hours. No one was allowed off base and, reportedly, there was a bad traffic jam at Tan Son Nhut Air Base in Saigon as well. Somebody must have been afraid of another unauthorized mission by the VNAF.

*My father never took part. He didn't belong to the military-political inner circle.

CHAPTER 5

SKYRAIDER DOWN

FROM THE LONE 7,800-FOOT RUNWAY AT THE OLD FRENCH barracks in Danang, it took from just ten to forty-five minutes to fly to the Demilitarized Zone, or DMZ, depending on whether it was in a jet fighter or a helicopter. Located forty miles south of Hue City, Danang would later become a major offloading point for the U.S. military machine, especially for Marines. With Khe Sanh to the northwest and China Beach just east, this was the I Corps, soon to become the second-bloodiest killing field in the Marines' history. And in 1964 the bleeding had begun in earnest.

Major John Braddon, USMC, thirty-four years old, arrived in Vietnam in January 1964, as part of Marine Medium Helicopter Squadron 364, or HMM-364. He was among the 16,000 or so U.S. advisers of all ranks and races who were sent to help in the war effort. He left his wife, Jean Anne, and four young children behind in Santa Ana, California.

HMM-364 flew twenty-four ugly but reliable single-engine CH-34 Sea Horse helicopters. The squadron had fifty pilots (nearly twice the size of present-day units) and over 200 Marines. The Marines came to train the VNAF on helicopter tactics that had been honed in Korea a decade earlier. The intention was to turn the helicopters over to the VNAF upon leaving Vietnam. Higher headquarters had made a premature announcement that all Marines would depart by June, the month that the United States was planning to end all direct participation in Vietnam.

Like most American advisers, Braddon knew his job and did it well, but he had mixed feelings about his Vietnamese charges. He told his Marines, "These are good Vietnamese guys. They don't speak the same language as we do. But they're members of our squadron, and we're going to treat them that way."

But ARVN soldiers had a shaky reputation. Braddon remembered some of them running back into his helo as soon as he had dropped them off in a landing zone (LZ). At times his crew chief had literally kicked them out of

Flight of two VNAF A-1 Skyraiders from the 514th FS, 1963. (Wayne Mutza Collection)

2d Lt. Pham Van Hao, VNAF Skyraider pilot, 1964. (Courtesy of U.S. Air Force)

the chopper. "Occasionally they would shoot at us as we lifted off," he re-called.

On April 27, 1964, HMM-364 was ordered to lift a battalion of ARVN soldiers into a VC stronghold known as Do Xa, south of the Ashau Valley and fifteen miles northwest of Quang Ngai. Held by the VC for a decade after the fall of Dien Bien Phu, it served as a "gate" for communist forces to enter central Vietnam via the Ho Chi Minh trail which ran along the border with Laos. Brigadier General Nguyen Don, the Viet Cong commander for central Vietnam, based his headquarters there.

ARVN Col. Nguyen Van Hieu,* the chief of staff for the II Corps commanding general, led the planning of Operation Sure Wind 202. The assault on Do Xa would become the deadliest heliborne assault made before U.S. combat troops arrived in any appreciable numbers. The U.S. Army provided five UH-1B Huey gunships to provide escort for the large Marine flight, which included two additional VNAF H-34s. The entire flight would ren-

---

*Hieu became a two-star general and a division commander in 1968. One of the better ARVN generals, he was mysteriously assassinated a few weeks before the fall of Saigon.

dezvous to refuel and load at the Quang Ngai airfield, 100 miles south of Danang, before proceeding to Do Xa.

U.S. Army Capt. Jack "Woody" Woodmansee, a 1956 West Point graduate and classmate of "Stormin' Norman" Schwarzkopf, was in his final month of a one-year tour in Vietnam. As leader of the Huey gunship detachment Dragon Flight, Woodmansee had clocked his share of combat time escorting marine helicopter units based in Danang. Formed in December 1963, his unit had also supported the U.S. advisory teams in I Corps and two ARVN divisions. At that time the U.S. Marine Corps didn't have armed helicopters; its doctrine called for fixed-wing aircraft for escort, but there were none in Vietnam.

At Danang, my father landed his Skyraider fighter-bomber on the western end of the runway. He had flown up with his wingman from Bien Hoa for the joint heliborne mission with the U.S. Marines. He had done this many times before, flying with the 2d FS (T-28s) and his current unit, the 514th FS.*

The weather had been perfect on that spring day as Braddon and his Marine flight flew to Do Xa. Braddon was the leader of a two-aircraft flight to act as search-and-rescue birds, ready to pick up downed aircrew members if necessary. He had a clear view of the entire flight from his position high above the large formation.

Approaching the LZ, Woodmansee's gunship flight raced 2 miles ahead and performed "recon by fire," stirring up antiaircraft fire from the hidden VC below. Red tracers from VC machine guns crisscrossed beneath the Hueys as their door gunners fired back—immediately silencing several gun positions. The lead helicopter crew chief threw out smoke grenades to mark hostile fire positions for the other four gunships as they emptied their Emerson kits, four 7.62mm machine guns controlled by the copilots, and two pods of seven rockets each. The crew chiefs and door gunners fired M14 rifles and tossed hand grenades from treetop height. This large H-34 flight was on its final approach when Woodmansee got on the radio and warned them off. "Give us some time to clean up this mess!" he shouted. The LZ was still too hot.

After another pass Dragon Flight was running out of ammunition, while the Marine flight leader was pushing to land the attacking infantry force. Woodmansee hoped to convince the marine pilots to fly back to Quang Ngai

*At the time, he also helped stand up the 518th FS, the VNAF's third Skyraider unit.

so that Dragon Flight could rearm itself. He really wanted to talk the Marines out of going into the original LZ altogether: almost out of ammunition, all he could do was call the FAC to have the VNAF Skyraiders pound the LZ while the helos flew back to Quang Ngai.

As soon as Woodmansee could see the LZ he knew it was suicide. Enemy guns were alongside mountain ridges surrounding the LZ on three sides, with only the westerly approach open. Numerous caves could be seen in the mountainside cliffs. The machine guns were emplaced a few hundred feet up the sides of these cliffs.

Woodmansee flew close to the VC gunners, no more than about 30 feet above them. He could see dun-colored pith helmets and green uniforms, unlike the black pajama-clad VC guerrillas he had expected. They had readied their shoulder-sling-mounted .50-caliber machine guns with concentric gun sights like the ones Woodmansee had seen on World War II ships. He expended what ammunition he had left to mark the LZ for the FAC. "OK, right where the smoke is, there's a .50-cal and a bunch of guys in a tunnel," Woodmansee said, and then pulled off to watch the aerial bombardment. He had the best view in the house as the first Skyraider began its steep dive.

"I got it," exclaimed the FAC, orbiting overhead in a small L-19 Bird Dog observation plane.

My father had been flying a narrowing gyre above the choppers when his flight of Skyraiders got the radio call to attack. He turned his plane toward the LZ and threw the switches to arm his bombs and guns. Rolling into a deep 40-degree attack dive, he let loose several 20mm cannon bursts and unleashed two 250-pound bombs. They struck the bottom of the hill to the north of the LZ but missed their intended targets. The VC gunners greeted him with a barrage: tracers flew like red fireflies over his white aircraft. Veering off the target, my father wrenched to his left and looked back. He saw the tracers chasing his flight of two planes, the rounds getting closer and closer to their marks.

Hovering safely away from the bomb bursts, Woodmansee told the FAC to move the Skyraiders up the mountainside. It was a tough mission; the VNAF pilots were trying to hit a pinpoint target with "dumb" gravity bombs on the side of a mountain, almost impossible to do under the best circumstances.

My father climbed back to a safer altitude to swallow his fear and make a second pass. The VC machine guns kept firing, taunting him to come back.

He put the stick down, leading the Skyraider into a steeper dive than before, cannons blasting away as communist tracers zinged up again from the ground. This time, another gun across the valley, on the south side, opened up, punching holes in the plane from the engine cowling across the fuselage. The gun could track the Skyraider all the way down its bombing run. Rounds also punctured the wings, and just missed the cockpit area. His bird was on fire. Now he had to make a decision—stay with the aircraft or bail out over "bad guy" territory 15 miles from friendly forces. He didn't have much time or altitude to decide.

Braddon was with the Marine flight when he saw the Skyraiders hit the target. He didn't know where they had come from but he knew the aircrafts' capabilities. (He had himself flown Skyraiders earlier in his career.) As he watched the attack, he saw a Skyraider pull out of its dive, smoke billowing from its engine. The VC guns kept pumping, hoping to finish off the crippled aircraft as it fluttered away from the LZ. Thick black smoke silhouetted the stricken plane against the cobalt sky as its pilot struggled to maintain a level flight path. Braddon immediately pushed his stick to the right and followed the smoke trail and radioed the flight leader that he was breaking off.

Woodmansee figured that Braddon needed an armed escort because they were all flying over enemy territory. He followed Braddon's H-34 and soon there were two U.S. helos chasing their smoking VNAF ally. None of this had been planned or practiced.

The other Skyraider rolled in on top of the VC, who began to scatter from the hills to track my father's plane. They were probably anticipating his parachute descent or his crash-landing nearby. The other Skyraider's pilot made several passes, shooting his 20mm cannons and providing cover while my father's damaged plane quickly descended from 1,000 feet where he had leveled out after his bombing dive.

Inside the cockpit seconds ticked away as it began to fill with smoke. The powerful Skyraider was losing power and altitude fast. As he struggled to see the instruments while controlling the aircraft, my father began to panic—but then his training kicked in. Emergency procedures ran through his mind in the English he had been taught, then quickly translated into action. He reached up and slid back the canopy to allow the smoke to clear. He could see fire emerging from the engine cowling. Behind the flames and surrounding him were hills and rocky terrain crenelated by 8,500-foot peaks. Flames then broke through the firewall and seared his face, scorch-

Hoa's downed Skyraider. Note .50-caliber bullet holes on fuselage. Do Xa, Vietnam, 1964. (Courtesy of Warren R. Smith)

ing his eyebrows. The world through his windshield was growing quickly in size: the engine quit.

Not knowing his exact altitude above the ground, my father decided to stay with the aircraft and dead-stick it to the flattest surface he could find. Thoughts of my pregnant mother and my sister ran through his mind as he quickly went through emergency procedures for engine failure and fire in flight. For the first time since he'd joined the VNAF a decade earlier, he thought he was going to die. He was twenty-eight years old.

He had no clue that U.S. helicopters were following him. He could hear his Vietnamese wingman making Mayday calls when suddenly a dirt airstrip flanked by tall hills appeared to his left. He quickly lowered his flaps to slow his heavy plane, gliding in at over 150 knots. Careful not to stall the aircraft or nose it over, he "slipped" the aircraft, stepping hard on one rudder and pushing the opposite stick to quickly descend so that he wouldn't overshoot his intended landing spot. With the landing gear still up, the Skyraider hit the ground hard, and its large propeller blades wrapped around the cowling before its oversized engine broke away, as designed. The right wing wrapped around a large tree and stopped the aircraft from nosing into an irrigation ditch. My father must have forgotten to lock his seat belts, for he lunged forward on impact: his head struck the dashboard, splitting both his lips, bruising his forehead, and cracking his sunglasses. His left knee hit the lower dashboard, hard.

The Skyraider skidded to a stop, kicking up dirt and smoke. My father quickly climbed out of the cockpit. He was dizzy, and his left leg was throbbing with pain. He could not believe he had survived the crash-landing. Minutes before he was piloting a 22,500-pound metal projectile at 300 knots, the engine's roar and the boom of gunfire deafening him. Now he sat in total silence on a loamy field. The VC who had seen him go down would reach him soon, he thought.

Braddon's H-34, empty except for a copilot, crew chief, and door gunner, had barely been able to keep up with the Skyraider even as it had lost altitude and airspeed. Woodmansee's Huey was even farther behind, hustling along at just ninety knots per hour. Glancing through his dirty windshield for enemy fire from below, Braddon had focused on the smoking Skyraider as it suddenly dropped below his window, disappearing from his view just before it struck the ground, kicking up red dust mixed with the black cloud of its own burning fuel. Braddon had just witnessed his first aerial casualty of the Vietnam War.

Landing his H-34 near the crashed Skyraider, Braddon could see blood on my father's face as he approached the helo under his own power. "The lucky guy made it out," he thought as his crew chief reached out, grabbed the Vietnamese pilot's arm, and pulled him in. No one said anything; the helicopter rotors were too deafening to even try to speak. The Skyraider pilot collapsed on an empty row of canvas seats, and without delay the crew chief radioed Braddon to take off. Not knowing exactly where he was, Braddon immediately lifted up and flew east at maximum airspeed to Quang Ngai. He called the base to inform the medics of an incoming casualty. Woodmansee trailed the H-34. Both U.S. pilots knew there was still much work ahead: to them, the VNAF pilot was done as far as this mission was concerned. The Americans would have no idea of his fate as they dropped him off at Quang Ngai and repositioned their helos for the second attempt on Do Xa.

Back in Saigon my mother held my sister while battling morning sickness.

Her brother came knocking on the door with news that her husband's plane had been shot down over Do Xa a few hours earlier—he did not know whether her husband was dead or alive. She felt dizzy, falling into her brother's arms as he helped her lean back onto a couch. She moaned as pain gripped her stomach.

USAF Air Commando Course, C-123 Class, 1966, Hurlburt Airfield. My father is kneeling in center with bandage on his pinkie. Ho Dang Tri is to his right. (Courtesy of U.S. Air Force)

CHAPTER 6

HERE COMES JOHNNY

My FATHER HAD BEEN FORTUNATE, BUT SO HAD MANY Skyraider pilots who also walked away from crash-landings over the years. It was one tough aircraft, designed to handle heavy enemy fire and hard landings. After Major Braddon dropped him off in Quang Ngai, a VNAF C-47 from my father's old transport group flew him to Danang. He recovered in a military hospital when VNAF commander Nguyen Cao Ky, his former CO in the transport group, was in the area visiting wounded soldiers. (By the spring of 1964, after a few more coups, Ky was on his way to becoming South Vietnam's prime minister.) He saw my father in the hospital and promptly authorized him to be flown back to Saigon to Grall, the top hospital in the country once reserved only for rich Frenchmen. My grandparents and my mother were able to visit him while he recovered nearby instead of in far-off Danang. No medical bill ever came.

But first, upon receiving the news of my father's arrival in Saigon, my mother went to the Tan Son Nhut morgue, looking for his body to identify. In those days, the Vietnamese military had a difficult time notifying families of injured or deceased soldiers: news coming from the front lines was sketchy, often incomplete and sporadic. But the duty officer redirected her to the city, and then her brother drove her to Grall, where they both ran to my father's hospital ward. They found him sitting upright on his bed smoking a cigarette and smiling. He managed to crack a quick joke. His head was wrapped with white bandages, both his legs were covered with dressings. My uncle recalled seeing "Hoa's two white buggy eyes and no brows amid a burned face."

There must have been a reason that I was not born fatherless. After her husband came home from the hospital, my mother kept his bloodstained flight suit for several years in our closet in Saigon. That was it for history. No one ever told us that a U.S. helicopter, a U.S. Marine helicopter no less, had rescued him. I had to put the pieces together forty years later.*

After the crash my father came home from the hospital a different man. Now he snapped at my mother over little things. It seemed to her that the crash had changed him, removing a certain lightness from his character. They argued often, even late into my mother's pregnancy with me.

My father was grounded for several months after his crash, as stipulated by VNAF regulations. No blame was assigned—his downed Skyraider was categorized as a combat loss. Now, for the first time in his career, he had a desk job, and he didn't know how to shuffle military paperwork.

My father earned two Vietnamese Gallantry Crosses and two Air Gallantry Crosses while flying close air–support missions, and his unit won the U.S. Presidential Unit Citation (PUC), the first awarded to a South Vietnamese military organization. The citation is the highest U.S. military unit award, given to units with outstanding performance in action.†

But when my father returned to the Skyraider cockpit, he wasn't the same aggressive pilot he had been. He was uncomfortable, his hands trembled on engine startups, yet he managed to keep his jitters to himself, at least for a while. Somehow, he was selected to join the 83d Special Operations Group (SOG), along with his 2d FS buddies Ly Ngoc An and Tran Ba Hoi. The unit was under the direct control of General Ky. Ultimately, the 83d SOG was to carry out air strikes against North Vietnam. Trained by the U.S. Navy in naval commando tactics, SOG pilots were to fly northward at night over the South China Sea at an altitude of 200 feet then turn at certain checkpoints and head toward land, above the 17th parallel. Practice missions were flown at night and often completed just before dawn. The war was expanding, and the growing number of VNAF fighter pilots would do their share by striking Ho Chi Minh's forces in their homeland.

---

*For his bravery at Do Xa, Braddon won a Silver Star and his copilot received a Distinguished Flying Cross, the first time that Marine Corps aviators had received such decorations in Vietnam. Woodmansee was recommended by HMM-364 for a Navy Cross, but Marine brass quickly disapproved. They apparently did not want to award the first Navy Cross in Vietnam to an "army" aviator. Both officers returned for second combat tours in Vietnam. Braddon became commanding officer of VMFA-334, an F-4 fighter squadron. Woodmansee spent a year as a White House fellow before going back to Vietnam to command another helicopter unit. He retired as a three-star general.

†In the Marine Corps, no unit would earn a PUC after the Vietnam War until the I Marine Expeditionary Force took Baghdad in April 2003 as part of Operation Iraqi Freedom.

On August 5, 1964, the USS *Maddox* incident* in the Tonkin Gulf led President Lyndon B. Johnson to authorize direct air strikes against North Vietnam.

Every combat flier in Vietnam, Vietnamese or U.S., wanted to take part in the retaliatory strike against North Vietnam. While the VNAF fliers were told that their propeller-driven aircraft wouldn't stand a chance against North Vietnamese antiaircraft defense system, the U.S. Navy continued sending its Skyraiders into North Vietnam from 7th Fleet carriers operating on Yankee Station. VNAF Skyraider pilots would only get their chance the following spring, after USAF, U.S. Navy, and U.S. Marine pilots had their opportunity. The fighting in the air was starting to shift to the Americans even before ground combat troops would arrive.

On September 27, 1964, the Year of the Dragon, I came into this world in a small room in Saint Paul's Hospital in downtown Saigon. A few weeks later, on a dark night over the Gulf of Tonkin, my father flew a training mission alongside An's wings. They were part of a large flight of Skyraiders practicing commando raids against makeshift North Vietnamese targets. With 200 feet on the radar altimeter, they had plenty of nose-up trim, the small aerodynamic adjustments that took pressure off the control stick. Airspeed exceeded 300 knots. There was no terrain to use for checkpoints. Over the black, horizonless ocean, navigation was by time and distance, clock and map.

The pilots' eyes feverishly flashed between the maps on their kneeboards strapped to their thighs, and their instruments—especially the altimeter. No help came from the dimmed cockpit lighting. Little chatter took place between airplanes. Pilots had to focus for hours and tensions ran high during the flight. Some pilots kept a death grip on the controls, the kind that held the stick so tight that knuckles would lock. The death grip could lead to overcontrolling the aircraft, and at low altitudes, pushing a stick forward just a quarter-inch for a few seconds would mean instant death.

My father was already tense before he got into his plane. Maybe he had gone back to flying too soon after his crash; maybe he was worn down by the war; maybe his mind was on my mother, my sister, and me. At the time little was known of the 83d SOG. Their pilots stood out, dashing young men wear-

---

*Controversy has raged for decades over whether the USS *Maddox* was actually attacked by North Vietnamese gunboats, as Johnson claimed, or whether the "attack" was simply promoted by his administration to justify his war aims.

ing black flight suits with fancy unit patches and polka dot purple scarves. All were volunteers, somewhat cocky, and believed they were invincible.

Their camouflage Skyraiders had no national insignia but bore the words *than phong,* or "kamikaze" (Japanese "divine wind") inscribed on both sides. Their leader, Ky, wore his signature lavender scarf.

According to An, on that fateful night my father heard an abnormal engine noise, louder than usual. Nothing seemed right. The plane was shaking. He couldn't tell if his engine was about to quit. (No one was talking on the radios—not even the U.S. advisers.) That engine noise increased. He was shaking by then, and sweat formed on his forehead, dripping down his neck. The flight was 50 miles off the coast of South Vietnam; the mission still had another forty-five minutes to go.

Finis. Xong roi. Done.

He pulled up from 200 feet and climbed to 3,000, took a deep breath, and tried to collect himself. He still had to fly back to Bien Hoa. He radioed his flight leader and dialed in the Bien Hoa military navigational beacon. An pulled up as well and quietly led the lonely flight of two back to land. After nearly three years of continuous combat, my father's days as a fighter pilot had come to an end.

Later in the Vietnam War, what befell my father would come to be called post-traumatic stress disorder (PTSD), a clinical psychosis that still afflicts tens of thousands of U.S. veterans. All he knew was that, for the time being, he couldn't fly anymore. For my father, flying was like riding a tiger: if he got off its back, he would be eaten alive. So he just stayed on and kept riding.

By mid-1964, ARVN losses had exceeded 13,000, on track to pass the 21,000 deaths the previous year. Civilian casualties hovered near 250,000.* With such losses, it was uncertain whether the South Vietnamese would be able to hold their own against a growing insurgency. I can't even imagine how life would have turned out had those young Americans not come to our aid. On the other hand, was it worth all the death and destruction seen in the following decade when the outcome may already have been inevitable?

---

*South Vietnam's casualty statistics are from *Street Without Joy* by Bernard Fall.

CHAPTER 7

NO ONE-YEAR TOURS

N OT MANY KNEW THE REASON WHY MY FATHER LEFT the fighter community. The 83d SOG's executive officer reassigned him to the Tactical Air Control Center in Saigon, but my father knew his career goal to command a squadron was in jeopardy. His superior was Col. Nguyen Ngoc Loan, one of the rare senior pilots who flew combat missions with the 514th as well. Loan, a French Air Force Academy graduate, was one of the few truly admired VNAF officers. He was small in stature but a tough individual who took a liking to my father.

On February 8, 1965, the VNAF made national history: General Ky handpicked twenty-four pilots from various squadrons and led the first air strike into North Vietnam. In this raid every Skyraider took hits and one was shot down. The mission boosted VNAF morale, and more important, improved the reputation of the VNAF among U.S. leaders. The Vietnamese would be rewarded with more aircraft and training.

By then my father had started to miss flying, and regretted his decision to quit a few months earlier even though it was made during a busy time in his newly married life. He wished he had flown north with his buddies. He asked for a transfer back to the Skyraider community, but it was denied. Colonel Loan, who also flew the C-47 to keep up his flight hours, made the decision that would restart my father's career, restoring my father's flying status but with one condition: my father had to go back to the C-47. My father was more than happy to oblige, getting up to speed quickly and regaining his aircraft commander status.

The war was evolving rapidly. Operation Rolling Thunder, the bombing of North Vietnam, had begun* and increased VC attacks on U.S. airfields in Danang and Pleiku required added security. Although there were still plenty of ARVN troops on hand to defend the bases, American ground troops were called in.

On March 8, 1965, two battalions of U.S. Marines from the 9th Amphibious Brigade waded ashore unopposed in Danang. Vietnamese girls donning white *ao dai* (traditional silk dress with pants) presented leis to the Marines in front of worldwide press coverage. Bui Diem, chief of staff for South Vietnam's prime minister, was required to write the communiqué "inviting" U.S. troops into South Vietnam—as the Marines were landing. At the time, a Gallup poll reported only one in four Americans thought "sending troops to Vietnam had been a mistake."

Lyndon Johnson wanted to show the North Vietnamese that he was serious, and he thought that the sight of U.S. Marines coming ashore would send a strong signal. That amphibious walk in the park marked the official beginning of the "Americanization" of the war and relegated the South Vietnamese military to the sidelines.

Now the U.S. military's footprints would be everywhere in Vietnam, from the buildup at Tan Son Nhut to Bien Hoa, Cam Ranh Bay to Nha Trang, Danang to Chu Lai. (It took about ten men at these massive facilities to support the one combat "grunt" out in the boonies who did the actual trigger pulling.) Command and control, logistics, supply personnel (known during the war as REMFs—"rear-echelon motherfuckers") made up most of the 3 million Americans who served in Vietnam between 1960 and 1975. Along with the men and materiel came the post exchange (PX), military stores (with surpluses that would end up on the black market), barbershops, bowling alleys, movie theaters, mess halls, and brothels. Certain parts of Vietnam, including Saigon, were transformed into the likes of Olongapo and Subic Bay in the Philippines; tawdry but welcome escapes for the U.S. military personnel (and civilians) and other foreigners.†

U.S. airmen, marines, sailors, and soldiers and the journalists who covered them arrived en masse. Everyone wanted a piece of the action, to get that

---

*The U.S. dropped three times the tons of bombs and used twice the artillery fire power used in all of World War II. Unexploded ordnance and land mines still pose a danger in Vietnam, probably the most bombed country in history.

†Some 80,000 Amerasians were born in Vietnam during the war, many left behind after the fall of Saigon.

combat tour, to send war dispatches from the front lines. Career advancements were on the line, and getting the Vietnam ticket punched was a must. It was the biggest game in town. Civilian contractors erected bases overnight, laid down runways, opened up harbors, paved dirt roads, and made millions in the process. Oversized military vehicles crowded dirty streets and forced civilians off the roads. Many thought it would take six months, maybe a year to "kick some ass, take names, and go home."

In faraway and dangerous outposts, Marine and army infantry (grunts) lived spartanly, often supplied only by helicopter. They occasionally gained a brief rest and recreation (R&R) trip to the rear. With General William Westmoreland's strategy of "search and destroy" while running up "body counts" of dead Viet Cong, the United States was seen as "winning the hearts and minds" if not the war itself. The U.S. Marines practiced their Combined Action Program, where a squad of Marines would live and serve within a village.

Even Australia, Canada, New Zealand, and South Korea eventually sent over 300,000 troops to fight. But more and more U.S. troops joined the war, peaking at 560,000 in 1969.* The personnel policy meant one-year combat tours; individuals rotated into units already in-country. Even though some volunteered for extended or additional tours, the mind-set of these troops and ARVN soldiers unfortunately differed greatly: there was no such thing as a one-year combat tour for the South Vietnamese military.

Western journalists landed well before the U.S. buildup. British author Graham Greene had written *The Quiet American* in 1955, keenly observing the unintended consequences of the arrival of Americans in Indochina. Bernard Fall, a French scholar and writer who had become a U.S. citizen, wrote *Hell in a Small Place* and *Street Without Joy,* notable books about the siege at Dien Bien Phu and the beginning of U.S. involvement in Vietnam. Fall later died while accompanying U.S. Marines on a mission outside Hue. (My father was mentioned in his second book, though not by name. He was in a footnote to history, recorded as, "4 helicopters and one AD-6 [Skyraider] are shot down, 18 other helicopters hit [over Do Xa].")

The American press put its flag up in Saigon, attending the popular routine known as the "five o'clock follies," the bitter name news writers gave to the daily command briefings during the war. The war gave meteoric boosts

---

*It took four years for U.S. forces to reach 560,000. During the 1990 pre–Gulf War buildup, it took just over four months to reach the same number.

to the careers of David Halberstam and Neil Sheehan, two of the most well-known journalists of the era and both Pulitzer Prize winners. Others were CBS newscasters Dan Rather and Morley Safer, who brought home the images of Marines burning the grass-roof village at Cam Ne with their Zippo lighters. Many of today's network news anchors made their brief "I was there" appearances. Some journalists spent as much as five years in Vietnam, like Richard Pyle of AP who became the Saigon bureau chief. His colleague, George Esper, held the record of ten years, finally getting kicked out after the fall of Saigon. The AP had the largest number of journalists covering the war, including Pulitzer winners Peter Arnett and Horst Faas, the photographer.

While I have been grateful for the many articles, books, and news clips generated by this august collection of chroniclers, I wasn't always sure which war they were covering. They certainly received much acclaim, especially considering that many other newsworthy and watershed events were taking place in the United States and the rest of the world during the Vietnam War. What they didn't write about was the war my father and his South Vietnamese colleagues fought or the reign of terror the Viet Cong brought to families like mine.

It took many years after reading many books, but I finally came to this conclusion: American journalists wrote about Americans and America's War in Vietnam for Americans back home. The history of what happened to the South Vietnamese remains in the hands of expatriates, but I don't expect any revisionists to come to our camp thirty years after the war. Careers were made on a certain style of reporting; positions were clearly staked out. Hindsight and regrets would undo everything, so nothing new will change those attitudes, but I am hopeful that future generations of reporters will be more open to different perspectives.

After the Americans arrived the fighting didn't stop for the South Vietnamese. My father continued ferrying troops to the front and hauling supplies to outposts. On many return trips his plane would be full of "silent passengers."

"You know they're there, you know their names. But they don't talk to you. And you can't talk to them," my father recalled.

Tin coffins with dead ARVN soldiers, usually from I Corps (many were picked up at Phu Bai), needed to be flown to Saigon where family members could properly bury them. Some of the corpses had already begun to rot on the tarmac in the broiling sun. Out in the fields the rains would cover the bodies in mud, then later wash away the sludge, exposing the dead to be found. There were so many stacked up; so first come, first out was the policy. The yellow flags with the red stripes were draped over each one.

As the transport planes rose above 8,000 feet or so the pressure changed— in unpressurized aircraft. The gases in the coffins would undo the lids, opening them slowly in gruesome waves. (The crew in back would watch in silence, as if the dead had acknowledged their deed.) Pressure changes speeded the decomposition of the bodies and thus made it difficult for families to identify the remains.

The smell of death got into the ears, hair, nostrils, and flight suits. My father tried stuffing his nostrils with cooking oil, and that helped a bit. But the stench finally was so strong that two or three showers didn't do the trick, and occasionally flight suits had to be thrown away. Yet he never refused a coffin mission.

"When I die, drape my country's flag over my coffin and bury me fast enough before I smell," he once said. My father got his final wish.

In January 1966 my father and several other VNAF pilots and crew members were selected to train in the United States. It would be his second trip to the States. The airmen were to be qualified on the C-123 (although this plane was not to be delivered to the VNAF until 1970) at the Hurlburt Air Commando School in Florida. The fast and new C-123, a twin-engine, short-field transport aircraft that looked like a whale, had replaced the C-47.

The United States was quite different from the one he remembered from his first visit. Now civil rights marches, drugs, and rock and roll music made the headlines; the antiwar movement was under way, and the press reported it daily. My father saw the news every day in his bachelor officers' quarters, and it never failed to predict bad things for South Vietnam's war efforts.

The VNAF crew had come to Hurlburt to learn the newest commando tactics. They were to return to Vietnam to fly covert missions into the north, such as dropping off agents and saboteurs the way the earlier, failed CIA-backed missions had done. Low-level navigation, night missions, parachute drops, and no-communication flights were to be the standard.

My father was definitely "back in the saddle."

By the 1960s there were thousands of nonmilitary South Vietnamese in this country, not counting the war brides. Most had come to study at universities, managing to avoid the draft back home. While American conscientious objectors fled to Canada and Oxford, some South Vietnamese men went to the United States or France. Some opted to remain in the United

States after their studies and several joined the antiwar movement with their new American friends.

It was a difficult nine months for my mother. She had turned thirty, alone with two small children, and was teaching full-time. Luckily, both sides of our families were nearby and both grandmothers and her sisters pitched in. Even though mail took weeks to get from the United States to Vietnam, she received many letters from my father, including numerous Polaroid shots from a new camera that he had bought at the PX. She sent back traditional black-and-white photos of herself and my sister and me at the Saigon zoo and in front of the Continental Palace, another familiar Saigon landmark.

Meanwhile, my father's old friends in the VNAF fighter community were suffering heavy casualties. The 514th FS lost a third of its pilots (nine out of thirty were killed in combat) in 1967 to enemy fire. That was the same rate as a U.S. Navy squadron operating from carriers on Yankee Station. The only time my mother saw my father cry was the night his friend "Stork," the squadron mate from the 2d FS, was shot down and killed. He often attended funeral services, in his uniform, and sometimes gave the bad news to the family and the eulogy at the funeral. (Two of his Lubbock, Texas, classmates also died. The VNAF motto became "Fly until you die.")

His good friend An had a near-fatal mishap while taking off with a full load of bombs for a mission in North Vietnam. Right after taking off from Tan Son Nhut as part of a large strike, An nearly died when his engine blew up. Fighting fire and smoke, he managed to set his Skyraider up for landing when the smoke overwhelmed him. Luckily his wings had been leveled and the impact brought him back to consciousness, and the 500-pound bombs had not yet been armed. (His plane skidded off the runway atop 3,000 pounds of explosives.) An lost a hand, however, and was badly burned. But once again General Ky took care of one of his pilots: he authorized An to be flown to the United States where he received world-class medical care. An entered this country without any immigration paperwork. His flying days were done; he would serve as a military attaché in Washington, D.C., and as a psychological warfare officer until the end of the war. During his recovery his VNAF friends nicknamed him An "Cut" or "One-Hand" An.

In May 1966, a young VNAF pilot from the 516th Fighter Squadron named Nguyen Quoc Dat was shot down on his twenty-sixth mission over North Vietnam. Hit by heavy antiaircraft fire, he too made a crash landing in the sturdy Skyraider and survived. Unfortunately, though, the North Vietnamese nabbed him immediately. They thought he was a U.S. flier, maybe an orphan adopted by a GI, since he was carrying a Texas driver's license from his training days.* And he had on "Jockey" underwear. He was taken to the Hoa Lo prison, or "Hanoi Hilton," where other U.S. POWs were being held. Nicknamed "Max" by fellow POWs, he would earn the distinction of becoming the only VNAF pilot held at Hoa Lo. Later that year, two Americans, Navy Lt. Paul Galanti and Marine Capt. Orson Swindle, would join Max in captivity. Orson was on his 205th, and last, mission, and Galanti his ninety-seventh. Assigned to kitchen and other menial duties, Max would sneak food and medicine to his fellow POWs. The Americans would never forget him. All three reconnected in this country after their release in 1973, thanks partly to the efforts of a Texas billionaire named H. Ross Perot.

Returning to Saigon in September 1966, my father rejoined the 83d SOG as part of its transport group. By then, the 83d had its full complement of Skyraider, transport, helicopter, and observation pilots, all handpicked. Yet before he got to fly into North Vietnam, the unit was disbanded and its pilots ordered back to regular units. Due to infighting and mistrust, President Thieu supposedly didn't want anyone, including Vice President Ky, to have the luxury of a special-operations air unit available for use to possibly unseat him. After all, VNAF pilots had taken part in coups before.

Around this time VNAF Skyraiders stopped flying bombing missions into the north altogether. For one year, they had been ordered to remain south of the 19th parallel, just north of the DMZ (at the 17th parallel), leaving those missions to U.S. pilots. It appeared that U.S. military leaders had grown leery of an overzealous Nguyen Cao Ky taking the war to the north beyond their control.

The Tet offensive of 1968 gave me my first taste of war. I have an early memory of a loud explosion and AK-47 gunfire that disrupted our holiday celebrations. My mother took my sister and me to my aunt's house in a safer part of Saigon. It was reported then that the VC had taken over the city. My father grabbed his personal weapons which he kept at the house, a U.S. M14 rifle, and several pistols, and remained on base for three weeks. We didn't hear from him during that time. Until Tet, and outside of occasional grenade attacks, Saigon had been fairly insulated from the war. Near the DMZ, U.S.

---

*VNAF and other foreign military pilots took their English language training at Lackland Air Force Base in San Antonio.

Marines courageously held their outpost at Khe Sanh, where ten NVA divisions surrounded the hills as the Viet Minh had the French at Dien Bien Phu. In Hue City, U.S. Marines and ARVN troops fought house to house in fierce combat and retook this old imperial capital. (It was then learned that the VC had murdered about 3,000 civilians, even though little of the atrocity was mentioned in Western press.)

On February 1, 1968, at the height of the Tet offensive, Brig. Gen. Loan, by then appointed by Vice President Ky as national police chief and head of the RVN equivalent to the CIA, executed a Viet Cong officer in front of an NBC television crew and an AP photographer named Eddie Adams.* In a fraction of a second, a South Vietnamese military hero would be forever transformed into a barbarous symbol of the war. Even though the Viet Cong had been decimated by ARVN and U.S. forces, Walter Cronkite still declared the war as "unwinnable."

---

*Already a well-revered photojournalist, Adams would win the 1969 Pulitzer Prize in photography. The picture made front-page headlines in leading U.S. newspapers the following day.

CHAPTER 8

ON OUR OWN

RICHARD MILHOUS NIXON'S 1969 INAUGURAL SPEECH CON-spicuously was devoid of the word "Vietnam."

Reducing the U.S. presence had been a Nixon campaign promise, but its corollary, Vietnamization, giving the Vietnamese greater responsibility in prosecuting the war, would take time to achieve. The need for U.S. advisers and B-52 bombardment never really went away. The invasions of Cambodia and Laos (an ARVN-led operation called Lam Son 719) in 1970 and 1971 to cut off North Vietnam's supply chain only created more uproar in the United States and the world over the war in Vietnam.

The VNAF finally received its first jets, in the form of a squadron of supersonic F-5s, and a year later, three squadrons of A-37 attack jets were formed. Maintenance on these high-tech aircraft proved more difficult than that for the propeller-driven planes and the necessary civilian-contractor support ("tech reps"), also used by the U.S. military, ensured dependence on the United States. Other South Vietnamese military services also expanded in capability with the goal of replicating the military philosophy, tactics, and structure of their great ally. Unfortunately, this meant inheriting the associated costs and complexity. By 1970 the South Vietnamese government remained totally supported by, and completely dependent on, the United States.

My father was on flight status for his twelfth consecutive year. While some of his peers had returned to the United States for the U.S. Air Force Command and Staff College, followed by a staff or instructor tour at the national military academy, he stayed and helped start another new unit, the 817th Combat Squadron or *Hoa Long*. The 817th flew the AC-47 "Spooky," or "Fire Dragon," gunship armed with three 7.62mm quick-firing miniguns designed to rain deadly fire onto an enemy on the ground. The USAF had left the gunships behind as it upgraded to the newer C-130 "Spectre" (still in service today in Iraq).

The "Fire Dragons" boosted morale for besieged ARVN troops, flew combat support missions for air base defense, and compiled a combat record comparable with that of U.S. squadrons.

While my father flew missions for the VNAF, my mother took care of my sisters and me at home with the help of a nanny who cooked, cleaned, and did general chores. My family had a television set (a rarity in Vietnam then), and we watched Neil Armstrong walk on the moon in July 1969. The United States seemed so far away, so advanced, and so incredible. And we saw the daily television reporting of the war. I remember reports of South Vietnamese and U.S. soldiers still bravely fighting the Communists and dying in numbers.

My mother would take my older sister and me with her on a Honda moped to school, masterfully dodging the Saigon traffic. We were attending Le Qui Don public school, across the street from the Presidential Palace.

We students were very competitive, and lots of homework was given out. I studied hard after school with the help of my mother at night. I loved to read. I borrowed anything I could, Vietnamese folklore, short stories, anything. One of my favorites was the biography of Saburo Sakai, the World War II Japanese ace who shot down sixty-four Allied planes. He was a descendant of the samurai, the ancient Japanese warrior class. He had risen from the enlisted ranks to become a pilot like my father. After the war, he lived a hard life, as did many Japanese veterans, before becoming a Buddhist acolyte and owner of a small print shop. Sakai also befriended various Americans he once battled in the air. He died in 2000, at age eighty-four, a month before my father passed away.

Looking back, it was strange to cheer for this famous pilot, a former enemy of the United States. I guess his story was familiar; he reminded me of VNAF pilots, Asian men flying prop-driven fighters. My friends enjoyed the book as well, which had been translated into Vietnamese and passed around among military brats. The VNAF pilots in the mid-1960s who had painted their Skyraiders with a "kamikaze" logo must have also read Sakai's book.

I remember watching the American Forces Vietnam Network, the English-language channel for servicemen. Between news broadcasts were episodes of *Twelve O'Clock High* (the television show in the 1960s, not the movie) and *Combat,* another show about World War II. (*Star Trek* was then on the air, too.) The GIs won most of the battles; the airmen braved walls of flak and held tight formations while dropping their bombs, but I didn't take to Captain Kirk or the weird-looking Dr. Spock with his funny ears; outer space adventure was beyond our realm. At the movies, my father and I saw *The Longest Day,* the 1962 epic of the 1944 Normandy landing, with Vietnamese subtitles. My friends and I would make drawings of the amphibious landing in Normandy, with parachutists descending onto the beach and ships congregating offshore. My mother took my sisters and me to two other American-made movies, *The Wizard of Oz,* which frightened me for days, and *Willy Wonka & the Chocolate Factory,* one of my favorites. For children, the universal appeal of candy and chocolate transcended nations and war.

Like every Asian movie buff of those years, I became an avid fan of Bruce Lee movies, spoken in Chinese with Vietnamese subtitles. He looked larger than life, and as a well-muscled Asian movie star with good looks, he became one of the very few "positive" Asians on the big screen. Of course, I didn't know of his previous American television role as Kato, sidekick to the Green Hornet. Later, during my Marine career, I first didn't understand why it seemed that every other Asian-American naval aviator I knew had a call sign of "Kato."

In early 1972 my family moved onto Tan Son Nhut Air Base, mostly for security reasons. Our new military home was much bigger than the house we had shared with my father's parents. It was about 2,500 square feet, a one-story dwelling on a 10,000-square-foot lot. It reminded me of U.S. military housing for officers (except for the Marine Corps, long notorious for outdated and substandard quarters). We lived in the field-grade officer housing section (my father being a major), which was across the street from former Prime Minister Ky's house.

I remember crossing the street to play soccer with my friends, children of junior officers, who lived down the street from Ky's house. But no kid would dare go near there. I was tempted once when urged by my friends but I did not accept the "mission"; a battle-ready tank sat outside his front door, though I never saw anyone in it. (After the 1971 election, when he failed to defeat Thieu for the presidency, Ky essentially sat out the remainder of the war as a private citizen.)

In February 1972 President Nixon visited China after his national security adviser, Henry Kissinger, had met secretly with the Beijing government. Both Nixon and Kissinger wrote in their memoirs of China's probable motives in seeking détente with the United States. By the end of 1969, North

Vietnam had expelled tens of thousands of Chinese advisers, "volunteer" workers, and soldiers, and had clearly begun to align itself with Moscow. Given the confrontations with the Soviet Union on the Manchurian border, therefore, Beijing most likely wanted the United States to remain engaged in Southeast Asia despite China's official support for the Hanoi regime. A shift in policy was needed, and the United States saw the potential in a new Chinese market after supporting China's entry into the United Nations.

In a declassified taped conversation from the U.S. National Archives in 2003, Nixon and Kissinger mulled over the situation in Vietnam in preparation for the presidential election of 1972.* It worried Nixon that "losing" South Vietnam (thus making him the first U.S. President to lose a war) would cost him his reelection. "If we settle it, say, this October [1972], by January '74 no one will give a damn," Kissinger coldly said to Nixon.

There were other reelection concerns for the Nixon administration besides *realpolitik*. Nuclear arms limitation negotiations were under way with the Soviets. The situation in the Middle East involving Israel and Egypt (the Yom Kippur War in 1973), along with the subsequent oil crisis, were looming.

South Vietnam, the "domino theory," "our ally," "stemming the tide of communism," no longer mattered as much. Détente with the Soviets and a direct channel to China meant that Vietnam remained the burr under the saddle of U.S. foreign policy. It was time for "a peace with honor" and the beginning of a treachery in Paris a year later. More bloody fighting would follow as the Saigon government "had to hold on," at least until the U.S. election in November 1972 was over (and ideally after the next in 1976). To Kissinger, U.S. support for South Vietnam only had to buy enough time for a "decent interval."

Several weeks after my family moved into its base housing, my father had me help him do a "home improvement" project. Next to our dining room was a cement stairway entry that led to an underground bunker, about 15 feet deep and big enough to hold twenty people. I hesitantly went down into the bunker while holding my father's hand. It was claustrophobic and creepy down there and it felt like being inside a tomb. The ceiling was made from

---

*Transcribed by Ken Hughes of the University of Virginia Center of Public Affairs.

pieces of pierced-steel planks, probably left over from military runway construction. I could see sunlight through the circular holes, so the bunker wasn't totally dark.

We went back up to the dining room and stood above the bunker, which was like a basement with an outside entrance. My father pointed to a pile of empty sandbags on the driveway. "See those bags? I want you to fill them up with dirt from our front yard. I'll stack them on top of the [steel] planks." He didn't need to explain to me why. Already at age seven, I had seen many sandbagged bunkers in South Vietnam. I assumed the probability for survival increased with the bags' protecting us unless we took a direct hit. It took me all day of shoveling hard dirt and rocky sand into those green bags. By evening, my father had neatly stacked three layers of sloppily filled sandbags atop our home bunker. We were going to be hunkering down like the rest of our fellow South Vietnamese.

By spring of 1972, my father had become executive officer or XO (i.e., second in command) of the 425th Transport Squadron. Earlier, as part of Nixon's Vietnamization initiative, the VNAF had received hundreds of airplanes, helicopters, and thousands of spare parts: the VNAF's inventory quadrupled to more than 2,000 aircraft and 60,000 personnel. C-123s replaced C-47s as the lead transport aircraft. My father, who had already qualified in the C-123 in 1966, took part in training new students. Along with USAF advisers, he helped bring two other squadrons on line, the 421st and 423d, before assuming his duties with the 425th, which was made up entirely of VNAF-trained pilots. Even though the VNAF had grown to be the fourth largest air force in the world, just behind the U.S., the Soviet, and Chinese forces, that would contribute to the overblown assessment of South Vietnam's true military capabilities. As an example, many of the older Skyraiders, and other aircraft, were put into storage due to a lack of spare parts but were still counted in the general inventory.

In April of 1972 North Vietnam launched a 130,000-man, all-out assault (also known as the Easter offensive) throughout South Vietnam. Retreating southern troops converged on the city of An Loc, 60 miles northwest of Saigon, with a handful of U.S. advisers among thousands of ARVN soldiers. Along with Soviet T-54 tanks and advanced antiaircraft cannon, portable, SA-7 surface-to-air missiles (SAMs) had made their appearance for the first time, which immediately knocked down vulnerable VNAF airplanes and helicopters. A combination of B-52 strikes and ARVN tenacity kept the attackers at bay during a siege that would last 70 days. The situation began to look alarmingly like Dien Bien Phu in 1954 and Khe Sanh in 1968. Without aerial resupply, the troops could not hold out.

The heavy NVA antiaircraft fire was the heaviest ever seen over the skies of South Vietnam.

On April 15, the aircraft flown by the commanding officer of the 425th was shot down, killing all ten crew members. The plane had been filled with antitank munitions and it instantly exploded when hit by antiaircraft fire. (At the funeral, as my mother recalled, the commander's wife and his mistress argued in public and created an unforgettable scene.) My father then took command of the 425th; at age thirty-six, and with over 7,000 hours of flight time, he had finally achieved his goal of becoming a commanding officer. He promptly canceled all leave and ordered every pilot in the unit onto the flight schedule, and he led the next mission. As he announced to the squadron, "You have to do your job or quit flying and turn in your wings. I'll go first, then the new XO, then the next officer in rank. Then we'll repeat the order. No sick call, no sick mother excuses. If your name is on the flight schedule, you will fly. If it's your turn to die, that's it."

Sorties were flown around the clock. Then four days later the 425th lost another plane and another ten crew members. Morale plunged. My mother said that my father came home then white as a ghost. It was a good thing our family had moved onto the base so that we could at least see him some of the time.

Once again USAF pilots came to help. Several U.S. C-130s attempted to resupply An Loc, and three were shot down within ten days—which led to the U.S. squadron commander's prompt relief and being ordered back to the States.

The siege ended badly for the North Vietnamese, who suffered around 100,000 casualties, or two times South Vietnam's losses. General Creighton Abrams (who had relieved General Westmoreland as U.S. commander) reported: "Overall, the South Vietnamese have fought well under extremely difficult circumstances. They have made great progress in this area [the integration of air, armor, artillery, and infantry into a coherent whole] during the past year in particular." A distinguished Vietnam historian, the late Douglas Pike, cited the defense of An Loc as "the single most important battle of the war." The South Vietnamese military had risen to the occasion and answered lingering questions about its resolve to fight. The ARVN repelled the assault albeit with the hold of U.S. air power. The revered General Giap was "moved" out of his job as overall NVA commander. Saigon gained another three years.

Despite withstanding the Easter offensive, South Vietnam suffered a public-relations blow when American actress Jane Fonda visited North Vietnam in August 1972. A photograph of "Hanoi Jane" in a pith helmet and peering through the sight of an antiaircraft gun was seen around the world. She ended her visit by broadcasting a radio message from Hanoi.

(Her apology in 1988 would not prove good enough for thousands of American Vietnam veterans. In 1999, when she was profiled in a television show named "A Celebration: 100 Years of Great Women," there was an outcry across the United States. Senator John Kerry would experience the same outrage, especially from the Swift Boat veterans during his 2004 presidential campaign, though he never expressed regret. Some Vietnam veterans don't easily forget and forgive. Both incidents demonstrate that the Vietnam War is still being fought in the United States, among Americans in an unrelenting generational and political divide. Now as then, the Vietnamese people themselves hardly matter.)

Nixon overwhelmingly won reelection in November 1972 over George McGovern, a World War II bomber pilot and ardent antiwar senator. All that was left now to save in Vietnam were 600 or so American POWs. That would be the top agenda item in Paris before the North Vietnamese withdrew from negotiations in mid-December.

At the end of 1972, the VNAF received C-130s from the USAF, replacing all the C-123s. Once more, in order to quickly attain greater capabilities, the VNAF sacrificed gaining familiarity with the new equipment. My father, along with five other sets of aircrew, rapidly underwent the instructor pilot and tactics courses at Tan Son Nhut and other airfields in Southeast Asia. Two C-130 squadrons were manned, and he took the assignment as XO of the 437th Transport Squadron.

Five days after North Vietnamese negotiators abruptly left Paris, Nixon gave them and their fellow citizens an "early Christmas present." Over 120 B-52 bombers raided Hanoi and surrounding cities assisted by hundreds of U.S. Marine and Navy tactical aircraft in Linebacker II, the deadliest nonnuclear aerial strikes ever known to mankind. Twelve days later, the North Vietnamese bowed. Nixon had spoken and carried a gigantic stick, and the Communists listened.

In January 1973, the Paris Peace Accords were signed and both North and South Vietnam took a much-needed respite from full-scale fighting. The NVA used the cease-fire to rebuild, but my family saw more of my father.

Three key provisions (or concessions) in the accords would contribute to the fall of Saigon in 1975. First, the North Vietnamese were allowed to keep 150,000 soldiers south of the DMZ. Second, the United States would retaliate if North Vietnam violated the accords. Finally, and most important, the United States would continue to aid South Vietnam unconditionally. The latter two provisions would never happen.

CHAPTER 9

THIS IS THE END

S ADLY, NORMAL LIFE ONLY CAME DURING OUR LAST TWO
years in Vietnam. My father was around more than he had been in
previous years; it would be when I felt closest to my father. His flight
time and overall VNAF training had been curtailed. A shortage of detona-
tors, fuel, bombs, and spare parts kept much of the VNAF fleet grounded.
My father's C-130 squadron rarely had more than two or three airplanes in
"up status" out of sixteen. Overall, the VNAF operated at less than 50 percent of capacity and morale bottomed out. The other military services also
faced cutbacks in ammunition and supplies and were ordered to ration what
they had remaining.

Some of my father's duties required him to drive his squadron's jeep onto
the flight line, stopping to inspect cargo, coveys of military personnel, and,
sometimes civilians. He took me on some of these drives. He'd pull right behind combat aircraft being armed for missions and get out and talk to the pilots. He drove underneath the wings of huge cargo planes so that I could
stare up at their engines, rivets, and fuel tanks, marveling at the size of these
machines.

My father came home from work one night and told my mother during
dinner that there was a Viet Cong being held at the base jail. I was eating at
the table so I overheard. In my young mind, the Viet Cong remained this elu-
sive mysterious enemy talked about on radio and television. To my surprise
the next morning, my father looked over at me sitting in the right seat of his
jeep and asked, "Do you want to see what a Viet Cong looks like?" I immediately nodded. We drove to the Tan Son Nhut prison as military policemen
saluted my father, who was by then a lieutenant colonel. We strolled through
the jail until we reached a desk in front of a locked door with a small win-

dow. My father said something to the guard as he opened the door. The Viet Cong captive stood up, looking at us expressionlessly. He was in his late twenties, had a hollow face and a rail-thin torso, and he wore a white T-shirt and black shorts. In my mind, it was completely opposite to my expectation. *The VC looked like us.*

During this short lull in the fighting, my father caught the fishing bug and he took me along half a dozen times on weekends. I would sit on the back of his Lambretta, hanging onto his waist with one hand and holding the fishing poles with the other. My arm would get tired from holding the poles, which bounced up and down at my side as we motored along unpaved roads. I was so worried about dropping them and disappointing my father that I bit my bottom lip and hung on, my arm numb with pain. On one trip, about ten of his friends and their sons rode on their scooters to the countryside where bomb craters carved out by B-52 raids had filled up with rainwater and become ponds. We were fishing for bluegills, catfish, or anything that bit. After a slow morning one of the men produced a hand grenade and dropped it into a fish pond. A loud explosion interrupted the tranquility as waves rippled across the water, and thirty seconds later dozens of fish floated to the top, some bleeding from their gills. A grenade proved to be the best bait any of us used that day, but I never tried it.

On another occasion my father took me fishing at a naval base on the Saigon River. He had graduated from simple bamboo fishing poles to more modern, Japanese-made open spinning reels mounted on fiberglass rods. He went after channel catfish, a Vietnamese delicacy but one not easy to hook. The bait was several 2-inch-long brown cockroaches that I had trapped the night before in our kitchen. I was given several small poles to fish around the pier pilings. As I gazed across the river waiting for action, I noticed a strange clump of brush moving toward the pier where we were fishing. It was floating against the outgoing tide. Suddenly, the Vietnamese sailors in the watchtower opened up their machine gun. Rounds flew over my head, striking the water around the vegetation, and finally blowing it to pieces. Empty cartridges were ejected onto the pier, clinking on the concrete. I dropped my poles, got on my knees, and covered my ears. Meanwhile, my father went about his business nonchalantly, casting with his pole as if nothing was happening around him. I didn't particularly enjoy my first "combat" fishing outing.

One of my biggest fears when growing up was swimming. Before I could go fishing with my father in deep water, I had to take swimming lessons at

Le Cercle Sportif, a popular former French retreat in Saigon. One of my uncles was a prominent lawyer in Saigon, so my parents would occasionally be invited as my aunt's guests. My mother remembered U.S. ambassador Henry Cabot Lodge in the late 1960s quietly reading a book on a lounge chair or eating in the dining room. The members were Americans, French, and well-off Saigonese. My father occasionally played tennis there while my mother supervised our swimming lessons after school.

The Communists had never planned to abide by the peace accords. Rocket attacks were soon resumed, and I was glad my father had reinforced our bomb shelter with sandbags. One night when my father was away flying, the air raid siren shrieked through the Tan Son Nhut night. Seconds later, the first incoming rockets landed close to our house, which was less than a third of a mile from the flight line. The concussion shook us right out of our beds. Our bedroom's broken wooden shutters flew open and shut with every blast. My sister Thi's job was to shut off the gas line. My mother grabbed a prepositioned flashlight. My job was simple—to run down the hallway into the bomb shelter in our dining room and grab a light with a long extension cord on the way.

The shelling went on for what seemed like hours, but in actuality was probably more like fifteen minutes. Before this attack I had been a macho nine-year-old, seasoned in war games with my friends and comfortable around military men and their hardware. And I had seen the war movies. Yet, in front of my sisters and my mother, I started bawling nonstop, asking where my father was. My sisters just looked at me without saying anything, while my mother tried to calm me down. I couldn't stop shaking until the attack ceased. (If only my father could have seen his boy cry like a little sissy.) I don't think my mother ever told him of this shameful episode.

In the middle of the so-called countrywide cease-fire, my parents entered on their first entrepreneurial venture: they decided to raise chickens and sell them to the vendors on the open market to make extra money. Later, as an American, it was unfathomable for me that my parents had to even pursue such an endeavor. My father was a lieutenant colonel, after all, and my mother worked full-time as a teacher. Yet we needed the extra money. America tried to make the South Vietnamese military into a replica of her armed services, but without any matching pay scales, or the elimination of endemic corruption and desertion. Inflation rocketed and unemployment increased after the U.S. military had departed.

My sisters and I chipped in to help, cleaning the chicken cages and picking up eggs each morning. It was fun for us children to have the feeling of living on a "farm" while our parents tended their chickens in flight suits and *ao dai* after returning from work. A few months later, my parents sold the remaining hens and got rid of the cages. It was simply too much work.

In August 1974 President Nixon resigned from office. The news sent a shock wave throughout South Vietnam, for he was seen as its last savior. To make matters worse, in the same year Congress reduced the amount of aid to South Vietnam by $300 million, signaling its impending abandonment. North Vietnam took notice and tested U.S. resolve under President Ford's new leadership. Ignoring the Paris Peace Accords, they quickly overran Phuoc Long Province in December without drawing a response from the United States. The new president mentioned "Vietnam" once in his state of the union address in early 1975.

My father finally took a staff assignment, leaving his C-130 unit to become the wing safety and standardization officer, flying missions only on occasion. For the final months of his career, he was not even attached to an operational unit. I am not sure he ever really knew the reasons why South Vietnam fell so quickly. He and other VNAF veterans told stories of aircraft flying half-loaded with fuel and bombs, and jet planes landing with blown tires that were never replaced. Clearly the VNAF was feeling the effects of U.S. disengagement, but the ARVN had grown to depend heavily on air support during the war. And without the high-tech and expensive support of the VNAF, the army could not hold out for long.

In March 1975, confident of U.S. indifference to the plight of South Vietnam, Hanoi unleashed an all-out assault to end the war. The province of Ban Me Thuot quickly fell and President Thieu (himself a former ARVN general) made the fatal decision to withdraw ARVN troops from the Central Highlands. Already paranoid about a coup, he desperately wanted elite units to defend Saigon, and so the northern regions were practically deserted.

Having family members nearby in a war zone was a luxury for the South Vietnamese that the average U.S. soldier did not have. That's what happens when you fight a war in your own backyard. But as the "family syndrome" came into play, the withdrawal to the south turned into chaos. Soldiers abandoned their units to return home to help evacuate loved ones amid confusing orders from Saigon. Troops and refugees crowded Route 7B, a single-lane highway known as the "convoy of tears," as NVA artillery shells rained down from above. This time there would be no An Loc. No heroic stand. No reprieve.

James Willbanks, a retired U.S. Army officer on the staff of the U.S. Army Command and General Staff College, wrote of the collapse of South Vietnamese forces in his book *Abandoning Vietnam:*

> The loss of materiel and equipment was staggering. Hundreds of artillery pieces and armored vehicles had been destroyed on the road or abandoned in Pleiku. Only a handful of armored vehicles, including just thirty armored personnel carriers, made it to Tuy Hoa. Nearly 18,000 tons of ammunition, a month's supply for a corps, was left in depots in Ban Me Thuot, Pleiku, and Kontum. Scores of good aircraft were left for the enemy at Pleiku.

At the end of March 1975, President Ford dispatched Gen. Fred Weyand, army chief of staff, to South Vietnam to assess the imminent collapse. A week later, he reported to Ford and sent a copy to the National Security Council. An excerpt of Weyand's report, highlighting his assessment and recommendations, said as follows:

> The present level of U.S. support guarantees the GVN [Government of Vietnam] defeat. Of the $700 million provided for fiscal year 1975, the remaining $150 million can be used for a short time for a major supply operation; however, if there is to be any real chance of success, an additional $722 million is urgently needed to bring the South Vietnamese to a minimal defense posture to meet the Soviet and PRC (People's Republic of China) supported invasion. Additional U.S. aid is within both the spirit and intent of the Paris Agreement, which remains the practical framework for a peaceful settlement in Vietnam.
>
> One of the most serious psychological and attitudinal problem at all levels, military and civilian, is the belief that the South Vietnamese have been abandoned, and even betrayed, by the United States. The Communists are using every possible device of propaganda and psychological warfare to foster this view. Much of this emotion is keyed on the 1973 Paris Agreement and subsequent U.S. withdrawal. It is widely believed that the GVN was forced to sign this agreement as a result of a private U.S.-North Vietnamese deal under which the U.S.

was allowed to withdraw its forces and get its prisoners back in return for abandoning South Vietnam. This sense of abandonment has been intensified by what is widely perceived as a lack of public U.S. acknowledgement of South Vietnam's current plight or willingness to provide needed support.

There is not and cannot be any guarantee that the actions proposed will be sufficient to prevent total North Vietnamese conquest. The effort, however, should be made. What is at stake in Vietnam now is America's credibility as an ally. We must not abandon our goal of a free and independent South Vietnam.

While sitting on the sidelines militarily, the United States began devising an evacuation plan for its personnel and several hundred specially selected Vietnamese at the recommendation of Gen. Fred Weyand. CIA agents and State Department personnel frantically worked around the clock inside the U.S. Embassy in Saigon as the sand ran out of the hourglass. Sensing the collapse, North Vietnam's generals pushed even harder, sending southward units previously held in reserve.

On April 10, Ford appeared before a joint session of Congress to appeal for $722 million in military aid and for $250 million in economic aid and refugee relief for South Vietnam. He received no applause as two Democratic freshmen congressmen (part of the 1974 post-Watergate class) walked out before he finished. Congress denied his request.

Like thousands of South Vietnamese military men, my father spent the last week in Saigon trying to get more family members out of danger. After my mother, my sisters, and I flew out of Vietnam, he hustled back and forth on his Lambretta from Tan Son Nhut to Saigon, trying to convince my maternal grandmother and one of my aunts to leave. Our exact whereabouts was unknown to him; he only knew we had been in good hands when he saw us depart on a U.S. C-130 on April 23.

The following day, President Ford gave a speech at Tulane University, declaring that "the war in Vietnam is over as far as America is concerned." Ambassador Martin notified Washington that the evacuation from Saigon of U.S. personnel and critical Vietnamese should soon commence. U.S. Marines had been flown off amphibious ships into the Defense Attaché Office (DAO) compound next to Tan Son Nhut in preparation for the evacuation.

Years later my father said he was no hero by remaining until the end, but he never told me why directly. In an interview with Bernie Edelman, he said "Officers cannot leave early or they're cowards. I could have left. But everyone will know what day I left. I would have that on my mind all the time. No one normal could do that." One of his colleagues told me at a VNAF reunion in 2004, "I saw your father the day before the last day. He was still wearing his khaki uniform, ribbons and all. Damn, he wouldn't leave."

My grandmother, an aunt, and a cousin were driven by an air force friend to Tan Son Nhut on April 27. (Many of my father's friends had congregated at our house to hide in our bomb shelter.) While waiting to board an aircraft, my grandmother wanted to see my uncle one last time, so she, my aunt, and my cousin left the base to return home. They, too, never made it out.

Meanwhile, in the political world Gen. Duong Van "Big" Minh had assumed power from a weakened Tran Van Huong, who had replaced Thieu a week earlier. (After the 1963 coup that toppled the Diem government, Minh had temporarily risen to power.) False rumors also surfaced about Nguyen Cao Ky's attempting to take power.

Under orders from the United States, the VNAF sent its fleet of F-5 fighters to Thailand to avoid their capture by the advancing North Vietnamese. Transport aircraft manned by VNAF pilots also took part in the evacuation, often flown by many of my father's colleagues and former students. On the evening of April 28, three captured A-37 jets flown by North Vietnamese pilots (led by the defector who bombed the Presidential Palace on April 8) struck Tan Son Nhut Air Base, damaging a number of aircraft on the ground.

By April 29, NVA troops on the outskirts of Saigon were lobbing long-range artillery rounds and rockets into the air base. My father and a dozen of his comrades clambered into our home shelter to wait out the heavy shelling. At daylight next morning, several of those in the bomb shelter left and caught the last VNAF C-130 flights out of the country (at this point the aircraft were skirting debris on the runways as they took off for U Tapao Air Base in Thailand). My father was last seen in the shelter talking on the phone to my grandmother. Two others of his colleagues fled to Vung Tau, the coastal resort, where they boarded departing Vietnamese Navy ships.

U.S. Marine Sgt. Ted Murray checked on his Marines shortly after the NVA barrage ceased. Two of them had died during a rocket attack: Cpl. Charles McMahon, Jr., and LCpl. Darwin Judge were the last two Americans to die in combat in Vietnam.

Murray recalled that fateful morning:

I saw first-hand the delays and the needless paperwork that people were put through before leaving. There was a Vietnamese woman who waited at the guard gate to the compound. Von was her name and her daughter was Van. I promised both of them on the 28th that I would make sure that they left before we did. But that night, the airport was bombed by the Dragonfly [A-37] aircraft that had been captured by the NVA. [Von] had gone home already. I don't know if she ever got a chance to get back in or not. . . . I was just a sergeant doing my job to the best of my ability and doing things that could have gotten many of us in trouble, putting people on planes without prior "authorization" from the State Department or anyone else. Why? Because I could. And that is one thing that I am extremely proud about.

Murray witnessed what were probably the final sorties flown by the VNAF. On the morning of April 29, an AC-119 gunship made a last effort, circling over Tan Son Nhut and firing its miniguns (which sounded like cloth ripping) into the advancing NVA troops. The aircraft had been in nearly constant combat source earlier that night, landing to refuel and reload several times before an SA-7 antiaircraft missile struck the gunship shortly after 7 a.m. The gunship exploded violently, and several open parachutes were seen descending to the ground. Two Skyraiders from the 514th and 518th FS (my father's former units) also took to the air and made several strafing runs. One would be shot down by antiaircraft artillery fire and the other by an SA-7. These last combat missions brought the illustrious history of a mighty air force, born and grown in war, to a sad ending.

Hundreds of VNAF fixed-wing aircraft fled to Thailand, while appearing like locusts on the horizon, VNAF helicopters rushed to land on the overcrowded U.S. fleet in the South China Sea, only to be pushed overboard to make room for others. General Ky flew Lt. Gen. Ngo Quang Truong* and a dozen others in his personal helicopter, landing on the USS *Midway* shortly after noon. Ky's aide-de-camp, Maj. Ho Dang Tri, one of my father's closest friends, refused to leave; Tri's entire family stayed in Saigon.

The price of freedom was no longer a factor. Rear Admiral Lawrence Chambers ordered the dumping of some $10 million worth of Huey helicop-

*Truong was I Corps commander and regarded by most Americans (including General Abrams) as Vietnam's best field commander and the "second coming of General George S. Patton," according to Ky.

ters to save one family. VNAF Maj. Bung Ly (with his wife and five children on board) successfully landed his O-1 observation plane—without a tail-hook—on the aircraft carrier USS *Midway*.

It would take fifteen years before another Vietnamese would land aboard a U.S. Navy ship then as a Marine helicopter pilot.

My father decided to go back to Saigon one last time to attempt to bring out my grandmother. When she refused he headed back to Tan Son Nhut and tried to reenter the base. As he drove through Saigon, he passed the remnants of an army scattered throughout the downtown area. Members of the 18th ARVN Division, the last unit fighting at Xuan Loc, had retreated to the city. Soldiers ran about in their boxer shorts, their boots and uniforms left on the ground. M16s were thrown into the Saigon River.

My father, too, had changed out of uniform and into civilian clothes. Weaving in and out of traffic, he pushed his Lambretta as fast as it could go. Trying to avoid capture by infiltrators and advancing NVA troops, he managed to get to Tan Son Nhut in hopes of catching a departing plane.

Unbeknownst to him, the airport had been shut down after the rocket attacks had rendered the runways unsafe and unusable. The U.S.-led evacuation had shifted to Option IV, an all-helicopter extraction at the U.S. Embassy and the DAO compound. Bing Crosby's "White Christmas," the signal for the remaining Americans to evacuate, had been played a few hours earlier. My father managed to get to the front gates of Tan Son Nhut where he saw once-familiar faces, now wearing Viet Cong uniforms. He changed direction and headed to the DAO compound where giant U.S. Marine CH-53 Sea Stallion helicopters began landing shortly after 3 p.m. He stopped his Lambretta and ran toward the fence to join the terrified crowd.

Amid chaos and confusion, a shirtless Marine wearing a flak jacket pressed the muzzle of his M16 against my father's chest, quickly discouraging him from any thoughts of entering the compound. My father stood back and watched the fortunate Vietnamese who had been allowed to enter. A U.S. Marine had rescued my father eleven years earlier, and now another would keep him from catching a flight to freedom. Stranded and dejected, he watched with shame as more South Vietnamese soldiers ripped off their uniforms and threw their rifles into the river to evade capture by the approaching communist troops. On the night of April 29 my father drove back to my grandmother's house to await his fate.

Through the rest of the afternoon and into the morning of April 30 Marine and Air America (CIA) helicopters lifted nearly 7,000 Americans, South

Vietnamese, and third-country nationals to navy ships offshore. Operation Frequent Wind became the largest helicopter-based evacuation operation ever conducted. At 4:59 a.m., a CH-46 with call sign "Lady Ace 09" piloted by Capt. Gerry Berry radioed the amphibious command ship USS *Blue Ridge,* "Tiger, tiger, tiger." That signaled the departure of Ambassador Martin from Saigon. Martin had remained only until a direct order from President Ford was given for him to leave the embassy. At 7 a.m., Berry flew the second to the last group of Marines out of Saigon. "You could see fires. The (South Vietnamese troops) were retreating into the city and some of them were still putting up a good fight, especially in the north end of the city," Berry told me years later. "I could see NVA tanks entering the city. After twenty years of fighting, it was a tough thing to watch."

At 7:30 a.m., CH-46 call sign "Swiff 2-2" ferried the last eleven Marines off the embassy rooftop. By 11 a.m., two NVA T-54 tanks had crashed through the front gates of the Presidential Palace. A crewman ran into the palace and unfurled the red communist flag from the front balcony. President "Big" Minh and his three-day-old cabinet officially surrendered to a military journalist, Col. Bui Tin.*

When the announcement to surrender came over the radio, an ARVN colonel in uniform stood at the base of the Vietnamese Marine Memorial, saluted, and killed himself with a single pistol shot to the head. Several ARVN generals also committed suicide at various posts in South Vietnam. Family members had to take away my father's pistol because they feared he would kill himself.

My father peeked out at the streets of Saigon as the NVA rode into town. His mind was foggy; his actions unpredictable. Twenty-one years of his military service had come to an end. Thousands of his peers had given up their lives for South Vietnam, including the dozens of personal friends who had been shot down during the long years of fighting. A strange quiet fell on Saigon that evening. My father remained at my grandmother's for a month and a half before he would report for "reeducation" along with other South Vietnamese officers. For most Vietnamese the fighting had finally ended. For

---

*Fed up with censorship and lack of democratic development in Vietnam after the war, Bui Tin moved to France in 1990. In his memoir *Following Ho Chi Minh,* Tin recalled the day of surrender. "On April 30, 1975, he [Nguyen Van Hao, head of the National Bank of South Vietnam] told me that South Vietnam's gold reserves [16 tons], which President Nguyen Van Thieu was rumored to have transported out of country, in fact remained intact and under guard in the national treasury in Saigon."

several millions, however, the dying and the suffering would continue in the years after Saigon's "liberation."

Bui Diem, South Vietnam's ambassador to the United States, remembered this about South Vietnam's final days:*

"Is it possible for a great nation to behave this way?" That was the question an old friend of mine asked me in Saigon when the news came in August 1974 that [the U.S.] Congress had reduced the volume of aid. He was a store owner whom I had gone to school with in North Vietnam, a totally nonpolitical person. "You are an ambassador," he said. "Perhaps you understand these things better than I do. But can you explain this attitude of the Americans? When they wanted to come, they came. And they want to leave, they leave. It's as if a neighbor came over and made a shambles of your house, then all of a sudden he decides the whole thing is wrong, so he calls it quits. How can they just do that?" It was a naïve question from an unsophisticated man. But I had no answer for it.

The South Vietnamese people, and especially the South Vietnamese leaders, myself among them, bear the ultimate responsibility for the fate of their nation, and to be honest, they have much to regret and much to be ashamed of.

Two weeks after Saigon fell Henry Kissinger, in his 1975 memo addressed to President Ford (declassified in 2000), wrote, "When the United States entered the war during the 1960s, it did so with excesses that not only ended the career and the life of an allied leader but that may have done serious damage to the American economy. When we made it 'our war' we would not let the South Vietnamese fight it; when it became 'their war,' we would not help them fight it."

The memo was never sent to the President.

*From his memoir *In the Jaws of History.*

CHAPTER 10

OPERATION NEW LIFE

OUR C-130 LANDED BEFORE SUNRISE. ASIAN SOLDIERS wearing khaki uniforms entered the aircraft and led us down the rear ramp. They spoke in their own language to one another, but used English with the USAF crew. My mother huddled the four of us together as we found our own way off the airplane. It had been a rough, cramped flight. Like most other passengers, all of us were still groggy from the long flight. Once outside, we lined up in front of a series of tables with stacks of paper on them. As the sun came up, we were provided with milk and fruit, and U.S. uniformed military personnel helped us fill out paperwork and answer questions. We were then told to get on a bus and proceed to a huge terminal to wait.

My mother fell asleep before we kids did. I watched some families leave the terminal, going back onto buses. The military personnel had brought us dinners on paper plates. I wolfed down my first U.S. military cafeteria meal in no time. It didn't matter if the mashed potato, green beans, canned corn, and breaded chicken tasted bland compared to a bowl of *pho,* white noodles sprinkled with *nuoc mam,* fermented fish sauce. The milk definitely needed sugar. I was used to drinking hot water mixed with French condensed milk, which was sweet as can be. After dinner my sisters and I finally fell asleep and woke up an hour later, to find that everyone had left the terminal. The other refugees hadn't bothered to wake us up. We were on our own. A young

U.S. airman finally tapped my mother on the shoulder and told us to grab
our belongings. A bus was waiting outside. We were the last family to walk
out of the terminal. My mother never forgot his simple good deed: it was her
first "live" impression of an American, and it had been extremely positive.

We stayed in the Philippines for just under twenty-four hours. Apparently there were many more inbound planes from Saigon, and we had to
leave to make room. President Ferdinand Marcos refused to accept the in-
flux of Vietnamese: he demanded that the United States get the refugees out
of his country as soon as possible. Later in the week, Vietnamese Navy ships
overflowing with refugees would be banned from docking in Subic Bay and
were forced back to sea. They had to sail directly to Guam, adding another
week of misery for those onboard. So much for the fellow Asian brotherly
love!

Travel conditions improved, though. This time, we filed into a C-141, a
four-engine jet transport with enough seats for everyone. There was no rush
to run aboard. Everything was calmer than our departure from Tan Son
Nhut the night before. The jet noise inside the cabin was deafening (there
was no padding), so the crew passed out yellow foam-rubber earplugs. We
began to feel safe, since enemy ground fire no longer threatened us.

We flew to Guam, while other refugees went to Wake Island.

The flight took less than two hours and we landed at sunrise again. Our
plane touched down at Andersen Air Force Base, ironically home to the
B-52s that had once pounded the NVA. There was hardly anyone at the terminal when we first got there; it was as if no one was expecting us. It turned
out our plane had been one of the first to arrive, so the actual refugee camp
(another bus ride away) was still getting ready. We were then driven to Camp
Asan, an abandoned area that had once been a Marine Barracks.

In less than twenty-four hours, 400 or so Marines and Navy Seabees made
the abandoned, faded-yellow Quonset huts habitable again.

Since we were in the first group to enter the camp, my mother had her
pick of fifteen or so empty barracks. Typical of junior enlisted personnel
housing, each Quonset hut held two rows of racks (twin-size beds) for about
fifty people. We slept separated by a 5-foot-wide path down the middle. The
first night on Guam I developed what turned into a recurring episode of bed-
wetting. I used the green issue blanket and white sheets to wipe up the mess
as quickly as I could. Then I ran out the back door to throw the blanket away
before anyone could see me. The evacuation had taken an emotional toll on

me, but I didn't know it then. However, I was old enough to know that boys my age no longer peed in bed.

Our week on Guam seemed like a month. Everyone was waiting for the "big battle" that never took place in Saigon. Denial was still the norm; there was talk of returning to Saigon when things "calmed down." More and more people arrived daily; buses ran round the clock. Those already in the camps kept waiting for new arrivals, hoping to see loved ones among the crowds. I ran into several schoolmates—some with their entire family and some, like me, without their fathers. We children congregated each night to watch American movies under the starry equatorial skies. The Marines had set up the camp to make our lives more comfortable, adding amenities each day, such as portable toilets and additional chow lines. A Vietnamese man, Tony Lam,* was designated the "camp manager" and served as the liaison between the refugees and the Marines. He spoke some English and was one of the very few among us who understood what the Americans were saying. The rest of us just followed gestures or Vietnamese slang that some GIs spoke.

The kids usually were first to line up for meals, and I ran to the head of the line three times a day. The military men were nice to the kids, always smiling. I couldn't understand them when they said something to me so I smiled back and gave them that reaffirming American "thumbs-up." Between meals our parents gathered near makeshift bulletin boards, where announcements and messages were left for incoming refugees.

Guam's beaches were rocky and shallow; the water was up to the knee or the waist from the shore to at least a mile out. I saw several teenagers wade out until they became dots on the horizon. Adults paced the beaches, staring out to the same horizon. The warm water soon attracted more bathers, including me. The beaches brought back memories of the coastal town of Nha Trang where my family took our second and last vacation. On our third day on Guam, I was scratched by something in the water. A few hours later, the infection had turned my right foot red and blue, and soon after a bluish coloring ran up to my thigh. My mother, as if she hadn't had enough on her mind, ran me over to the clinic, where a navy doctor squeezed some pus out of my ankle and gave me some medicine. I spent the next two days, mostly by

---

*Tony Lam also later served as "camp manager" at the Camp Pendleton refugee camp in California. In 1992, he became the first Vietnamese American to be elected to public office in the United States.

myself, resting in our empty building during the day, fighting a slight fever and feeling exhausted. Sometimes hours went by before someone came to check on me, and it was lonely.

More and more refugees arrived, and soon Camp Asan became full; tents were erected to handle the overflow. Chow lines took longer, so we began lining up sooner, usually holding places for the adults. Those with large families usually caused a ruckus, since they would take up more spots in front of families already in line. There were conflicts between adults and among the children, but the Marines and Seabees quickly broke them up. Each day my mother would run to the bus arrival area, hoping to catch a glimpse of familiar faces. The new arrivals piled off buses, exhausted and traumatized, just as we had looked a few days earlier. My mother would return to our hut each night looking disappointed. Not only did she not find my father, she hadn't run into any of our other relatives. She did, however, see several of my father's VNAF colleagues reunite with their families, and that made her even more sad. A USAF adviser who knew my father stopped by the camp many times to check with the VNAF pilots to see if anyone "had run into Hoa." No one had.

Shortly after noon on April 30, 1975, a crowd of mostly women and elderly refugees burst into tears. They had been huddling near the camp's operations center listening to the BBC. My mother was among the crowd. "The Communists have entered Saigon. It's all over." The radio announcement quickly spread throughout the camp. Our worst fears had been realized.

The next day my family left for its new life in the United States, fortunate to be among the 1 percent of the population that had escaped. The tropical scenery of Guam had given us a temporary illusion of Vietnam, but we had to move on. As in the Philippines, more refugees were arriving and we had to vacate our quarters to make room. My mother wanted to stay longer, in hopes that my father would catch up; we were told that families would be able to connect in the United States. As our plane rolled down the Andersen runway, I noticed two rows of dark-green jets, neatly parked, with no crewmen in sight, and no bombs to be loaded. They were the B-52s the South Vietnamese had thought were coming one more time.

We stopped in Hawaii at Hickam Air Force Base to refuel. As the plane descended, I remember staring out the window and seeing the tall buildings on Waikiki's beaches with the Diamond Head volcano at one end. Pearl Harbor was full of gray ships. When we touched down, I also saw many military planes including more parked B-52s. Hickam resembled a quiet Tan Son

Nhut with the mighty U.S. forces sitting idle. We made one more stop at San Francisco International Airport and finally arrived at Little Rock, Arkansas, nearly a full day after leaving Guam. Another bus took us to Fort Chaffee as its gates swung open to take in some 24,000 refugees over the next three months.

In the mid-1970s, Arkansas was well known for hogs and Tyson Foods. Vietnamese loved eating pork, including the ceremonial head, and we were desperate to quickly find things in common with our new hosts.

Life at Fort Chaffee began as at Camp Asan, minus the beaches and the uncertainty of the war's outcome. The base had row after row of wooden barracks, more sturdy than the Quonset huts on Guam. A soldier must have seen my mother and four young kids milling about the camp, for he assigned her an end room with a door lock so that our family could have some privacy. That was especially good for me, since I still could not stop my bed-wetting habit.

Citizens from nearby towns donated clothes and volunteered at the camp, teaching English to the refugees. One family in particular came to our aid. Retired Army Lt. Col. Dick Clohecy, a Vietnam veteran, and his wife Gloria met my mother one day when she was at the donation center looking for clothes for my sisters and me. The weather was cool in Arkansas compared to the tropics of Guam and Vietnam, so we needed more layers. Dick and Gloria lived in Gravette, a small town nearby on the Arkansas-Oklahoma border. (The nearest "big city" was Tulsa, 100 miles away.) I don't know how many people lived in Gravette in 1975 but the 2000 census showed 1,800 with 91 percent whites and less than $30,000 in income per household. The Clohecys had two teenage girls, so it wasn't that they were retired and had nothing better to do. They brought clothes, especially boys' pants and jackets for me, and came back weekly during our seven-week stay.

Outside the camps, public sentiment against Vietnamese refugees ran high even though at the time we did not directly feel it. The book on Vietnam had been closed for most Americans until the refugees arrived in unprecedented numbers; only the Cuban refugee resettlements had even come close in size, and the news reported the country split on what to do with the refugees.

In a May 1975 *New York Times* article, West Virginia Senator Robert Byrd commented that "barmaids, prostitutes and criminals" should be screened out as "excludable categories." Delaware Senator Joe Biden "charged that the [Ford] administration had not informed Congress adequately about the number of refugees." As if anyone actually knew during the chaotic evacuation. "They are better off in Vietnam," sniffed George McGovern in *Newsweek*. At the time unemployment in the United States hovered near double digits, so perhaps this had something to do with feelings against refugees.

In Larry Engelmann's 1997 *Tears Before the Rain: An Oral History of the Fall of South Vietnam,* Julia Vadala Taft, formerly in charge of the refugee re-settlement effort, recalled such opposition:

> "The new governor of California, Jerry Brown, was very concerned about refugees settling in his state. Brown even attempted to prevent planes carrying refugees from landing at Travis Air Force Base near Sacramento. . . . The secretary of health and welfare, Mario Obledo, felt that this addition of a large minority group would be unwelcome in the state. And he said that they already had a large population of Hispanics, Filipinos, blacks, and other minorities."

After a few weeks my mother began attending English and general classes about the American society. That left me free from sunrise to sunset, wan-dering all over the camp. There was an open grass field, and we kids congre-gated there to play soccer after meals. I got into games with kids around my age, playing goalie. Once, when I dove for an incoming ball, a charging player continued kicking after I had gathered the ball, until I was lying on the ground bleeding from my mouth. Luckily I lost no teeth. I stayed away from our barrack as long as I could, until the bleeding stopped, and ran back after dark. My thin mother, who had lost 15 pounds in the weeks since we left Vietnam, was livid when she saw the swelling on my lips. She took me inside, and unlike anytime before, screamed and slapped me until I cried. "Your fa-ther is not here so you better listen to me. Do what I say and don't talk back. I don't have time for this." She cried too.

By now U.S. military food was tasting great to me. I had never eaten so much before: even creamed chipped beef on toast or (known forever to GIs as "SOS"—"Shit on a shingle"), peanut-butter-and-jelly sandwiches, bur-gers, hot dogs, and cookies and cakes. I didn't particularly like tasteless corn flakes, not until somebody told me to put two teaspoons of sugar into the milk. Once in a while the mess hall would serve fish, but it didn't taste like the salty and flavorful catfish dishes in Saigon. Ice cream was the fa-vorite for the kids in the camp, and the GIs brought it out at night when we huddled to watch B-grade movies under the stars; the films didn't have Vietnamese subtitles, so the crowd would chuckle when the Americans laughed.

At Camp Talega, in the northeastern training area of Camp Pendleton, a former concert promoter, but now a refugee, Nam Loc, strummed his guitar and composed a tear-jerking song titled, "*Saigon Vinh Biet,*" or "Farewell Saigon."

Saigon oi, I have lost you in my life,
Saigon oi, my best time is far away.
What is left is some sad memory,
the dead smile on my lips, bitter tears in my eyes.
On the street, is the sun still shining?
On our path, is the rain still falling?
In the park, is my lover still there?
Going under the trees? Smiling or crying lonely?
Here, I am the bird losing her way.
Day by day my time just passes by
the life of an exile is painful.
O Saigon I call you
Saigon oi, I will be back, I promise!
My lover, I will keep my word always
Although here, passion begins at night,
the city lights are bright,
but you still are in my mind.

We refugees were extremely fortunate. Our biggest supporter, outside of Julia Vadala Taft, was the U.S. president. In May 1975, President Ford visited the camp and soon after refugees began leaving to start new lives across the country. I don't recall any other politicians, antiwar protestors, esteemed journalists, or celebrities visiting Fort Chaffee.

During our stay at the camp, more families were reconnected and those who arrived later found notes from loved ones who had been settled. But there was still no news of my father's whereabouts. More and more familiar faces showed up at the camps, mostly VNAF families we knew, but no one had seen my father.

The first English terms I picked up in the camp were "GI," "Salem,"

"Coke," and "sponsor." A sponsor (I pronounced it "spun-ser") was our ticket out of camp, for he or she signed the paperwork that allowed families to leave. The refugee task force's goal was to resettle as many refugees as it could within a few months of arrival.

One of my mother's brothers had escaped on one of the last planes out of Saigon: Uncle An, his wife Aunt Ly, and their daughter Dien were the only relatives we had in this country. They had studied in the United States in the 1960s and had been able to connect with one of Aunt Ly's classmates, who served as their sponsor. They left the refugee camp in early June and moved to the Los Angeles suburb of San Fernando Valley.

While my father had had the foresight to get us out of Vietnam early, my mother made an even more critical decision while we were in Fort Chaffee. Three of her sisters were living in Paris, and my mother was fluent in French. My older sister Thi and I had studied French since the second grade. My two younger sisters . . . well, they didn't speak any of it at all, but in some ways it would have been much easier to choose France as our destination. After talking with one of her sisters, my mother decided not to go to Paris and took a risk in choosing this country. Later she admitted, "I felt you kids would have much more opportunities in the United States, especially with your education. The French never saw Vietnamese as equals."

My uncle began posting ads for sponsors in newspapers in California but received no response for several weeks. His own sponsors, Ron and Bonnie Counseller, had two small children and couldn't have possibly taken on my family as well. My mother started to get nervous; other families, with both parents, began to leave in droves. She worried that a mother with four young children could be perceived as an extra burden on an American family. Finally, after three weeks, we found a sponsor. A man named Edward Minton called my uncle and we were on our way to the Golden State, despite the concerns of the governor and secretary of state. Our destination was Oxnard, "just north of Malibu." That was a local joke, we learned later: there was a world of difference between the two. Life had been a roller coaster for nearly two months, but the future looked as promising as it could get.

The last time the U.S. government had put so many Asians (this time 125,000) in camps was shortly after Pearl Harbor, and that was for a completely different reason. Japanese Americans had unconstitutionally been rounded up for internment at various camps even though they were U.S. citizens. In 1975, we Vietnamese refugees were just—refugees. Yet we received better treatment than our Asian-American predecessors and we got out of the camps after months, not years. How could a refugee ever pay back such kindness?

Top left: *New Americans. My refugee family in Oxnard, California, 1976. (Author's Collection)*
Right: *A Little League All-Star with my mother and youngest sister Thu, 1977. (Author's Collection)*
Bottom left: *(from left to right) Mark Adams, Mike Hiji, James Stewart, John Gadd, and I at our high school graduation. Oxnard, California 1982. (Author's Collection)*

CHAPTER 11

BASEBALL, MEMORIES, AND MOM

NAVY PETTY OFFICER EDWARD MINTON, HIS WIFE, THREE young daughters, and a son awaited us at his home, outside the Port Hueneme Naval Construction Battalion Center (CBC or Seabee) in Oxnard, California. His was a small, one-story house, with four bedrooms and a white picket fence. Slightly overweight and wearing thick, standard-issue GI black-frame glasses, Minton had a huge, warm smile. His wife hugged us, but her daughters were standoffish. We sat down and ate some sandwiches and attempted to communicate. The Mintons gave us one of the bedrooms, and we immediately fell asleep on top of the bedding. The next morning the Minton girls woke us up and began chatting, apparently more receptive to our presence than the day before.

In the mid-1970s, Oxnard was an agricultural working-class town of 150,000, nestled on the coast between Los Angeles and Santa Barbara. The early inhabitants were Chumash Indians who made a living near the beaches. Apparently a sugar beet factory owner in the 1800s, Henry T. Oxnard, frustrated by his dealings with bureaucrats, named the town after his family. His factory soon attracted many migrant workers to the area, including Chinese, Japanese, and Mexican immigrants. By World War II, a military base, Point Mugu Naval Air Station, was established just north of Malibu and 7 miles from our first apartment. After we moved there, once in a while, I would recognize a C-130 coming in for a landing. But the days of roaming the flight line with my father were long gone.

A few days after arriving, Minton took me with him to work at Port Hueneme. I had expected to see a military base like Tan Son Nhut, with planes and tanks; instead, we went to a kitchen, where he took me into a large refrigerator full of slabs of beef hanging from iron rods. Minton worked in the food service side of the U.S. Navy and his job was as a meat cutter. There I stood, lost inside a freezing room full of cow parts, wondering when I could go home. But he kept smiling and hacking away at the meat; neither one of us could say much to each other.

After a few days with the Mintons my mother decided we would be better off in town; there were simply too many of us living too close together for comfort. After we had spent a day at the county welfare office, Edward Minton drove us to a small rickety apartment on Aleric Street (rent at $175 a month), which was on the second floor, part of a rundown building with six units. There we kept to ourselves the first week, too scared to go outside. Our neighbors kept staring at us, and one family, in particular, had a single mother and five kids. They all had black hair, dark skin, and round eyes. They didn't look like the "other Americans" I had met in the refugee camps or the Mintons. They didn't speak English either, but they kept waving to us every time they saw us peeking out through the blinds.

Aleric Street hosted many hookers and pimps, drug pushers and sellers, all going about their business in broad daylight and at night. Years later, the city eventually changed its name to Cuesta del Mar Drive but that didn't erase its reputation from my memory or from that of anyone else who lived in Oxnard back then.

On our third night on Aleric loud explosions were heard after sunset. Rockets whistled and small firecrackers popped in our neighborhood like sporadic gunfire. I could hear people yelling and laughing outside. The noise continued for half an hour before subsiding, just as the incoming rounds had in Saigon (minus the concussions). I ran to the window and caught a glimpse of bright and colorful flashes in the distance; then a glow appeared low on the horizon, behind rows of apartments. I ran back into my bedroom (my mother and my youngest sister shared one of the other bedrooms) and I pulled the covers over our heads. My mother turned off the lights and we kept quiet. After a while the explosions faded and the yelling stopped. The next day we learned about the commotion: Fourth of July fireworks.

As for our friendly neighbors? They were Mexicans.

Welcome to America.

There was a convenience store down the block. My mother would occasionally walk there, and I would tag along. When she pulled out food stamps to pay for the groceries, the clerk would spitefully stare at her whenever she purchased any candy or goodies. One early evening, I noticed pretty women all dressed in short skirts, faces glistening with makeup, hanging out in front of the store, which stood on the corner of Hueneme Road, a main road a few blocks from the ocean. Strutting in their miniskirts and high heels, they smiled and puffed their cigarettes on the sidewalk. Men pulled up next to them in beat-up cars and drove away with the women. "Mom, what are those pretty ladies with red lipstick doing out there?" I asked. My mother grabbed me and said nothing. After that my sisters and I weren't allowed to go outside anymore after dark.

A month after arriving in Oxnard, my mother signed us up for summer school at a nearby elementary school. My sister Thi was eleven, I was ten, and my sister Uyen was six. My youngest sister, Thu, who was two, remained at home. My mother had already spent several weeks trying to teach us English by forcing Thi and me to copy words from a children's book she'd found. But it was all to no avail. We wrote page after page, trying at least to gain familiarity through writing out our new language. Although reading and speaking English weren't yet possible, I soon discovered I could do arithmetic faster than my American peers. I completed multiplication exercises on the blackboard faster than they did. For the first time in my life, I enjoyed competition, especially when winning out over peers (and gaining approval) in front of a strange audience. When the school decided to help us with language training, a U.S. Vietnam veteran who allegedly spoke Vietnamese was hired to help us with our studies. He couldn't understand us, and we could barely make out his broken Vietnamese slang, so the situation worsened. After a week he was let go. Our English as a second language, or ESL, lessons never materialized, and we had to swim or sink, learn English or make no friends. (Actually, French was our second language and English third.)

There were many boys my age in our neighborhood. Soon after arriving, they grabbed me to go play hide-and-seek in an alley behind our house. We communicated with one another by pointing, giving thumbs-up signs, drawing things in the dirt, tugging shirts, and using simple statements like "aaeeyy," "cool," "hey man," and "run." (The television show *Happy Days* and its lead character Fonzie were big hits. However, it took me a year to understand the meaning of "sit on it!") Two of the boys took my right hand and shaped my palm into a closed fist. Slowly, they pried open my middle finger, which also loosened the other knuckles. After several tries, they succeeded in raising my right arm with only my middle finger extended. All three of them jumped up and cheered and joined in the ceremonial graduation. There I was, bonding with my new American friends (a Mexican, a Japanese American, and a white kid) telling the world how I felt, even if I didn't yet know what the gesture meant. That first cultural lesson remained with me for a few days as I proceeded to flip everyone off in my neighborhood. An adult finally told me to stop, happily before I got a beating.

Once regular classes began in September 1975, I entered the sixth grade in Mrs. Dorothy King's class at Art Haycox Elementary School. Mrs. King was in her late fifties, and close to retirement. She spent extra time with my English lessons, often speaking more precisely and slower than she did with the other students. I remember her being protective of me, seating me toward the front of the class and scowling at students who mocked me. It didn't take long for the other students to call me a teacher's pet.

During recess one day I watched my peers play a variety of games. I decided to try my hand at one that I knew—marbles. In Vietnam boys shot marbles with two hands, one hand holding the marble on the tip of the other hand's middle finger, bent back like a slingshot. American kids flicked their marbles with their thumbs. I managed to win a few marbles while the other kids tried, without luck, to duplicate my style.

I learned that Bruce Lee was as popular an actor here as he was in South Vietnam. Boys often asked me if I knew kung fu or karate, then proceeded to motion with their hands to mimic the martial arts legend and yell something they thought resembled Chinese: "Waahh! Yaaa! Oueeiue!" I usually ad-libbed a few hand chops accentuated with a kick or two, then stopped, doing just enough to make the others wonder. It worked; no one challenged me to a fight until the end of the school year. However, one day after school, a popular kid named Javier, just slightly bigger, decided to find out. He followed me and a group of fifteen or twenty students tailed along. I knew my first "true" test in this new land was about to be given. Javier had started by pushing me in the back as I crossed the schoolyard on my way off campus. He mocked me and laughed. "You don't know any kung fu, man. Let me see you try some on me." The other students, several of whom I'd befriended, didn't cheer Javier. They just stood back and watched as Javier and I pushed each other around in a shouting match. I managed a broken reply, "I no chicken. You want fight. I fight." The shouting match went on for about five minutes as the spectators grew impatient. Most likely, they just wanted to see how the new kid from Vietnam would hold up.

His first punch landed on my shoulder, but I didn't even feel it because I was so pumped. Javier just stood as if he was waiting for me to cry. I leaned forward and struck him as hard as I could, on one of his shoulders as he had done to me. (In those days, a punch to the face was a serious move and this fight hadn't gone that far.) Javier then kicked me in the stomach. I fell backward, but quickly sprang to my feet and gave him the old one-two kick-and-punch combination that would have made Bruce Lee proud. The crowd grew in size and cheered for both Javier and me. The other kids weren't against me; they just wanted to see a good old-fashioned schoolyard brawl. Javier and I traded blows for a few more minutes, then we both simultaneously stopped to catch our breath. He looked at me probably to gauge if I had had enough. I realized he didn't want to lose face, either, so I held up my hands, palms open, signaling a truce. Javier and his group walked to the other side of the field as I gathered my books and went down the alley toward our apartment.

I had withstood my first challenge here, and a tie was all I needed.

In the spring of 1976, several kids in my neighborhood grabbed me to go try out for the Little League baseball at the Seabee base. I hardly knew what baseball was, but I decided to join them, without telling my mother. I hitched rides with my friends, since my mother hadn't yet received her California driver's license (she had learned how to drive in Vietnam when our family owned a Volkswagen Beetle for a year). Most of the kids already belonged to a team in the base's six-team league. They either were children or relatives of the coaches or they had participated the previous year.

I joined the "majors" with eleven- and twelve-year-olds. New kids had to attend a tryout where coaches would select several players to fill their rosters. At the tryout I borrowed another kid's glove and waited for my turn at bat. One of the coaches in the league threw batting practice as a small crowd, mostly parents and players already on teams, sat and watched prospective benchwarmers. My turn to bat finally came. I stood at the plate and held the bat with a reverse grip. I was right-handed so I held the bat the most natural way to me. As a result, I could hardly bring the bat around and badly missed the first few pitches. I could hear the hisses in the bleachers. They were probably wondering, "Where the hell did this boy come from?"

The kid playing catcher was nice. He told me to reverse my grip but that didn't help either. I could not time my swing and didn't even make contact despite ten or so pitches. The coach sent me to right field, which I later found out was the position for the worst players. Even there I failed to catch any fly balls, and, to make matters worse, managed to trip over myself chasing a fly ball, resulting in much laughter in the stands.

I didn't think I made any team, but when I got home one of the kids told me to call Chuck Morse, head coach of the Indians. Apparently he had "drafted" me. I knew I hadn't dazzled anyone during tryouts, but I just wanted to hang around my friends at the baseball field and to wear that Little League baseball uniform. I began to develop a desire to belong to something, to be identified as somebody, and to be accepted. In Vietnam athletics weren't nearly as high a priority as academics. There was no Little League, or soccer league, or Pee Wee Football. For me, though, team sports were my entrance into America. But I didn't like being laughed at by my peers or, worse, by their parents. Proving doubters wrong would be the thrust of my life for many years, starting at ballparks and on playgrounds.

Coach Morse was a swell guy. He must have been in his late thirties or early forties. He was overweight and never took off his dusty black windbreaker and filthy baseball hat, which had the initial "I" for Indians, his team. He had a son, Chuck Junior, who was a year older than me. Coach Morse drove a beat-up, dirty white van with no seats in the back. Several long bags full of bats and balls rested in the back, along with bases and cleats. He showed up at my door one day and briefly met my mother before taking me to practice. Apparently he won her trust in supervising me after school.

Even though Morse looked like what people today would call "white trash," I thought he was great. For two seasons he picked me up and drove me home on most game days. I rode my bike to the field for practices, which was about 3 miles from where we lived. He probably even paid my league fees, because I knew my mother didn't have the money. He treated me better than he treated Chuck Junior, whom he often scolded on the field and forced to run laps dragging a weighted bag belted around his waist. I can still hear his deep voice, yelling, "Jiminy Cricket, Pham! Bend your knees! Get down closer to the ball! Jesus H. Christ!" He didn't yell that much at me and when he did, it didn't matter. *What the hell was a Jiminy Cricket anyway?*

I managed a .ooo batting average that season, but my worst experience took place during the last game, when Coach Morse stuck me in right field.

It was a bright Saturday afternoon, and the Indians had finished the season second to last. We had several good players who had made the all-stars, but by the end many of our best players had already left to hit the beaches for the summer.

I was playing right field when a rare pop fly headed my way. Judging its flight path, I ran underneath it, certain I was going to make this catch in front of a large crowd that was waiting for the championship game scheduled to play after ours.

Suddenly I felt my feet scrabbling under me as I looked up at the bright sky, attempting to locate a small, quickly falling, dark baseball. I raised my oversized mitt (which was too large for my hand) and it nearly blocked out the sky. I was about to make the catch when suddenly the ball disappeared. I then felt a heavy pain in my chest as I fell on my back. There was a hush in the crowd as Coach Morse ran toward me.

The sun was so bright that I had a difficult time seeing the faces of the adults now surrounding me. I could hardly breathe, but gathered enough strength to sit up after a few minutes. I sat there for a moment, not so much because of the pain, but because I was too embarrassed to get up and walk off the field.

Although that playing field back in 1976 wasn't exactly level, I was glad just to get onto one. The opposing pitchers weren't going to slow down their pitches for me, and the other teams' batters wouldn't hit the ball any slower or softer. I had to catch up.

(To hurt my fragile ego further, the public announcer never did say my name correctly. It was always "Kwang Fong or Kwung Fang.")

To improve, though, I also spent that summer playing baseball in the alley behind our apartment. The neighborhood kids and I decided to use a tennis ball in case we accidentally hit somebody's window. Since it traveled faster than a baseball, especially on hitting the pavement, my timing improved as well. I had the other kids pitch tennis balls to me, and we traded places in pitching and hitting. I was going to be prepared for the next season. I was tired of being laughed at.

I also watched the Los Angeles Dodgers on local Channel 11 whenever I could. Even though I didn't play first base, my favorite player was Steve Garvey, the sturdy first baseman with the good looks and a hot blonde wife: they seemed the Ken and Barbie of baseball. He became my first sports hero, and I wore his number 6. I was quickly buying into Mom, apple pie, and the all-American look even though in reality, I was a short, Asian benchwarmer living in a single-parent household eating rice for dinner.

Between sixth and seventh grade I got my first job, delivering a daily newspaper after school. The *Press-Courier* had been Oxnard's daily for many years, and my route took less than an hour each day because there weren't many subscribers in my Aleric neighborhood. My pay was $20 to $30 a month, depending on my ability to sign up new customers. I learned a little about selling as I knocked on doors and pitched the paper. It was also a chance for me to practice my English, speaking to adults by myself.

(President Jimmy Carter took office in January 1977. His first official act was to pardon all Vietnam-era draft dodgers, including those who fled the country (not including deserters or those who had gone absent without leave from their military units). For Americans, this act either marked the beginning of the healing or the continuation of division of that generation. With a signature, Carter "forgave" thousands of Americans. Years later several articles included the future President Bill Clinton in this group, although he was never charged with draft evasion.)

Baseball was on my mind again as my second baseball season rolled around in spring 1977. So was the laughter of those parents the previous spring. This time I was ready. Coach Morse put us through two weeks of practice as he tried me at nearly every position. By our first practice game against the Reds, the previous season's league champions, I had cracked the starting lineup, batting third and playing second base. A boy named Nathan, one of my closest friends on the team and a left-hander, batted clean-up and played first. And he had been one of my biggest supporters the previous season.

That game marked the beginning of the "new" Quang, Quang the athlete. In the first inning a runner stood on first with one out when I came to the plate. Only a handful of parents had come out to the practice game, but I recognized their faces. I didn't waste any time. The pitcher went into his windup. As he released the ball from some 40 feet, I saw its seam stitches more clearly than I ever had before. I belted the first pitch over the left fielder's head into some weeds. The sparse crowd clapped as I rounded first base, still in shock over my first-ever hit. The coaches (also acting as umpires) decided to hold me at second base, ruling my hit as a ground-rule double. The runner scored. I had earned my first run batted in as well. It didn't matter that it was a practice game. I had ended the dry spell, thrown the monkey off my back—pick a cliché! On my next at-bat I laid down a perfect bunt along the third-base foul line after receiving a signal from Coach Morse. (Like Buddha, his bunt signal usually included a rubbing of his ear and belly.) I also fielded several ground balls to second base without making an error.

Tied for first place, the Indians made the one-game championship playoff that year. I had started the entire season at second base. Late in the championship game, with the bases loaded, I hit a single up the middle and two runners came home. We held on to win the game and received individual championship trophies. I was elated, and to top things off Coach Morse, having coached the league champions, became the head coach for the CBC All-Stars. He selected me to play in the All-Star Series.

After the season I thanked Coach Morse for all he had done for me. He laughed and jokingly said, "Pham, just have your mother cook me a good Vietnamese dinner sometime." My mother never invited him over. I think she was a little scared of him, and he was married. I never saw him again after that. I wonder if he ever knew how much of a difference he made in a young boy's life.

CHAPTER 12

MY COMING-OUT PARTY

IT WAS THREE YEARS AFTER COMING TO THE UNITED STATES before I finally felt comfortable speaking and writing English. Reading comprehension would take a little longer. I had achieved a 3.8 grade-point average by the end of my freshman year in high school, receiving As in college preparatory classes, including Spanish. I guess my Vietnamese didn't meet the college entrance requirement for a foreign language.

My mother worked several jobs during the day while completing her associate degree in accounting at night. I remember hardly seeing her during those years except on the weekends. After she got her degree, she accepted a new position working in the back room of a small bank. My older sister also found a part-time job at the local shopping mall. I worked various part-time jobs, from a clerk at a local state government office typing forms to a janitor cleaning toilets and picking up trash at a local accounting company. With the income we were now all bringing in, my family was able to move to a nicer part of town on the north end of Oxnard.

Finally, gone were the days of having to use food stamps and receiving welfare checks. Although grateful for these services, I was embarrassed every time I went to the grocery store clutching food stamps. Even the federally subsidized school-lunch program didn't feel comfortable. I would use the allowance my mother gave me to pay for "discounted" lunches (20 cents), which I hoped would make me appear to other children (paying the full 50 cents) as if I weren't poor. *For Christ's sake, I was the son of Lt. Col. Pham Van Hoa.** I can't describe that feeling of low self-esteem and shame but I was

---

*I would learn that I wasn't the only Vietnamese refugee who was hung up on my pre-April 1975 status.

glad public assistance was there: without it our family would not have been able to make it here. My mother worked overtime so our family could jettison that stigma of poverty even though, in reality, we hovered right above the line.

My family made friends with only one other Vietnamese family (although there were several Vietnamese at my schools) during our first several years here. I played with one of the boys, who was a few years younger. We visited each other's house only once a month, and after a while we went our separate ways. Since the nearby navy bases brought Filipino sailors and veterans to the area, we went to school with many of their children, but only to toil in their shadow. The Filipino kids were called "Flips," while we garnered an acronym that pretty much marked us in the minds of the other kids.

"FOB" was short for "fresh off the boat." FOBs often didn't speak proper English (choppy, incomplete sentences lacking action verbs, and with no "s" in plurals); looked as if they were still traumatized (as if many Asians displayed much emotion anyway); and wore mismatched clothes from Goodwill stores or the Salvation Army. Most of all, FOB boys had the same haircut, the supposedly universal Asian "bowl cut." For my sisters, they dreaded the "à la garçon" bob. For me, becoming a Marine would not be the first time I had had a bad haircut.

There were other Asian-American students at my school: several Chinese and *sansei* kids, third-generation children of Japanese-American farmers and ranch owners (the Mexicans picking strawberries and other crops from the formers' fields). I made friends with some although I overheard some of the *sansei* boys refer to us Vietnamese as "those fucking FOBs" on many occasions. (It was bad enough having whites, blacks, and Mexicans make fun of us.)

During those days in Oxnard popular jeer aimed at Mexican students was "la migra," meaning "Immigration Service" or "Border Patrol." Heads would quickly turn when the taunts were screamed, then laughed about by ruthless pranksters of all colors. (At least I had a green card.) No doubt the Vietnamese refugees received special treatment and help from the government to immigrate and resettle, in contrast to some other immigrants. Maybe America felt badly about the events of April 1975 and was making things right for us few fortunate escapees.

By 1977 the plight of the Vietnamese "boat people" had caught the world's attention. Conditions in postwar Vietnam were horrendous: discrimination, human right violations, famine, and poverty had driven many to flee across the high seas in the years after the fall of Saigon. The refugees risked their lives in leaking, overcrowded fishing boats, and so U.S. Navy warships operating in the region were ordered to pick up refugees at sea.

Then, in late 1978, Vietnam invaded Cambodia and overthrew Pol Pot's regime (by then, about 2 million Cambodians had died in the "killing fields"). In early 1979 China and Vietnam fought a two-month border war. China had supported Pol Pot. So, facing discrimination and retaliation from the government, many ethnic-Chinese Vietnamese (the bulk of the entrepreneurs in the Cho Lon district in Saigon) fled by fishing boat. Thus over 60,000 of them ended up in refugee camps throughout Southeast Asia. Hostility grew as the boats continued to come to the shores of Asian neighbors, some boats being forced back to sea.

I wondered if the *Mayflower* pilgrims and the immigrants who came through Ellis Island were also called "FOBs."

Another jeer I often heard was, "Go back to Vietnam!" I wanted to yell my comeback, "I can't!" but I never did. Nobody would understand anyway. That's the difference between a refugee and an immigrant. *Hell, even the 15,000 or so who emigrated before the fall of Saigon could no longer go back.*

The United Nations estimated that more than a million people left Vietnam between 1976 and 1985, and as many as 300,000 died from drowning, hunger, sickness, thirst, and attacks.

In my spare time I continued my fascination with the military and aviation. With money from washing neighbors' cars and selling raffle tickets, I bought model airplane kits even though I wasn't very adept at putting the plastic parts together. *My* planes always ended up with extra glue, visible on their fuselages; their insignia were slightly crooked, and the propellers often didn't spin because parts were broken or somehow lost during assembly. Still, I could rattle off the types of airplanes that were flown in World War II by U.S., British, German, and Japanese pilots.

The only planes I knew my father had flown were the C-130 and C-123 transports. My mother kept a photo of my father's Air Commando training class, taken in the United States in 1966, along with pictures of him in Texas. I also had one headshot of him smiling and wearing a flight helmet with U.S. Air Force inscription. I knew transport pilots didn't wear helmets; I also knew bomber pilots didn't wear helmets because I had seen *Twelve O'Clock High.*

I rode my bike to the annual Point Mugu airshow featuring the Blue Angels, the U.S. Navy's flight demonstration team. I watched in awe their display of aviation precision, those beautiful blue jets soaring so close to each other. Other planes participated in the show, including vintage aircraft and modern fighters reenacting dogfights and strafing runs. Then, one time, a blue-gray aircraft appeared, a sleek, dual rudder, twin-engine fighter, with a short probe on its nose and "MARINES" painted on its fuselage. The plane looked like a space-age aircraft in contrast to the other jets at the show, even the A-4 Skyhawks flown by the Blue Angels. The crowd of mostly aviation enthusiasts was mesmerized, and so was I. The announcer finally said, "To your right coming in for landing is the McDonnell-Douglas YF-17, our latest fighter."*

I attended the same Point Mugu airshows regularly, even while I was in college. I remember walking up to pilots and asking them about their airplanes, the maximum speeds, and the weapons they carried. I remember my first meeting with a U.S. fighter pilot, the commanding officer of the navy's Top Gun squadron. He was speaking to a crowd of attendees, talking with his hands to demonstrate maneuvers and how he had shot down enemy aircraft. He then proceeded to pull out some books to sell, which were his memoirs! I later found out that he was the first ace in Vietnam and a future congressman.

I did, however, buy *Marine Air: First to Fight* from a former pilot named John Trotti. In the book were color photographs of Marine planes and helicopters and their pilots. I particularly liked the green camouflage color of the pilots' helmets. Marine pilots struck me as being different from air force or navy pilots. On the television series "Baa Baa Black Sheep," the pilots got into fistfights (like *Crazy* Hoa), won their dogfights with Japanese pilots, got drunk often, and always ended up with the navy nurses.

I would occasionally pull out my father's B-25 flight school yearbook from Class 1959-E at Reese Air Force Base in Texas. Along with his photos and records, the book was in one of the bags he gave us the night we left Saigon. My mother stored most of his documents in her bedroom closet but I kept the yearbook. It was the only item I could understand because it was like my high school yearbook. But I couldn't comprehend why my father had been training in the United States or why he was wearing the flight helmet. There were several pages of crumpled VNAF documents with short Vietnamese phrases and abbreviations typed on onion paper. I had no clue what they meant, nor was I interested in asking my mother.

*The YF-17 was the prototype of the F/A-18 Hornet, widely used in U.S. Navy and Marine Corps aviation since the 1980s.

My favorite part of his yearbook was the "A Student Pilot's Day" section, a chronology of black-and-white photographs with captions.

0500	Another day . . . [alarm clock]
0530	Breakfast, Hurry! [coffee, juice and toast]
0620	Flight Briefing [poring over flight plan]
0700	You Fly First!? [walking to airplane]
1200	On Final [cockpit view of runways]
1230	A Moment's Rest [lunch]
1300	Mail [opening mailbox]
1305	To Class [carrying brief case]
1400	Notes, Notes, Notes! [writing copiously]
1530	Ten Minute Break [smoking]
1625	P.T. [physical training]
1730	Dress for Supper [coming out of shower]
1815	Supper [food and smoking]
1900	Relax [pinball]
2000	Study [flight charts, maps]
2200	Dear Nancy [writing home]
2300	Lights out [alarm clock]

Back then, never once did I think I could do what my father did, achieving pilot's wings in a foreign country. Nor did I ever envision myself as a U.S. pilot even after I had attended the military airshows and seen the war movies and TV shows. FOBs couldn't possibly become fighter pilots, although I was really a FOP or "fresh off the plane." It also didn't occur to me until much later that all of the U.S. military pilots I saw were white—at the airshows, in the aviation books, and in films.

For Christmas in 1980, my Uncle An gave me Frank Snepp's *Decent Interval: An Insider's Account of Saigon's Indecent End Told by the CIA's Last Chief Strategy Analyst in Vietnam.* It was the first of many books on the Vietnam War that I would read. It took me years to finish the book; each time I would cringe at reading about the deceptions that took place before the fall of Saigon. Defying all censors, Snepp wrote the book just two years after the South Vietnamese capital fell. The CIA took him to court (all the way to the U.S. Supreme Court, where he lost) and he had to forfeit some $200,000 in royalties. Most of his marvelous writing was over my head at that time, but even then I began to sense there were more reasons why my family and thousands of Vietnamese had had to flee our native country. Our motherland hadn't just been "lost overnight."

After getting cut from the JV baseball team, basketball became my new athletic obsession. I bought a rim and bolted it onto a 3-by-3-foot piece of wood. I then hung it about 10 feet high in the alley behind our apartment complex. The apartment manager wasn't thrilled about that but she didn't say anything, since I allowed other kids to use it. The men in our neighborhood who worked night shifts also weren't too pleased with the sound of bouncing balls early on weekend mornings.

I shot hoops nearly every day. I practiced the fundamentals by watching varsity players do their warmups. I made sure I could do layups, pushing off on the correct foot as well as not traveling with the basketball. I shot free throws after school and played one-on-one with my new friend, Mark Adams. He was assured a starting position as the small forward. He often imitated Larry Bird of the Boston Celtics with his fade-away jump shot and pinpoint passing. I preferred the flashy guy with the big Afro—"Dr. J."

Oxnard High School was the ultimate melting pot. We had blacks, whites, surfers, "loadies" (or partiers), rich, poor, Mexicans, Japanese, Koreans, Chinese, and several Vietnamese. Our team exactly reflected the school's composition. Amazingly, all the players got along and we even hung out together outside of basketball. We didn't take shit from anyone, especially from the rich kids at nearby Thousand Oaks and Westlake high schools. We even had a small bunch of groupies who rooted for us at every game, at home and away (that is, when they weren't drunk or high on dope).

I was on the verge of getting cut from another sports team. My inability to bring the ball up court against a full-court press in practice proved to be my Achilles' heel. But my man-to-man defense and offensive skills otherwise held up. My make-or-break chance came during the fourth and final practice game against Santa Barbara High School. It would be an insignificant moment in the history of Oxnard High School athletics but unforgettable for me.

Late in the third quarter I was sitting near the end of the bench, second farthest from our coach, Rick. The varsity team and their head coach (Coach Smith) sat behind the scorer's table, just 20 feet away. Rick had already announced that he would post the final roster the next day. I had on my sweatshirt, and was ready to end my short-lived hoop dreams when he called me over. "Pham, you're going in for Dan as the two."

Boy was I glad I didn't have to run the point. I could hear my teammates trying to pump me up. A few minutes after I entered the game, a loose ball rolled past me and toward the scorer's table. Without hesitation, I headed for the floor, diving headfirst, but did not come close to even touching the ball which had ended up under the bleachers next to the scorer's table. My head banged into one of the table's legs; my vision temporarily went blank. My skin peeled off my knees. Everything seemed to slow including Coach Smith's voice. "Are you OK, Pham?" he asked while looking down at me. He extended his hand and I grabbed it, pulling myself off the floor, expecting laughter to cascade down from the stands. Instead, I heard Coach Smith and the varsity players enthusiastically say, "Way to hustle, man! Go get 'em!" Coach Rick ran over and gave me a pat on the back, smiling proudly.

On the next inbound, our team got a steal. I ran down the court and the point guard fed me the ball on the left wing. I came to a jump stop, put the ball in the air from about fifteen feet and—nothing but net. Our bench jumped up and down and I ran back on defense, fully charged. A few plays later, I got a steal and scored on a layup. Another jump shot followed. We lost by about twenty but on the bus back to Oxnard after the game, I felt I had turned the corner.

The next day I paced the hallways, anticipating the final roster which was to be posted after school. I could hardly wait, pestering Mark about my chances. He just laughed, reassuring me that the small bump on my head, a souvenir of the previous game, had earned me a spot on the team. Still, my heart pounded as I approached the locker room.

Twelve kids made the junior varsity team; my name was second to last.

By the fourth game of the season, with a 0–3 record, Coach Rick shuffled his lineup and announced a new starting point guard. Me. I never lost my starting job (despite many turnovers) and was often appointed as one of two team captains Rick selected before each game throughout the season. We finished 0–16, losing by ten to the league's champion, Westlake High, in the season's finale.

At the team banquet Rick made some remarks about our winless season. He said that the team had improved throughout the year and that was important. He decided not to give a most valuable player award (which would have gone to Mark). Instead, he held up a plaque and said something like, "Throughout the season, there was one player who rose up and took charge even though he hadn't become a starter. He was vocal at practice, in games, and during time-outs. He hustled and he played hard. He made me proud. I am pleased to present the 1981 team captain award to . . . Quang Pham."

In less than three years of high school, I had gone from a studious geek, speaking broken English, with a bowl haircut to a sort-of jock (OK, junior varsity still counted) and basketball team captain. I still had the bad Asian hairdo but there was something special in the air that day for this sixteen-year-old high school kid. I felt as if I belonged, that I had been accepted. For the first time since I arrived in this country, I could compete in the classroom and on the basketball court. As if my ego needed another boost, I found the girl that I had a crush on, a varsity cheerleader and a knockout, and asked her to an upcoming school dance. Used to rejections, I was not expecting it when she smiled and nodded, "I'd love to go with you." I hadn't even thought of the consequences since she had just broken up with her boyfriend, a good friend of mine and a varsity football lineman. I was lucky he didn't beat the pulp out of me.

"Bird Dog" became my new nickname for a short time. I didn't know what that meant until Mark whispered something to the effect that I "had moved in" on the lineman's ex so soon after his breakup. To me, she and I were just friends, but it was obvious I still needed much cultural training.

A couple of new Vietnamese students enrolled at Oxnard High School, but I never spent much time with them except for a quick hello once in a while. I had become a "somebody," but in reality I was really no different from the latest arrivals from Vietnam. Except that most had their fathers with them. At school I hardly ever ran into my older sister, Thi, who by then had become a senior with many boys vying for her attention. Some of them tried to befriend me, and I took advantage of their bribes to get close to her. I borrowed their Pontiac Firebirds, or asked them to buy me new rock-and-roll records in exchange for passing notes to Thi.

In the fall of 1981, just before my senior year, my mother bought our first home with help from my Uncle An and Aunt Ly. It was a small four-bedroom house on Doris Avenue two miles from the high school. The mortgage took most of her salary, so we basically lived on Thi's part-time wages and my monthly newspaper delivery check of some $400. My mother had incredibly achieved the American Dream of home ownership after just six years, and starting with nothing.

I still remember waking up with her every day at 4 a.m. to deliver the *Los Angeles Times*. Afterward, she would go to work at her bank and I would go to school, often nodding off by the early afternoon. My mother taught me how to drive with a stick shift, the way my father had taught her in a Volkswagen a decade earlier. The newspaper route had come from a friend who was two years older and already had his driver's license. He first had hired me as his "assistant." After two months, he decided it wasn't worth losing his beauty sleep over and was about to quit when I offered to take over the route.

We delivered newspapers to about 200 customers—she'd crisscross the streets in the wee hours, while I sat in the passenger seat throwing the rolled-up papers with my right hand. (The other "paperboys" were grown men in their forties and fifties, holding another job to make ends meet.) For those few months, I spent more time with my mother than I had since we left Vietnam, but I don't remember much of our conversations though since we were hardly awake those mornings.

My three years of delivering the *Los Angeles Times* brought our family extra money for the mortgage, and got me up early enough to attend morning basketball practices, leaving my afternoons free to play in games after classes. It was particularly difficult, however, to wake up on Saturday mornings after Friday night games and postgame parties. But my boss, Mr. Hendrickson, called my house every morning for three years, often two or three times, to get his young employee out of bed. He was my backup in case I was sick—which rarely happened. The route was for seven days a week, 365 days a year, and in three years I only missed a few days.

As an added benefit, my job enabled me to read the front and sports pages every day before school.

One day after school I came home and smashed all my model airplanes, and I threw them all away. I ripped posters of warplanes from my bedroom walls. I had come to feel that the model-building hobby was for geeks and nerds. I had become "somebody" now, a team captain and a varsity basketball player. I had only three things on my mind as I prepared for my final year of high school: babes, basketball, and my Volkswagen Bug.

As the only boy I had my own bedroom, while two of my sisters shared one and my youngest slept with my mother. That special treatment would not go unnoticed by my sisters, especially Thi. My mother had also imposed different standards on us—Thi had to come home by 10 p.m. while I could stay out until 11, which she greatly resented. We occasionally crossed paths at high school parties but she was the one who had to leave first. (She also got grounded when she came home with cigarette smoke on her breath.) Thi added another nickname to my long list, "Mama's Boy."

During our later high school years, my mother paid a lot more attention to Thi and me. Thi could not have boys visit her or call the house, with the exception of her attending the senior prom, while I violated my curfew twice before I was grounded, thus missing a huge party after our football team upset our cross-town rival.

On one occasion, I came home with alcohol on my breath after driving back from a party. I could taste it so I figured my mother would be able to easily smell it. That was *the* rule I could not break. I was hoping my mother had gone to sleep so I could sneak in through the garage as I had done before.

My mother stood like a madwoman in the living room when I staggered through the front door. She had been wide awake, her hair all mussed, her eyes already red from crying. Without saying a word she slapped me so hard that I saw stars. I could barely see my sisters in the background and their blurry faces. Nobody had ever struck me that hard, even after all those street fights with the other boys. She hit me again. Tears welled up in my eyes as I became angry. My chest tightened in angry response and my fists were clenched.

My mother must have seen the look on my face and my tensed body. She backed off. I could see my sisters looking down from the stairwell, their faces smiling at "Mama's Boy" crying again. My mother began to weep, covering her face, "If your father was here, you would not get away with this. God, in Vietnam, I would not have to put up with you undisciplined children. You uneducated and disrespectful imbeciles. Please send me back to Vietnam, God." That's when my sisters began to cry as well.

We children had heard her cries many times, but a reference to my father would bring a stop to every argument, his presence felt from some jungle camp 12,000 miles away. We all quietly retreated to our bedrooms.

My mother never struck me again after that, and I never drove home drunk again (at least while I lived with her).

I don't know how my mother ever did it, coming to the United States by herself and raising four kids. But it also never occurred to me that we were a single-parent household. Unlike the other kids with single parents in my neighborhood and in school, my father hadn't left us, we'd left him. As the years went by, though, my hopes of seeing my father again began to vanish, leaving room for me to go on with my life. My Vietnamese cultural knowledge and language were slowly slipping away.

CHAPTER 13

ABANDONED ALLY

Vietnam 1975–1982

J UST AFTER THE FALL OF SAIGON MY FATHER REMAINED IN hiding. Uncertain of the new government's intent, he kept mostly inside my grandmother's house in the Ban Co area of Saigon.

Saigon was then littered with U.S.-made military equipment and uniforms of ARVN soldiers who had escaped Vietnam or disappeared into hiding. Shredded papers were strewn across the streets, remnants of documents from the U.S. Embassy and other government buildings. Whole blocks of the city resembled ghost towns. In congested areas downtown, "liberators" from the north continued to pour in via every entry point into the city. The reek of diesel exhaust from tanks and trucks fouled the humid air.

My father stripped himself of everything linking him to the VNAF, the Saigon government, or the United States. He destroyed his ID card and ripped his names off his uniforms. He had given my mother most of his official documents the night we left Saigon, but he didn't know that my Aunt Nhang also kept some photos of my family in a secret box in my grandmother's house. Looting was in full swing as crowds gathered to cheer arriving NVA soldiers, hoping for possible amnesty down the road.

Old Glory and the South Vietnamese yellow flag with its three red stripes disappeared on May 1, 1975. Red flags with single gold stars now flew in front of the former Presidential Palace (renamed Reunification Palace) and on the antennas of tanks and armored vehicles clanking through the streets. The Communists promptly renamed Saigon Ho Chi Minh City (although to this day many residents and expatriates still refer to the old "pearl of the Orient" by its maiden name). The next day, communist cadres, broadcasting over loudspeakers and local radio stations, announced roundup points for former South Vietnamese government and military officials. Posters of the faces of South Vietnam's senior officers were posted at the Ben Thanh Market. The same procedures were carried out throughout the country, in every province. The *Who's Who* in South Vietnam would become "Hanoi's Most-Wanted."

Joining my father in the reeducation camps were thousands of VNAF veterans, about 90 percent of whom had stayed in Vietnam. They included Lt. Col. Nguyen Cau (call sign "Dupont"), a former C-47 navigator and commander of the "Monkey Mountain" radar center east of Danang. Cau spent the most camp time with my father, nearly a decade, and in six different facilities in northern and southern Vietnam. Other fellow inmates were "Piggy," who had been one of my father's wingmen in the 2d FS back in 1962, and Maj. Ho Dang Tri, "Tri Toc," a navigator and former aide-de-camp to Gen. Nguyen Cao Ky. Three decades later they all provided me with firsthand recollections of their years in captivity. My three uncles gave me their perspectives on the reeducation camps in the south.

In all, about a million South Vietnamese were sent to hundreds of reeducation camps throughout Vietnam. The detainees included thousands of journalists, judges, politicians, propagandists, teachers, and religious leaders. Although most of the civilians underwent three-day lectures, about 100,000 were sent to long-term reeducation.

Many ARVN soldiers (airborne troops, rangers, and Vietnamese Marines), especially those stationed in Military Regions I and II closer to the DMZ, never had a chance to escape. The three uncles had been captains in the artillery, infantry, and signal corps, respectively, and they, too, were sent to the reeducation camps. Somehow they would never cross paths even though prisoners were kept in groups according to rank.

Infiltrators, those who worked clandestinely for North Vietnam during the war, revealed their true identities and began shouting that "the new Vietnam would be good for everyone." For the first time since anyone could remember, the open market was empty—anticipation of a bloodbath kept everyone in their homes. Communist troops looted Tan Son Nhut, carrying out air conditioners, bicycles, refrigerators, and typewriters. Rumors of revenge on the "puppet" regime and "infidels" floated from door to door. Communist officials continued broadcasting over old Saigon radio stations and loudspeakers: "It's time to forgive and forget. The war is over. Turn yourselves in for reeducation. There's only one Vietnam."

Soon after victory, communist cadres called for ex-VNAF pilots to return to Tan Son Nhut and another location in the city. My father reported along with about 500 other men; they were uncertain how the new government was going to treat them. North Vietnam certainly did not abide by Geneva conventions, as evinced by their treatment of U.S. POWs, and if the victors were seeking revenge, the only enemies the Communists could get their hands on now were South Vietnamese.

The South Vietnamese were told that their pending incarceration would last between three and thirty days, depending on rank. Enlisted members attended a three-day reeducation course, the shortest, and were then released with official certificates of approbation. Lieutenants and captains were to report for ten days; majors and above prepared for thirty days.

After reporting to Tan Son Nhut, the prospective internees turned in all identification and arms that they still possessed. In longhand writing they answered a detailed questionnaire about their lives since 1945. There was no way they could lie on the questionnaires: a former captain in the VNAF administrative headquarters had been a Communist agent, and he knew everything about everybody. Cau estimated about 1 percent of the VNAF was VC. After completing the forms most were sent home to wait for further instructions.

My father was ordered to assist the cadres for two weeks. As one of the first flight instructors in the C-130, he and other crewmen translated its flight manual from English to Vietnamese. The cadres forced him to teach communist pilots how to operate this newest and biggest transport plane in the VNAF inventory.

According to USAF sources only ten C-130s could be flown out to Thailand and Singapore, so fourteen of them were left behind, and it was later revealed that the Communists operated about three of them, until spare parts ran out.

An armed cadre sat in the cockpit between my father and his new communist copilot. There was only enough fuel in the aircraft to fly brief training missions and not enough to flee to Singapore or the Philippines. My family and I did not know why my father didn't try to attempt to escape or to overwhelm the cadre member. Years later I was told that he'd had one chance. On one of the flights a junior cadre agreed to defect to Thailand with the crew; however, one of my father's crew members aboard didn't want to flee, since his family would have been left behind in Vietnam. My father turned the plane around and landed at Tan Son Nhut.

Yet successful escapes such as these did occur on at least two occasions. One C-47 pilot was able to convince his Communist copilot to flee to Ubon, Thailand. They flew at extremely low altitude and barely made it before their fuel tanks went dry. A helicopter crew also successfully defected.

It didn't take long before the cadres got fed up with flying lessons, so my father was transferred to other duties. Along with other detainees, gripping small brooms, he swept the parking lots and runways at Tan Son Nhut, where he had made thousands of takeoffs and landings. The summer heat was unrelenting on the asphalt runway and PSP ramps, a portent of harsher labor in the years ahead. Still, his famous humor did not go unnoticed.

He reported one day for sweeping duty wearing an extra dose of Aqua Velva aftershave lotion from his last bottle. He didn't want to "waste" the remaining drops. The cadres apparently weren't fond of his scent, so they gave him some extra hours of sweeping as punishment for being a wiseguy. An "enlightened" fellow VNAF officer told my father, "You're not used to manual labor, are you? To them [the Communists], that means glory." My father retorted, "If we did hard labor, we wouldn't have energy left to fly airplanes!" This was not a response designed to win Communist hearts and minds. And it didn't.

The cadres then ordered all the prisoners to stop speaking foreign languages, especially English. *Be proud of our mother language!* To that my father angrily countered, "American airplanes, American fuel, American training. If we spoke Vietnamese, we may make a mistake in communication that would make flying very unsafe. Even the Russians speak English when they're flying. It's the international aviation language."

There was no resistance to the massive incarceration. Like the others, perhaps still in shock over the rapid fall of Saigon, my father's mind was full of defeatist thoughts. Since he was a southerner, he hadn't been exposed to the nefarious communist ways, but his colleagues born in the north were leery because they had been made to witness executions, rapacious land reform, and other instruments of communist rule.

After they locked their heels in front of the victors on June 15, 1975, the South Vietnamese were required to fill out dozens of long forms listing all of their previous military assignments. They also had to write denunciations of their earlier allegiances. Cadres with nothing else to do compared the forms with previous versions (and with the knowledge of turncoats). Those who lied would be punished by beatings.

A few days after officially reporting to what amounted to a military police station, my father's prisoner group was trucked to Camp Suoi Mau (Spring of Blood) near Bien Hoa, his former duty station fifteen miles northwest of Saigon. His "thirty-day" sentence was quickly absorbed into his first year, consisting of hours of classroom propaganda on the "new way of thinking" and endless denouncement of the "puppet regime" and the "American imperialist dogs." Communist ideology and labor were praised throughout daily eight-hour study sessions. "How many kids did you kill, Mr. Hoa?" cadres would dully intone. "How many villages did you torch with napalm? How many bombs did you drop?"

While at Camp Suoi Mau my father wrote a letter to my grandmother dated March 27, 1976:

HT 1248/K-5-A8
Dear Mother,

I received permission to write you, sister Nhang [my mother's sister] and family. I am continuing my studies and it is going well. I will overcome all difficulties to be "reeducated" in order to become a citizen in our new society. The camp manager has allowed us to write and ask our families to send necessary items. I don't really know what to request except medicine and dry food. The clothes you sent were adequate, as it is getting hot again. I hope my brothers and their families continue to live near you for support. I will try my best to graduate from reeducation soon so I can return to society a better man. Please say hello to everyone.

Your Son, Hoa.

In his letters, my father was necessarily vague. He never mentioned his immediate family living in the United States. If his captors had learned that his wife, son, and daughters had escaped to this country, they may have held him longer. Once his responsibility, our freedom became his liability.

In the summer of 1976 a few senior prisoners were flown to the north on C-130s, while thousands more were sent crammed onto teeming cargo ships. My father boarded the *Song Huong,* packed in with about 1,000 other prisoners. The ship, named after the Perfume River at Hue City, in central Vietnam, and once used to transport pigs, would make numerous trips ferrying prisoners along the coastline of Vietnam. It took four days to steam from the port of Saigon to a small port in Nghe Tinh Province just north of the DMZ.

Conditions on the ships were horrendous. Men slept in the cargo hold and often got sick. With detainees living literally atop one another, many fell ill from having to lay in feces and vomit. To compound the prisoners' utter humiliation, the cadres forced them to wear the old Vietnamese Ranger "tiger-striped" camouflage uniforms.

After disembarking and stumbling ashore shortly after midnight, they were kept in an old warehouse built of corrugated tin and wood. Guards with dogs patrolled throughout the night to prevent escape. In the early morning the hungry, exhausted men were walked through a gauntlet of angry locals. Six- and seven-year-old children, schoolteachers, old men, and women spat on the prisoners, pelted them with rocks and cursed, "You blood-thirsty imperialist dogs! Do you know how many of our people you have killed? You are nothing but puppets of the Americans!" Cau and many prisoners believed the angry protests had been staged, so they just laughed and marched to their destination. How would these children know who they were?

The prisoners were then placed on a train headed toward the provinces of Son La (in the northwest corner of Vietnam near Dien Bien Phu and the Laotian border), Hoang Lien Son (near the top of Vietnam and the China border), and Lang Son (in the northeastern corner). They were locked inside cattle cars for two days. Years later Cau had a difficult time speaking about this: "It was like the Holocaust. First, we thought they were taking us to our graves. But soon we realized we would not be killed right away. They needed to profit from our labor." The cadres repeatedly announced through megaphones: "We're lenient. We're going to give you a chance to be reeducated first."

When they arrived at the provincial train depots, the prisoners were divided into subgroups and squeezed into the backs of trucks. The guards secured the canvas tarps to prevent attempted escapes. The trucks got them closer to their destination, but the last 15 miles was done in a forced march to their respective camps deep in the mountainous jungles. Hundreds of camps and subcamps ran along the base of the Hoang Lien Son Mountains where Mount Fansipan, the tallest peak in Southeast Asia, rose to over 10,000 feet. The French had called Fansipan and surrounding mountains the Tonkinese Alps. This mountain range also marked the border with China. Escape by foot was impossible, according to Cau. Unlike the south, which had only a "wet and a dry season," the north had all four distinct seasons: during summer, the humidity neared 100 percent; in winter, snow fell.

My father and Cau were herded to Son La, a sizable, ethnically mixed village 200 miles northwest of Hanoi and, incidentally, the site of a concrete French jail built in 1908. Opponents of the French colonial regime and, later, counterrevolutionaries were incarcerated under harsh conditions, including Le Duan, a founder and head of the Vietnamese Communist Party after Ho Chi Minh died in 1969. Numerous camps were established 2 to 3 miles apart, with each housing some 300 to 400 prisoners. Colonels and high-ranking civilians were held there; my father went to Camp 3, Cau to Camp 1, two of the most remote camps.

The lies of the Communists became apparent as my father's sentence went from thirty days to three years. The three-year sentences were the standard to "reeducate" former high-level officials, combining indoctrination and hard labor. Policy being to establish a self-sufficient army throughout Vietnam, the People's Army of Vietnam (PAVN) formed Group 776 to run the northern camps. The PAVN was determined to "grow" its own food at the expense of its prison camp detainees; death by hard labor and starvation didn't matter.*

Dropped in the middle of forests, the prisoners had to build their own camps, some from the latrines up. At night, guards barricaded the prisoners with fences built from bamboo trees and wood. No movement at night was allowed, so prisoners had to relieve themselves where they slept. Hard labor, malnutrition, and sickness inevitably led to many early deaths. Those who tried to escape and got caught were beaten to death with rifle butts and clubs; others were shot at night. No reasons were ever given.

The prisoners grew their own food, which was also provided to their guards. Daily rations included an occasional bowl of rice, salt, and six inches of starchy manioc root, which Cau said tasted like cardboard. Surplus rice was sold in the nearest markets by the guards to line their own pockets. The prisoners also caught whatever they could to eat, from rats to snakes, from scorpions to snails. Many died from amoebic dysentery from eating raw food.

In 1997, *Golf Digest*'s Tom Callahan reported that Lt. Col. Vuong "Tiger" Phong, a former ARVN province chief, died in September 1976 (from starvation and/or stroke) only a few months after arriving in the Lang Son labor camp. Ten months earlier, back in the United States, retired Special Forces Lt. Col. Earl Woods had nicknamed his newborn son Eldrick after "Tiger"

---

*Based on an interview with Robert DeStatte, formerly a senior analyst in the Defense Intelligence Agency's Special office for POW/MIA.

Phong (Woods had given Vuong this nickname because of his bravery in battle). Lieutenant Colonel Phong, possibly the most famous of all reeducation
camp detainees, died never knowing that his nickname would be given to a
world's top golfer.

In a 2003 interview with Michael Arkush for the VVA Veteran (Vietnam
Veterans of America), Earl Woods remembered his former ally: "He was a
courageous fighter and leader who was really nondescript," Woods said. "All
he wanted to be was a schoolteacher. Neither one of us were these robotic,
rigid professional soldiers. We had a job to do and we were doing it." When
Saigon fell in 1975, Woods "vowed that if I had a child, I was going to nickname him Tiger in the hope that he would be on television and 'the other
Tiger' would make the connection that he was my kid and would get in
touch with me. I don't know how I knew but I just knew that my kid would
be somebody great. I just knew that all the time."

After eighteen months of chopping wood and hauling burlap bags of rice
back to his camp, my father began to wonder how long he could go on. He
and other prisoners had dwindled to skin and bones, but their declining condition was of no concern to the cadres. "You've lived off the people. Now it's
your turn to live off the land and do something with your hands. You are the
lowest form of life in our country."

My father experienced his worst days in the camps sometime in 1977. His
body was bloated, his face and hands were swollen. He struggled to take just
three steps. He had been stricken with beriberi, a disease of eighteenth-century
sailors caused by a lack of Vitamin B1. Left untreated, beriberi could be fatal.
For reasons he could never figure out, the cadres then fed him a bowl of rice
with sugar and let him rest. Recovery was slow at first but his natural vitality
kicked in. Two days later, he was ordered back to work in the jungle.

(While my father was literally fighting for his life in a prison camp, I was
a twelve-year-old refugee just beginning to stand up to the teasing and bully-
ing I got in large doses. Vietnamese mystics might interpret my newfound
boldness to the courage and energy transmitted from my abused, faraway father. Once this spiritual transfer was completed—and I had decided to stop
taking shit from American kids—my father's mission had been accomplished. So his energy and his health returned.)

As a grown man and a U.S. Marine I know this could never have happened, but whatever it was, as a yellow boy in a strange land of blacks,

browns, and whites, I appreciated whatever caused me to stop running away and backing down.

Prisoners were allowed to receive up to two packages a year weighing a maximum of 1 kilogram (2.2 pounds) each. Families sent vitamins, sugar, and medicine for flu, diarrhea, and infections, although there was always a question of whether the packages would reach the prisoners, who were moved to different camps every few months. My Aunt Nhang recalled those years:

> Whenever we got an address for him, it would change within months. He kept moving and there was no way we knew. The cadres allowed us to ship him one kilogram. I packed hand towels, cold and stomach medicines, soap and toothpaste. We had to go to a certain location and wait all day to ship the boxes. We sat on the ground. I didn't know when he would get the boxes so I never sent food. I don't know if he got every package. He was in many camps.

This shuffling of prisoners was done to keep them from becoming familiar with possible escape routes and to prevent them from getting to know one another well. False rumors, constant movement, and starvation were the control measures employed by the cadres who were afraid of prisoner revolts or escape attempts.

Ho Dang Tri recalled an episode when he ran into my father as prisoners were shuffled from camp to camp:

> On a cold day, we were gathering near a fire pit. The cadres were watching closely; they didn't want the prisoners from different camps to communicate with each other. I looked away and said to your father, "Hoa, why are you so skinny?" Your father replied, "I wouldn't talk. You think you're fat or something?" We laughed at our misery. Cadres then ran over and asked us about the exchange. We denied it, of course.

When China invaded Vietnam in early 1979, my father and his fellow inmates were nearly "liberated" by the invading troops. As the Chinese attacked along the China-Vietnam border, very near the labor camps, the internees were moved farther south to Hanoi to Camp Nam Ha, known to former U.S. POWs as Ba Sao. Nam Ha had three subcamps. Nam Ha A was the most humane, and Nam Ha C was for detainees soon to be released. My father and Cau were sent to Nam Ha B, the worst subcamp.

Even so, conditions in the camps closer to Hanoi were better. Death rates were lower, although sickness was still rampant. For the first time, visitors were allowed and on the occasion of Tet, Liberation Day, and Ho Chi Minh's birthday, the prisoners received a small portion of water buffalo meat. Buffalo skin was distributed the rest of the year, which needed to be boiled for ten hours before it could be eaten.

Many of the prisoners died between 1977 and 1979, mostly from executions, starvation, and untreated sickness. "They [the guards] kept the discipline of the camp by playing on our stomach," Cau sighed.

In 1980 one of my uncles (a former captain) was released early from the camps. His wife had died, so he had to come home to take care of his children. Then Amnesty International inspectors visited two camps outside of Hanoi-Ta Son and Nam Ha, and conditions improved after their departure. The outside world was finally able to see that Vietnam's victors had memorialized their win with fundamental human rights abuses. During the five years after the fall of Saigon, Vietnamese expatriates had little information on the plight of their loved ones. Information came from rescued "boat people," who would tell human rights advocates and journalists about those still in captivity. This in turn piqued the interest of specialists from the Defense Intelligence Agency (DIA), who flew to Southeast Asian refugee camps to further investigate possible U.S. POW "live sightings" reported by refugees.

Also in 1980, courtesy of my Great Uncle Minh's driver and his truck, my Aunt Nhang and one of my cousins visited my father for the first time since his captivity at a camp in Vinh Phuc Province. (Great Uncle Minh had served in the Communist Party during the war and had risen to become a minister in the Ministry of Propaganda.)

Despite his connection with a high-ranking communist official, my father remained in Nam Ha until 1982, on his third three-year term. With few exceptions, he and his fellow prisoners remained in custody without formally being charged, without trial, and without protection from criminal abuses by the guards. In 1982, my two other uncles were released from their camps in the south.

CHAPTER 14

QUANTICO-BOUND

Some people spend a lifetime wondering if they made a difference.
The Marines don't have that problem.

—President Ronald Reagan

IN THE FALL OF 1983 I PACKED MY BUG AND DROVE AN HOUR south of Oxnard to Westwood, home of the University of California, Los Angeles (UCLA) Bruins. I had spent the previous year at Ventura College (a community college) even though I had the grades as I simply forgot to apply to UCLA in time. No one had informed me that four-year college applications were due in November. I never once met with my high school counselor one-on-one; he was only pitching me vocational schools anyway.

On my last day of work delivering newspapers, I arrived early to thank the men who had folded my newspapers for three years. They couldn't believe I was actually headed for UCLA; college was beyond them. My boss, Mr. Hendrickson, thanked me and wished me luck. The next day my mother stood in the driveway and cried as I drove off to start my new life, leaving her with my two younger sisters in Oxnard (Thi had left home the year before for college).

There were many Asian Americans and foreign students from Asia at UCLA, nicknamed the "University of Caucasians Lost among Asians." Others called it "JewCLA." The funniest nickname, though, that I heard for UCLA originated with a decorated Vietnam veteran years after I had graduated. He referred to it as the "University of Corrupted Liberal Ass-holes."

Hollywood had powerful influence on me in those years, and I found that a major benefit of attending UCLA was its proximity to Hollywood studios. World-class movie producers like Francis Ford Coppola and George Lucas had graduated from UCLA and nearby USC (University of Southern California) film schools. World premieres took place in Westwood theaters, just a few blocks from campus. Screening tickets were plentiful and so was on-campus filming.

Vietnam War movies began to emerge in the late 1970s and early 1980s, mostly angry and bitter portrayals of veterans and the controversial war: for instance, *The Deer Hunter, Coming Home,* and *Apocalypse Now.* I can't say I enjoyed them. (Where were the real South Vietnamese?)

No other movie from that period touched me more than *The Killing Fields,* based on the true story of journalist Sydney Schanberg and his Cambodian guide, Dith Pran, during Cambodia's takeover by the Khmer Rouge. I squirmed in my seat, as I envisioned my father working in the fields like the suffering Cambodians in the movie.

A few weeks after the 1984 election, I drove to the Los Angeles Convention Center to attend a ceremony to become a U.S. citizen. After nine years of repeatedly checking the "no" box in numerous questionnaires asking whether I was a U.S. citizen, I finally could check "yes" and skip writing my "alien number." I hadn't done anything special to warrant citizenship, but in the United States, I only needed to stay out of trouble with the law and wait. (Of course I had to pass an oral test about U.S. history and government selected from 100 questions, and had to demonstrate some fluency in speaking and writing English.) Without preparation, many native-born inhabitants would fail the oral part of the exam. For my father and thousands of elderly immigrants, the oral test was later a gigantic obstacle, with many taking a crash course before the exam.

There must have been 10,000 people of all colors and creeds standing on the convention floor. A judge came out and within minutes, all of us had become citizens of the United States after taking our oath of allegiance.

I hereby declare, on oath, that I absolutely and entirely renounce and abjure all allegiance and fidelity to any foreign prince, potentate, state, or sovereignty of whom or which I have heretofore been a subject or citizen; that I will support and defend the Constitution and laws of the United States of America against all enemies, foreign and domestic; that I will bear true faith and allegiance to the same; that I will bear arms on behalf of the United States when required by the law; that I will perform noncombatant service in the Armed Forces of the United States when required by the law; that I will perform work of national importance under civilian direction when required by the law; and that I take this obligation freely without any mental reservation or purpose of evasion; so help me God.

I wondered whether native-born Americans had to take a similar oath, or that their allegiance was naturally assumed. I didn't dare to raise the question; I was just happy about no longer having to check the "no" box.

I drove back to campus feeling indifferent about my new citizenship. There was no celebration. I didn't change my name, like some immigrants who adopted American-sounding first names. I still looked the same, and didn't get a patriotic tattoo on my arm or put a flag decal on my rear car window.

A few weeks later my mother called and asked me to come home. When I got there she pulled out a watercolor portrait of my father with the inscription, "To my friend Hoa, Camp Nam Ha, 1984." The portrait had been given to my aunt in Vietnam and she immediately mailed it to my mother. In the portrait I could see my aging, stoic father in a white T-shirt, then into his third term of reeducation. He no longer looked like a fighting man, at least superficially. The delicate sketch was the surest proof that he was still alive.

Sometime in 1985 I came across an ad in the campus newspaper that read "many Asian extras needed for upcoming major motion picture. No experience required. Three days with good pay and meals. Call for more information." How could I pass up this chance for fame and fortune? How could any student who attended UCLA? This could be my "breakthrough."

I rang the Los Angeles number. After several minutes a woman came on the line. I eagerly spouted my name and my availability and asked her if she could tell me a little about the movie. "I can't tell you the name of the project or the director. But I can tell you that it's going to be a major 'Vietnam' movie. We need extras to play the enemy. You know, the Viet Cong." I quickly slammed down the phone, my Hollywood dreams instantly vanished.

By the first quarter of my second year I had surged above a 2.0 GPA. Besides economics classes, most of my electives were political science courses, as well as two art classes and nuclear arms control seminars. In the mid-1980s, UCLA hosted its share of social issues demonstrations, ranging from protestors railing against the apartheid in Africa to prophets declaring themselves as Jews for Jesus. You could not get through the main campus thoroughfare, Bruin Walk, without hearing about somebody's misery or society's injustice. I blocked out most of the propaganda, taking the offered fliers just to be nice, but only to toss them as soon as I got to my next class. No one raised hell about the human rights abuses in Vietnam then. None of the issues struck a chord with me until one day in April 1985, on the eve of the tenth anniversary of the loss of my former country.

I was scurrying across campus, late for class, when a harried student pressed a leaflet into my hand. It read, "Come Help Us Celebrate the 10th Anniversary of the Reunification of Vietnam." The crumpled flier had a picture of the tank crashing through the Presidential Palace gates in Saigon and the unforgettable helicopter on top of a Saigon building awaiting a chain of humans climbing a dangling ladder. I had become very familiar with both images.

I tore up the document, wadded it into a tight ball, and threw it in the surprised student's face. He was a white kid with unkempt long hair and had on clean but wrinkled clothes. He looked like a sanitized Vietnam War protestor from the 1960s.

"What the hell is wrong with you, man? Go to hell!" I thought about knocking a few of his teeth loose but I just walked away. How could he have possibly known anything about Vietnam?

Later that night, I stayed up and watched Ted Koppel's "Nightline" broadcast from Saigon (now Ho Chi Minh City). Henry Kissinger and Le Duc Tho exchanged their thoughts via a satellite connection. Neither had seen each other since signing that sham agreement. Kissinger seemed bewildered while Tho would not stop talking long enough to give his interpreter a chance to speak. I still understood enough Vietnamese to begin to realize how this Communist had "operated" in Paris. Then the satellite feed broke off and Koppel disappeared, leaving Charlie Gibson to continue the interview.

Later Koppel characterized the episode as having been the "worst 'Nightline' ever." I disagreed. It was fun to watch Kissinger squirm. I couldn't help but wonder if Tho was as dominant a figure back in 1973. There was no peace and no honor, and no Nobel Prize should have been awarded.

Watching the aging diplomats trade barbs that night, I thought about my father and wondered what he was doing in the reeducation camps. I had no idea where he was, and I missed him dearly. I must admit, though, that in the midst of my kaleidoscopic collegiate life, I had forgotten about him. But thanks to the never-ending American nostalgia for Vietnam, I had kindly been reminded. And I have not forgotten since.

A few months before the Bruin Walk flier incident, I was eyeing a summer internship at a Fortune 500 company during a campus job fair when I saw a Marine Corps officer recruiter. With the haircut, neatly pressed short-sleeved tan shirt, and blue trousers with red stripes, he stood out among the blue suits.

The job market was tight for everyone then except engineers. Under Reagan, defense spending had jumped dramatically and aerospace companies were interviewing every engineering graduate they could get their hands on. I didn't have the grades for the engineering program so I made economics my major. I knew nothing about John Maynard Keynes and Milton Friedman except that my debts kept growing every month. "Econ" became the major of choice for many nontechnical UCLA students like me.

The recruiter was poster-perfect. Tall, tanned, handsome, standing erect at his booth in the same aisle as IBM, Procter & Gamble, and Boeing, he was doing better business attracting sorority girls to his table than prospective officer candidates like me. I noticed that. The recruiter was talking to several other students, so I timidly sneaked behind one of them and grabbed a pamphlet. He saw me but continued with his conversation. As I walked away while skimming through the literature, a crisp and loud voice sounded off, "Hey young man, come here. What are you going to do when you graduate? What are your plans for the future?"

I turned around as he put out his hand. "What's your name? I'm Doug Hamlin, captain of Marines." "I . . . I . . . I just wanted to have the airplane pictures."

(I was stupefied. This was what I had aspired to do all my life. And I just didn't have the nerve to say it. Quang Pham from Oxnard/Saigon a Marine pilot? No way.)

"That could be you in that F-18 cockpit in three years," said Captain Hamlin in his sales pitch. He sensed my curiosity and he was good at this. "If you qualify for the PLC Program and make it through OCS," he finished.

I stood there for fifteen minutes telling him my background, and he shared his with me. Doug Hamlin had been his fraternity's president at the University of Michigan. He had joined the Corps in 1980 and was assigned to the local recruiting office in 1983. He had served with the 1st Marine Division (2d Battalion, 9th Marine Regiment) at Camp Pendleton as an infantry officer and was a quarterback on the battalion football team.

He went over the Corps requirements, and I felt intimidated. "To pass the Marine Corps Physical Fitness Test, you have to run three miles in under eighteen minutes, do at least twenty pull-ups and eighty sit-ups in under two minutes. You need to graduate with a 2.0 GPA and have at least a 1,000 on your SAT. Any major is fine. (Well, three miles in under twenty-four minutes, ten pull-ups, and sixty sit-ups before OCS. Plus you need to pass the Aviation Qualifications Test and a flight physical. You have 20/20 vision, correct?)

"Remember, Quang, you can go into business anytime. This is your one chance to do something for your country as a Marine officer." I had bought his sales pitch, but it would be another year before I would attend the longest summer camp of my life.

I spent the summer of 1985 working as an intern in San Diego for the General Dynamics Corporation. John Gadd's stepfather, Mel Barlow, was general manager of the electronics division, so John and I preferentially got our jobs. (John was my best friend in high school.)

I could not stop thinking about the Marine Corps and Captain Hamlin's words. The General Dynamics complex was in Kearney Mesa, a few miles from the Miramar Naval Air Station, and during two weeks in July, F-14 Tomcats would be launched in the morning, followed by a smaller plane in close pursuit. Bored with my summer assignment after only a month, I was mesmerized by the planes, so I asked questions around the office. Nobody knew what they were doing. A year later, I would find out the planes had been part of the filming for the movie *Top Gun*.

My junior year sped by in a blur. By December 1985, after meeting all the academic requirements, I made up my mind to attend OCS, with no obligation (as reemphasized by Captain Hamlin). I had been thinking about my citizenship and how joyless I had felt after the swearing-in ceremony. I remembered the quiet, studious Asian Americans in the physics laboratories, and although I respected their goals I wanted more than a secure job. I wanted to contribute, to belong, and not disappear into the working world as another faceless minority member—a perpetual foreigner with mediocre grades. I wanted to do something to make my parents proud, beyond making money, to know that their sacrifice had been worth something. I wanted to be a *real* American because I could no longer be a true Vietnamese, since my country of birth no longer existed.

At the time, the reasons for taking what for me was a highly unlikely step seemed clear enough. Even though I was then closer to completing a college degree, I had basically been drifting. Nothing seemed permanent for me. I could chase girls, drink beer, and play pickup hoops with the rest of my buddies, but I'd begun to see those things as temporary, rootless. I wanted to do something meaningful, make my new citizenship momentous.

Perhaps not having a father in my life made me look for stability in institutions—and the Marine Corps was *the* most institutional of institutions, with "210 years of tradition unimpeded by progress."

Mark Adams, my high school buddy and roommate, thought I had gone crazy. So did most of my friends, especially the Asian Americans on my intramural sports teams. "Why the fuck are you going into the Marine Corps? There are plenty of jobs in L.A. Aren't they a bunch of rednecks?" But I ignored them all.

On New Year's Eve of 1985 some friends and I went to the Rose Parade, and then the Rose Bowl game. We stayed up all night and the next day watching and celebrating UCLA's victory. That would be the last night I would party so hard in college; the next week I began my self-paced training program in preparation for OCS, still five months away. Three miles equaled twelve laps around the Drake Stadium track where Olympic-caliber athletes trained. The 1984 Olympics, held in Los Angeles, had given the athletic facilities at UCLA a major upgrade.

After the first two laps around the track I had to stop. I couldn't breathe. I hadn't run laps in nearly four years. After a five-minute halt to regain my breath, I resumed my run and managed to eke out eight laps. I then went over to the pull-up bars and then did sit-ups, which were the easiest. It was clear to me that my faint hope of succeeding at OCS required much more discipline than suggested by the relaxed officer candidates in the color photographs of the recruiting brochures. I had to be ready by June.

The Marine OCS program that I would join had been around since the 1930s; it was the number one route for Marine officers candidates. This Platoon Leaders' Class, or PLC, became known as the "Please Leave the Corps" program later in my career as PLC members received reserve commissions (and rushed out of the service). Thus, many would leave after three years except for aviators who owed four and a half years of service for the flight training that cost more than $1 million. Those who wanted to remain on active duty longer had to compete in a process called "augmentation." Naval Academy and most Reserve Officer Training Corps, or ROTC, graduates automatically got regular commissions, regardless of their academic grades. (It was known that only a few top OCS graduates would receive a coveted regular commission, and I had no such hopes.)

In early June I saw the movies *Top Gun* and *Platoon,* and both psychologically prepped me for induction into the armed forces. I could not help remember the references to the Vietnamese in *Platoon* and in other Vietnam movies: "Charlie," "dink," "gook," "slope," "zipperhead." I believed then that the GIs were referring to their Viet Cong enemy and not their allies in the south. But I would find out otherwise. (Dehumanizing the enemy was the norm; "Jap" was used in World War II. In Iraq, the locals are known as "hajis.")

After I took my final exams at UCLA, Mark Adams drove me to L.A. International Airport. I had carried exactly one backpack and one bag, per the instructions sent to me by Marine Corps Headquarters. About twenty-five of us showed up at the USO Terminal, coming from all walks of life in Southern California. Pictures of famous veterans and Bob Hope hung on the wall. Flags, photographs of airplanes and tanks, and recruiting posters adorned the walls. I felt patriotic and couldn't stop looking around me. The room reminded me of my bedroom in Oxnard, minus the flags.

Most candidates were college students, and several had already graduated. Three were prior-service enlisted Marines in the reserves. The recruiters, including Captain Hamlin himself, showed up to give us a final pep talk. I knew they had already filled their recruiting quotas, so it was up to us candidates to make it on our own.

Hamlin asked us all to say a few words about ourselves. Several candidates mentioned that their fathers had been Marines. A few, like me, were hoping for flight school. The confidence displayed by these young men was remarkable. I particularly recall a pock-faced bodybuilder from San Diego. He stood over 6 feet tall and had already cut his hair fairly short. He was built like a linebacker, packing about 220 pounds, or eighty pounds more than me at that time. This candidate stood up, veins standing out on his neck and muscles bulging from his polo shirt, and barked, "My goal is to finish as the number one graduate from OCS."

Even though I wanted to scream to these guys, "I am here because my father was one of the best pilots in the Vietnamese Air Force. Because he stayed behind until the end and he's still in prison. Because he had fought for twenty-one years. Because I feel I owe it to him to make him proud of me—wherever he is, whether he's still alive or dead."

Instead, I mumbled, "My name is Quang Pham and I come from Oxnard and my goal is to become a Marine pilot." No one said a word to me after my self-introduction. We boarded the plane and flew to Washington National Airport. A black Marine sergeant in green trousers and short-sleeved khaki shirt greeted us as we departed the plane. He was courteous, but spoke in a commanding voice. We grabbed our bags and followed him outside to an old white school bus with "United States Marine Corps" inscribed on its side. The humidity in the air slapped me in the face, hinting at the impending physical challenges awaiting us at Quantico.

As soon as the bus driver closed the door and pulled away from the civilian-filled terminal, our world changed. The courteous sergeant spoke again, but now in a thick Southern drawl: "What the fuck took you girlies so long to lollygag through my airport? You better move quicker than that or you'll be going home tomorrow! Now sit the fuck down and don't say a fucking word. Look straight ahead. There is nothing for you to stare at out the windows."

I had a hard time understanding him at first. Having grown up in California most of my life, I hadn't come across any black people from the South, so I had to strain to pay attention. The bus finally exited I-95 toward a wooded area, where it was still light as we came to a stop outside the Quantico base gate. A sentry exchanged some words with our bus driver. Our bus slowly rolled through the gate, above which I could barely make out the inscription, "Crossroads of the United States Marine Corps." I didn't understand what that meant but I could guess it was basically "make or break." My soft civilian reality quickly changed when the bus came to a halt on what seemed like a large hardtop basketball court.

"Get out of this fucking bus! Get on line! I say get on line, candidates!" screamed two drill instructors who had just climbed aboard. I grabbed my backpack and ran down the aisle, nearly tripping over the seat legs. Once outside, I saw dozens of other young men also being yelled at and I felt more comfortable with the harassment. *Hey, I can handle this. I saw* An Officer and A Gentleman. *Oh yeah, that was the Navy.*

The staff had us running back and forth, aligning our suitcases neatly then repeating the sequence endlessly. We would not get any sleep during the first thirty-six hours in Quantico. Looking back, the barking and yelling would eventually teach us to follow orders from our superiors, under stress and without hesitation. Discipline was the primary goal for the individual and for the team. OCS employed techniques to expose the physically and mentally weak, and to wash them out over a ten-week period. In Vietnam, such blind discipline, even in response to illegal orders, had led to atrocities in such places as Cam Ne and My Lai, the latter an Army atrocity. "Burn all dem hootches! Waste 'em motherfuckin' gooks! Get some!"

Of course I knew none of this back then. Now candidates can simply visit an official Marine Corps OCS website and download the "gouge," as the inside scoop is referred to in the military. (I also wish Captain Hamlin had given me the "gouge" about our treatment before I got to OCS but he hadn't—probably on purpose.) When I checked into Charlie Company, I wasn't the only one without the gouge. The military brats probably had gotten the gouge from their fathers or uncles. The prior-service types had already been through boot camp, while OCS was a serious boot camp for college "pukes" like me. During the Vietnam War, and long before, regular troops called OCS graduates "ten-week wonders."

As I stood there dumbfounded and in shock, another big, black sergeant got in my face. "Fang, Fong, Fam! Whatever your fucking name is! What the fuck are you doing in my Marine Corps? Are you a Viet Cong spy?"

I was stunned. I didn't know what to say. "No, sir!"

"Don't be calling me fucking sir. I work for a living. It's Sergeant Instruc-

tor to you, candidate P-Ham. That's it. Go ahead and cry. We don't want ba-
bies around here!" He towered over me, leaning into my face.

Tears came to my eyes; I couldn't even speak. I was ready to quit right
then and go home. It was immediately obvious to me that I needed the Marine Corps a hell of a lot more than it wanted me.

With TBS classmates after 25-mile hump. From left to right. John Pettit, Chuck Protzmann, Bob Plantz, me, and John Pryce. (Courtesy of Frank Quattrocchi))

Second Lieutenant of Marines and Captain Doug Hamlin at commissioning ceremony. UCLA, 1987 (Courtesy of Thi Pham)

Solo flight in the T-34 "Turbo Weenie," Corpus Christi, 1989. (Author's Collection)

CHAPTER 15

THE FEW, THE PROUD

O N T H E B U S R I D E T O Q U A N T I C O , I C O U L D N O T G E T T H E recruiting slogan out of my head, "Yeah, I've got what it takes." A J. Walter Thompson recruiting commercial had been run in the 1980s, featuring an ironsmith hammering raw molten iron, forging it into a Marine sword. A bass voiceover crooned off a macho patriotic pitch: "We begin with raw steel . . . mold it with muscle, shape it with fire and sweat. Polish it to razor-sharp perfection. Maybe you have what it takes to be one of us—the few, the proud, the Marines."

All I could think of while standing at attention in front of the OCS barracks was how to get the hell out of the fire. Plus I had to go to the bathroom ("head") since the staff had ordered us to drain two canteens of water within minutes to keep us from becoming a "heat casualty."

Before OCS, I hadn't yet learned about the Marines' illustrious combat history aside from episodes of "Baa Baa Black Sheep" and John Wayne's Sergeant Stryker in *The Sands of Iwo Jima*. Most of the Vietnam War movies had revolved around the Army's experiences. Soon I would study the scripture of the Corps combat record in Vietnam.

In the face of overwhelming challenges and unclear objectives, Marines had fought valiantly in their longest war ever. They were as courageous as their "greatest generation" predecessors who had assaulted Pacific islands, hopping from one bloody battle to another. My mother had told me that "the VC were scared of the Marines. They were vicious." She was wary of my military venture but never tried to talk me out of it. Before I departed for OCS she added, "During the war, we never saw Marines in Saigon. They did all their fighting up north."

Yet the debacle in Southeast Asia would burden the Corps as it did the United States. And I felt the brunt of it, real or imagined, during my first four weeks at OCS.

Historian and retired Marine Col. Allan R. Millett determined that the Corps had 101,574 killed and wounded in Vietnam, almost 4,000 more casualties than in World War II. It was only in the number of dead (19,733 to 12,983) that World War II held the greater number.* Vietnam was not a simple "civil" war as depicted in history books and pundit columns. There was nothing civil about it.

When your name is Quang Pham and you check into Charlie Company (or C Company) at U.S. Marine OCS eleven years after the fall of Saigon, you don't expect any breaks. When the elite outfit you're trying to join has lost thousands of young men in the Quang Nam, Quang Ngai, Quang Tin, and Quang Tri provinces, you don't expect anyone to pronounce your name correctly, even if it was known how. I hoped these guys who were going to make my present a hell and determine my future realized that the war was over.

I was called a "VC" at Quantico, even though I had nothing to do with the U.S. debacle in Vietnam. I was only a kid, on the U.S. side, on the losing side, but to my Marine instructors I symbolized that loss and shame. My father was still paying for that loss at a prison camp. All I could do was remember that his predicament was infinitely worse than mine.

We candidates handwrote our biographies with emphasis on our accomplishments, which also inadvertently revealed our "potential" weak points as well: for example, if you didn't mention that you had leadership experience, then it could be assumed that you had poor leadership skills. My file contained my enlistment contract and OCS application with "MINORITY CANDIDATE" stamped across the top. (That hadn't been there when I signed the original paperwork.) On the second line, my birthday and my place of birth, "Saigon, Vietnam," were typed.† That's how the staff knew about my background. I didn't think the "minority" stamp was necessary if anyone had bothered to look at my face, my name, and my birthplace.

---

*Medical evacuation by helicopter (medevacs) played a major role in reducing the number of those killed in action (KIAs).

†In 2004, I received my military records from Marine Corps Headquarters and I interviewed my recruiter, Doug Hamlin, who had become one of my closest friends. When I pushed him for answers, Doug admitted that he and other recruiters worked to a quota system for minority and female officer candidates. Doug thought he would get more Asian-American candidates, especially at UCLA. He didn't.

The fourth platoon, my training platoon, was commanded by Capt. Barry Amos, an infantry officer who had washed out of flight school. His dislike of aviation types became evident the first week. "Let me see who my air candidates are. Raise your hand. Ah . . . Pham, I knew you'd be an Airedale." In the Marine Corps, everyone is first and foremost a rifleman. The infantry or the "grunts" made up the Corps and always would. The aviation candidates called Amos a "fallen angel" and "Captain Sunshine" for his cynical attitude. Gunnery Sergeant Robert Ramirez was the fourth platoon sergeant, and Sgt. Martin Anderson, the sergeant instructor, rounded out the staff. Both were physically shorter than average but were as lean and mean as Marines come.

Captain Amos also wanted to know if there were any "legacies" in the platoon. "Raise your hand if your father is a colonel or above." There was a line in the OCS application to list all "relatives who served or are serving in the armed forces" by rank, name, and service. I didn't write anything on my application. Somehow, I instinctively put up my hand thinking that my father would have been at least a colonel by 1986. Amos looked at me and sneered, "Colonel or above *in the U.S. military!*" (Sergeant Anderson did later threaten, "For many of you, that family military tradition will end this summer!")

After the first thirty-six hours of no-sleep shock treatment, I settled into the platoon's squad bay. It was a long linoleum-floored room, with bunk beds ("racks") neatly aligned. The training staff had private rooms. There was one communal bathroom (the head) with four toilets next to each other, a dozen sinks, and showers. In the middle of the squad bay was the rifle rack of securely locked M16s.

Fourth platoon began with sixty candidates, including twelve prior enlisted Marines, seven or eight aviation candidates, five minority members, and four lawyers. The candidates came from all parts of the country, although more came from the Midwest and the South. We had one Harvard graduate and a tough young candidate from Lebanon.

Candidates ran the gauntlet of uniform issue, reams of paperwork, and, yes, that first Marine haircut for three dollars that took less than three minutes. Soon we all had fuzzy "grapes" on our shoulders, some more lopsided than others. We wore camouflage-patterned utilities (cammies) with no rank and no Marine Corps emblem (eagle, globe, and anchor). We hadn't earned the title of "Marine" just yet. Our names were stenciled in black on white strips sewn onto our left shirt pockets.

Within the first week six candidates had dropped out for various reasons.

One was physically unfit and several had developed cellulitis from blisters on their feet (even the simple act of marching around the OCS parade deck had disqualified a handful).

The OCS staff graded its candidates in the following categories and their associated importance: academic 25 percent, physical fitness 25 percent, and leadership 50 percent. Peer evaluations, better known as "spear evals," came from candidates ranking one another in the top third or the last third in each squad (fifteen to twenty candidates) and in the platoon. Long before reality shows became big television hits, OCS candidates voted the "unsats" (unsatisfactory performers) off Quantico. The instructors acted as hosts; candidates played the "survivors." Those who made it through would receive lieutenant bars.

On the third night, we were ordered to drink two quarts of water but prohibited from making a head call. My bladder was about to burst, so I got up and ran back to my wall locker to relieve myself in my boots. The next morning I took the boots to the head and washed them before anyone could notice. Someone who slept near my rack had ratted me out on a spear eval. I had to squirm on the carpet in front of Amos to explain my predicament. He called me "unsat" and informed me that I had been ranked among the bottom three men in the squad that week. "What was I supposed to do? Hold it in or pee in my rack?" I thought the nark was a chickenshit. From that point forward, I learned to watch my back.

Integrity was the most important leadership trait. "Integrity violators" got the boot from OCS, with no second chance. That meant cheaters, liars, and thieves were automatically sent home. OCS was the first place that taught me about ethics. (I had not been a regular church attendee or Bible reader, and my mother never spoke about ethics at home. Her Confucian, later Catholic, discipline was enough.)

The OCS staff was the crème-de-la-crème, best from the Fleet Marine Force. Our company commander, Major Van Fleet, was a "mustang," once an enlisted Marine with combat experience in Vietnam who had earned an officer's commission. The Corps loved officers like Van Fleet, usually good with troops, gruff but approachable, firm but fair. The OCS commanding officer, in a colonel's billet, usually became a general officer. Ours was Col. Robert B. Johnston, a tough-as-nails two-dollar-steak colonel, also a highly decorated Vietnam veteran and originally an immigrant from Edinburgh, Scotland. He regularly finished the Physical Fitness Test in eighteen minutes, completing all three events: three-mile run, twenty pull-ups, and eighty sit-ups. He outperformed candidates twenty-five years younger than he was. It was motivating to see him run past us. In the Corps setting the example was paramount.

Every morning, reveille began before 5 a.m. A quick run through the chow line preceded physical training (PT). By sunrise the entire company of six platoons, including the female platoon, would assemble in front of a "colour sergeant," a senior enlisted member on exchange from the Royal Marines.

"Good morning, Charlie Company. Are you ready for some Marine Corps PT? Oohhrraahh! We will do three sets of UBDs (upper body development course) followed by the Fartlek Course (a 3- to 4-mile trail, consisting of nearly one dozen exercise stations, designed to build endurance). I will count the cadence, you will count the repetition. We will do twenty side-straddle hops. Reaaddy. Exercise! One, two, three!"

"One!" the number one echoed in the Quantico woods, screamed by 300 motivated (and mostly) bald candidates.

"One, two, three!"

"Two!" There was an enormous rush in my body listening to the bellows, synergized by the camaraderie.

After warming up platoons took turns running the trails, some days individually, some days in formation. Anyone who fell out of a formation run received a bad eval. Too many bad evals meant packing your bag and going home early, still with a peculiar haircut.

Major Van Fleet led us on a run once and he sang my favorite "Jody":*

Ho Chi Minh is a son of a bitch.
Got the blue balls, crabs, and the seven-year itch!
Gimme some, PT
Good for me, good for you!

Mama and Papa were lying in bed
Mama rolled over and this is what she said
Gimmme some, PT
Good for me, good for you!

Leaders in the platoon quickly emerged. Predictably, they were the prior-service members. They had the best polished boots, the most squared-away

---

*"Jody" was the mythic name of the SOB who would be "sneaking" your girlfriend or wife while you were off learning to be a Marine, soldier, sailor, or airman. I first thought "Jody" was a girl.

uniforms, the cleanest rifles. They also had an impressive military presence that I lacked, especially in public speaking. Until OCS, I had felt fairly comfortable with my English-language fluency. Yet I remained timid. I never had to bark orders to strangers or sing cadence or reply under stress. I had to think on my feet, react to obscene screaming, and make decisions in a satisfactory manner amid chaos. Outside of my childhood, my only exposure to the military had been airshows, movies, and television. The staff called the California contingent "Hollywood candidates." I could identify with that; there weren't any bases near Bel Air, Brentwood, or Beverly Hills.

Sometimes, under stress the left side of my brain reverted to my native tongue and my reaction was to say something in Vietnamese. It was a strange phenomenon and it only happened under the constant strain at OCS. The candidate who slept on the rack above mine, a lawyer from Texas, heard me mumble "something in Vietnamese" while I was tossing and turning. I was probably cursing at Amos.

The fourth week was the one I really had to survive. A fifth-week board would convene to determine the fate of the unsats. It seemed as if the staff took turns each week picking on certain candidates to push them to their outer limit. But it was in the fourth that the company went on its first forced march (or "hump"). Every candidate carried an M16, plus forty pounds of assorted military gear and a helmet. For me "humping" was a brand-new torture. A mile into the hump, I experienced pain in body parts I didn't even know I had. My neck ached from the weight of the steel helmet (Kevlar helmets came in the next year). My shins and my ankles felt as if they were going to snap with each step. The accordion effect, as the formation continually stretched out and then became compacted during the march, forced the rearmost platoon to run part of the hump to catch up. I couldn't fathom how Marines had charged up beaches in World War II or patrolled endlessly in the jungles of Vietnam. I was beyond exhaustion after only 3 miles, and nobody was shooting at me.

The motivating jodies helped relieve the pain and focused my mind on something else:

Gimme that ole' Marine Corps spirit
Gimme that ole' Marine Corps spirit
Gimme that ole' Marine Corps spirit
Cause it's good enough for me!

It was good at Belleau Wood
It was good at Tarawa
It was good at Inchon
And it's good enough for me!

Several candidates fell out of the hump and trailed the platoon. Afterward they all reported to Captain Amos. They were headed to the fifth-week board to face disqualification. I thought I'd be joining them, too, the way Amos spoke to me every time I had to face him.

(One time Amos closed the door to his office and had me stand at attention staring straight ahead. "Pham, I read your bio. I thought maybe you could talk about your father during the 'impromptu speech.' But you're too . . . too emotional. My brother was a B-52 tail-gunner in Vietnam and he got shot down. What do you think about that, huh?")

He was probably right, but I couldn't possibly have told my father's story then. I didn't fully understand it, myself, and nobody understood or cared anyway. Despite my resolve, my vision blurred with tears: I was so upset that I could not control my emotions. I wanted to yell back, "Fuck you, I didn't kill your brother!" I tried to keep my cool, maintain my composure. But somehow, in the heat of the moment, my voice cracked and tears ran down my cheeks again. "Get the hell out of here, Pham."

As soon as I left his office, I wanted to punch myself for letting him get to me again. I didn't know if he was lying about his brother or if he was just "working" me over.

After four weeks candidates were given a twenty-four-hour liberty pass. I had made friends with Mark Henderson, an unassuming aviation candidate from Boulder, Colorado. His father had flown combat missions in Vietnam and reached the rank of colonel in the air force flying F-16s. We hitched a ride to nearby Quantico, a typical service town with restaurants and stores that catered to Marines and not much else. Q-Town looked like one of those old towns in Western movies. Candidates circled the downtown, got haircuts, and ate pizza. Then Mark and I decided to take the train up to Washington, D.C. After walking around Georgetown, we checked into the Key Bridge Marriott in nearby Arlington. We turned on the television, blasted the air-conditioning, and ordered room service. Even hotel food tasted so good after four weeks of Marine Corps chow. It was heaven. After frantically setting our alarm clocks and calling the front desk for a wake-up call, we quickly passed out. Returning to OCS late would result in major problems.

The fifth week did not begin well for many candidates in fourth platoon. One of the prior-service Marines, and first-ranked candidate in the platoon, had tripped on the obstacle course and had to be taken away by an ambulance. I had passed all my multiple-choice academic examinations and tackled all PT challenges—but I had developed a major case of hemorrhoids after our second hump. So it was back to sick call to see the doc, and the news was not good. "Candidate Pham, you need to get those removed. That means NPQ (not physically qualified). You can come back next summer," the navy physician on duty advised.

I froze. There was no way in hell I was going to go through this again.

I begged the doctor, "Sir, can you give me anything to relieve the itching? I've got another hump next week."

I had made up my mind. They're going to have to drag me out of OCS. Dead. I'm halfway home.

"OK, Candidate Pham, go to the dispensary and apply this ointment and use the suppositories every few hours. Got it?" (My platoon buddies reminded me to take my medicine: "Hey Pham, don't forget to take your butt drugs!" Nothing in any basketball locker room I'd ever heard approached the personal nature of OCS "pimping." But at least they cared.)

The hemorrhoids kept me up at night. I would lie awake thinking about my father and about the South Vietnamese soldiers who had died in Vietnam. I would be ashamed if I ever let them down. The negative perception about the ARVN would be cemented. The U.S. media and military would continue their bashing: *The ARVN was corrupt, inept and unwilling to fight. Now their kids aren't good enough to join our ranks.* Gunnery Sergeant Ramirez's voice echoed in my mind: *There is no room for marginal candidates, let alone marginal officers. I ain't gonna let none of you weaklings lead me!*

I was angry yet grateful that I was there in Quantico, proving that I had the mettle to join the ranks of the best. In hindsight, that's all anyone can ask in this country—an opportunity and not a guarantee.

We saw quite a few Hollywood movie clips and training films. It became a wash of images of Marines bayoneting and flame-throwing Japanese on South Pacific islands, Communists in Korea and more Communists in Vietnam. Under the dimmed classroom lights, I would recoil while my fellow candidates screamed *Oohhrraahh!* and *Get some!* I did it too to go along with the crowd. This fixation on the Asiatic as the enemy was not the Corps' fault.

It was not racism, it was reality. Our simulated field training exercises were from lessons learned in the last war, the Corps' experience in Vietnam. *Five NVA soldiers with a machine gun at grid coordinate AB234784. Your mission is to destroy the enemy by fire and maneuver and close combat. Fix bayonet! E-tool! Oohhrraahh!*

The military training was hurtful but truthful. That's one thing the Marine Corps never hid from us or the public. The Corps built men and killers and was extremely good at it. That was what parents of young enlisted Marines expected—competent lieutenants who would not get their sons killed in combat. Our motto, *semper fidelis,* or "always faithful," was constantly drilled into our heads.

Several candidates were dropped by the fifth-week board, though. My bunkmate, the lawyer candidate who was doing fairly well, developed bad shin splints and was sent home. I asked him if he was returning the following summer after graduating from the University of Texas law school. "Hell, no!" was his reply.

Every time we lost candidates the platoon had to reconfigure the squad bay. Empty racks were disassembled, stored away, and the remaining racks reset at proper intervals. The staff wanted not a trace of failure within our sight. The departing OCS candidates transferred to the R&S Platoon and no longer wore cammies; R&S did not stand for Reconnaissance and Surveillance as in the Fleet Marine Force. Here R&S meant failure, that is, Rest and Separation, where the unsats and "shitbirds" waited for their out-processing. Although R&S candidates still had fresh "high and tight" haircuts, their slumping shoulders, their broken bearing, spoke volumes about their fate. Every time we ran past the R&S platoon, Sergeant Anderson would shout: "I look to my right and who do I see? A bunch of sick, lame, and lazy."

Captain Hamlin and the other recruiters visited their far-flung OCS candidates at the halfway mark. I couldn't wait to meet with him in private to "choke" him for sending me to my summer hell. He remained confident of my success, however, far more than I was. I was curious about what he knew about what lay ahead for me. He just repeated, "Focus on the present, tackle one obstacle at a time. You'll get through it."

Something miraculously ignited inside me during the sixth week. The fuck-fuck games appeared funny to me now (and racial epithets had ceased after the initial welcome). My forty-pound pack, M16, and assorted combat gear felt lighter during longer humps. The obstacle course was easier, the endurance run less painful. I had cut six minutes off my initial time. I was still struggling in every aspect of OCS except in taking written examinations (and Motrins and suppositories).

After the reshuffling of the squad, Candidate Tim Pierson became my new bunkmate. He was a prior-service Marine. He pushed me every time I struggled, sometimes yelling in my face, "Come on, Pham! You can do it! Just think about finishing!" Based on his facial expressions during PT, I could tell he was having a hard time as well. Yet he had been ranked one of the top three in my squad. "Come on, Pham. You've got to understand. They're just fucking with you. You're gonna make it. Hang in there."

The first instance of favoritism I saw in the Marine Corps happened at OCS. A twelve-year gunnery sergeant, a salty and cocky fellow, suffered a stress fracture in his leg. He was given crutches and placed on light duty (no PT). He was permitted to continue the course and observed the rest of us while we went through the remaining small-unit field exercises and PT. Standing in the back of a corpsman's truck trailing the company runs (in case candidates needed medical assistance), he still had the balls to "motivate" us. "Come on, Pham, don't fall out!"

I wanted to tell him to shut the fuck up.

The staff allowed him to finish and graduate with the rest of us even though he technically had only completed 70 percent of the PT. I guess those stripes and rockers of his rank insignia meant something after all. But I had thought *all* candidates were being "screened and evaluated" fairly. I hadn't known that Marine officers who had graduated from the Naval Academy were also exempt from OCS.

Female candidates, naturally, had separate PT standards.

The company took all its major remaining tests in the ninth week: a second small-unit leadership exercise and a final obstacle and endurance course culminating in a 15-mile hump. As the company came to a halt after finishing our "Bataan death march," I knew I had survived. Those who fell out were doomed. Our sole black candidate, from South Carolina, nice fellow, had flunked several written exams. He kept to himself throughout the course. I was rooting for him, but to no avail. He and six others were dismissed at the ninth-week board. (The bodybuilder candidate was dropped at the seventh-week board.)

Henderson and I took a cab to the Key Bridge Marriott again the moment liberty was sounded on the Saturday before graduation. I was elated but I was still paranoid about being summoned to a "last-minute" secret board by

Amos. After dropping off our backpacks at the hotel, Henderson suggested that we visit The Wall across the Potomac, in Washington, D.C.

It was eerie to stand before the inscribed names of the 58,000 Americans who had died in Vietnam. What would their lives be like now, had they lived? I did not know a single one.

Out of the sixty candidates who began training with fourth platoon, thirty-five graduated. Two of the five minority members had made it: the Lebanese candidate and I. All four lawyers were dropped. Bill McGuire (a friend from Oxnard) and his mother Jane drove down from Alexandria, Virginia, to attend my graduation. I was glad to see familiar faces in the bleachers. Mark Henderson's father showed up in his air force blues with shiny silver pilot's wings.

I hadn't invited my mother and sisters. Maybe I didn't think I would make it. But as I marched with my platoon past the bleachers and reviewing stand to the Marine Corps Hymn, a monumental sense of accomplishment coursed through my body. I had overcome the toughest challenge I had faced in my new country up to that point. I had represented my father and former country well (albeit in the bottom third).

My feelings unavoidably turned to the man who wasn't there. My father would have loved this moment, I thought. The discipline and focus on close-order drill helped me hold back tears of regret. *Crazy* Hoa—now you got company, sir!

As the "eyes, right!" command was given, I could think of no greater joy, knowing that I had passed possibly the hardest screening and evaluation of any military organization in the world. Just as the lowest ranked graduate of medical school is still called "doctor," my place in the bottom third of my class meant I would be called "sir" if I decided to join the Corps. (Even Chesty Puller didn't kick ass at OCS, and look where John McCain ended up in life after finishing fifth from bottom at Annapolis.)

Graduating from OCS was one thing, contributing to my new country was another matter. I had undergone training the summer between my junior and senior years at UCLA. I had to return to finish my degree and decide on my future. With my OCS diploma in hand, I landed at LAX with a "high and tight," packing eight additional pounds of lean and mean muscles (almost surpassing the buck fifty mark). I now saw the world as a Marine sees it. I went on a run on Sunset Boulevard around the campus perimeter. The hills of Bel

Air next to UCLA looked like a "military crest" at twilight. I saw "avenues of approaches" and "cover." Every other civilian I ran into appeared unsat and overweight. Bruin Walk was a world away from Quantico's Brown Field.

My senior year in college was a blur, submerged beneath waves of memories of OCS, The Wall, and the bronze statue of Frederick Hart's three soldiers, arms around one another, searing my memory. I thought of their deaths. (To me, it was not for nothing. Even if they hadn't believed in the cause, at least they went honorably. I wondered how they would have viewed their portrayals by history and Hollywood.) By the end of 1986, I had made up my mind that I had to do something to make up for my survivor's guilt. I wanted to contribute to a cause, so I called my recruiting office and advised it of my decision to accept my commission the following summer.

Before I was to become a lieutenant, two headlines piqued my curiosity in the organization I was about to join. The Iran-Contra affair began making news in late 1986, and Marine Lt. Col. Oliver North, Annapolis 1968, was involved. I was intrigued. I didn't know Marines worked in the White House involved in foreign policy. I had taken college political science classes and so I followed the scandal closely. North was well-spoken, and his testimony was credible. But the more I read, the more troubled I became. No one had told me at OCS about Marines conducting "arms trading" and secret funding for the contra rebels fighting in Nicaragua. Could it be the disclosure of another secret war like Kennedy's early involvement in Vietnam?

In April 1987, a drawing of a Marine with a black eye (wounding the Corps reputation) made the cover of *Time*. Sergeant Clayton Lonetree, stationed at the U.S. Embassy in Moscow, was suspected of passing secrets to a beautiful Soviet agent. It was shocking news that served some of my college friends well who had been skeptical of my career decision in the first place. U.S. Marines are not supposed to do these sorts of things. Integrity, integrity, integrity. I had learned, along with many around the world, that the Marine Corps was the best fighting organization in the world. At least that's what they kept telling me. But there was no war going on. Marines weren't used to being political players; no former Marine had ever occupied the Oval Office.

As my college graduation and commissioning day neared, I didn't know who to ask to administer my oath of office. Military fathers usually participated in the ritual, or an instructor or a family friend. I had made friends with the UCLA Navy ROTC staff and midshipmen, so the Marine instructor had invited me to participate in their ceremony. I gladly accepted just to be a part of a special day with twenty-five other new navy ensigns and one other Marine lieutenant. I called Doug Hamlin, who had resigned his commission the week I returned from OCS, and was now selling advertising for *Guns & Ammo* magazine. (He was still in reserve.) Doug gladly obliged. On a sunny, warm June afternoon, in front of my mother, my sisters, and two dozen friends, I repeated the "I do solemnly swear to support and defend the Constitution of the United States" oath like millions of Americans before me. I wondered if my father would ever learn that his only son had followed in his footsteps, not in Vietnam but here.

*A Communist cadre "reeducating"
former South Vietnamese officers, 1975.
(Courtesy of Marc Ribaud/
Magnum Photos)*

*A rare picture from Communist
prison camp taken by my Great Aunt
Phu. My father after a day's hard work in
the prison camp, Vietnam, 1985.
(Author's Collection)*

CHAPTER 16

NO BAD DAY

ONE OF MY FATHER'S FELLOW PRISON CAMP DETAINEES had a son who had fled to Germany. The man always spoke about his own pending release and the day he would rejoin his family in Europe. Months went by, then years, but the man kept hoping. One day he had a stroke and died in his sleep while lying next to my father. After witnessing his friend's death, my father lived by his newly adopted motto, "No bad day."

Late in 1982 the prisoners held in the north were transported to southern Vietnam on trains. My father and his peers (Cau, "Piggy," and Tri) had originally believed that their release was imminent. But they had been lied to again. When the trains stopped in Quang Tri, just south of the DMZ where U.S. Marines had fought fierce battles fifteen years earlier, crowds surged around the train station. The prisoners raised their hands to show they were handcuffed to each other. But this time the residents cheered, cried, and threw fruit and snacks to the prisoners. Most of the prisoners broke into tears. They saw that not all South Vietnamese had forgotten their plight. They were still part of the history of their former country, though it could no longer be called Viet Nam Cong Hoa (South Vietnam) in public.

Cau was taken to Camp Z30-C and my father to Camp Z30-D. Both were in the Rung La jungle, about 100 miles north of Saigon. Reserved mostly for senior officials and "difficult" prisoners, the inmates of Z30-D were forced to carry on the dangerous work of clearing the mine fields around their camp.

In 1984, my father was sent back to the north to Camp Nam Ha while his friends remained in the south. All three of them were released in 1985 and eventually resettled with their families in the United States by the early 1990s. My father's mundane labor routine would continue for another three years.

With its economy still in shambles ten years after the war Vietnam's government finally decided to place the economy over ideology. Adopted in 1986, the *Doi moi* reforms meant Vietnam would reach out to its former enemy, the United States, for a jump start. It marked the beginning of the "new" Vietnam. Analogous to the POW "bargaining chips" at the 1973 Paris Peace Conference, Vietnam had something the United States still wanted— a full accounting of those Americans missing in action (MIA).

In the United States, POW/MIA advocates continued lobbying the White House, Congress, and the Pentagon to account for their loved ones. They met with Vietnamese Foreign Minister Nguyen Co Thach in New York. Newspapers reported that the Hanoi government had asked for $4 billion in exchange for dozens of "live" U.S. POWs. In early 1987, President Reagan phoned retired Army Gen. John Vessey Jr., a former chairman of the Joint Chiefs of Staff, to ask him to assume the role of special emissary to Vietnam for POW/MIA affairs. Vessey landed in Hanoi in August 1987 with orders not only to find out if there were any living U.S. POWs left in Vietnam, and get them out, but also to obtain the release of former South Vietnamese military and political leaders from the reeducation/prison camps.

When General Vessey raised the question of releasing former South Vietnamese military officers and political officials, Deputy Foreign Minister Nguyen Dy Nien told him that it would be too difficult. "It just couldn't be done at this time."

On the way to the airport after a three-day meeting, which had led to some agreement on the U.S. MIAs, Vessey was asked by the escorting officer from the Vietnamese Foreign Ministry whether he thought his trip was successful. Vessey quickly replied, "No, I don't."

"Why?"

"I was told that we wouldn't be able to get any movement on getting the former ARVN officers out of the prison camps."

The officer stopped at the airport before Vessey was to board his aircraft. He made a call and connected Vessey with Nien, to whom he again expressed his disappointment. Nien then conceded, "We will do it then. We will make it happen."

Nien added, "We couldn't release the ARVN prisoners from the prison camps because they would disrupt the country and possibly form a rebellion." (If Nien had visited the camps and seen the men of "skin and bones," the word could not possibly have occurred to him.) Vessey quickly interrupted, "We'll take every one of them into the United States." Nien reaffirmed, "OK, under that condition, we'll let them out."

Two months later, on September 30, 1987, my father was released after nearly 4,500 days in captivity. His fellow prisoners did not rejoice, believing this was yet another lie. My father scrounged some money and went to a bar near the train station. He told no one of his release. He treated himself to a small glass of rice wine and some peanuts before boarding. He soon got sick from the wine and threw up. After more than twelve years without a drink, his system couldn't handle the alcohol.

My great-aunt sent a telegram to my grandmother in Saigon (now Ho Chi Minh City) about my father's release. A few days later when my grandmother, aunts, uncles, and cousins greeted him at the train station, they hardly recognized the tall, brash, handsome air force pilot he had once been. His hair was now gray, his skin sunburned and wrinkled from working in the fields. But his signature smile remained the same.

They cried together like so many other families at the station. After an abbreviated reunion several cadres took away the newly released prisoners: they had to go register with the local police—and stay behind bars for two more days. After his release, my father was told to report on a weekly basis all his activities including his movements (restricted as they were), his contacts, and conversations, especially if with foreigners. Being released did not yet mean he was free.

Here is how Ho Dang Tri spoke about his years after his release.

The cadres prohibited us from working jobs that required interacting with outsiders, especially tourists. Senior officers were not allowed to work as barbers, *cyclo* drivers, or street vendors. They knew we spoke French and English and were afraid of us telling our story. They repeatedly interrogated us about our contacts with outsiders. Everywhere we went we had to report the people we met and their location. Weekly check-ins: "Who did you meet, what did you talk about, etc." After a few years, they did away with this rule.

While the U.S. involvement in Vietnam engaged six U.S. presidents, it would take another five administrations to untangle its aftermath. The last prison camp detainees (some held since 1975) were released in 1993, but taking their place were the artists, political dissidents, religious leaders, writers, and anyone else who spoke against the Vietnamese government. In December of 1992, President George H. W. Bush awarded General Vessey the Presidential Medal of Freedom for his accomplishments as special envoy. In 1993, Vessey made his final visit to Vietnam, and reported to President Clinton that all living American POWs and political prisoners of the former Republic of Vietnam were released.

CHAPTER 17

TRAINED TO KILL

GOVERNMENT RED TAPE DELAYED MY ORDERS TO THE Basic School (TBS) in Quantico, Virginia. Captain Hamlin's recruiter replacement informed me that the Gramm-Ruddman budget reduction legislation meant I would not be reporting to TBS until "further notice." The emotional high of my commissioning was followed by months of lull. I had quit my accounts receivable job; my $12,000 in student loans would become due six months after graduation. I had moved back to my mother's apartment in L.A. She had moved from Oxnard when she took a new job.

Meanwhile, I had no job and no life in Los Angeles.

The recruiter left a message suggesting that I resign my commission and forgo my five-month-old oath because there was no funding for training. I didn't call him back but, instead, applied for a position as an associate financial analyst with a national firm. I was hired and immediately joined a training class in Glendale. Naturally, my military orders arrived. I had to report to TBS by January 2, 1988, to join Bravo Company, Basic School Class 2-88. I went to my new civilian boss and promptly quit. I was not ready to trade my dream—my coveted flight school slot—for an entry-level corporate pencil-pushing job.

Snowflakes covered the road leading from I-95 to Camp Barrett. TBS sat across the highway from OCS, still within the confines of the base at Quantico. (The FBI Academy, and not much else, was nearby.) Thick woods, nothing like those in Southern California, ran unimpeded to the edges of the long, dark, winding road. I managed to hit an icy spot and spin 360 degrees twice in my new VW Jetta. Luckily, I struck nothing and no one saw me, or

I could have lost my flight slot right then and there. The Asian bad-driver stereotype nearly came true.

TBS was nothing like OCS. It had no entry gate, so there was no alcohol checkpoint for young lieutenants returning from liberty in Georgetown or Old Town in Alexandria. (If there were, the Corps would be short of young officers.) An alcohol-related driving offense was considered a career ender, but even here there were exceptions made for a few lucky "water-walkers."

TBS marked the biggest difference between the Marine officer corps and those of other services. Every new officer (except some pilots during the Vietnam era) graduated from TBS, including aviators, lawyers, supply officers, and administrative types. Since every Marine is a rifleman, officers had to be prepared to lead a rifle platoon if necessary. Real infantry officers would continue their studies with an additional nine weeks of the Infantry Officer Course following TBS. About a third of the class, including me, was headed for Pensacola, Florida, for flight training as an aviator or a naval flight officer ("backseater").

Bravo Company lived in Graves Hall, with two lieutenants per room in dormitory-like bachelor officers quarters (BOQ). Married lieutenants rented off-base housing but kept a room in the BOQ as well. Graves Hall was named after 2d Lt. Terrence C. Graves, a Medal of Honor winner killed in action in Vietnam in 1968. Graves was twenty-two when he died. A color portrait of him hung on the first floor.

Our days were packed with a meticulous training syllabus refined by a staff, as at OCS, that included the best officers in the Corps. Unlike OCS, we were accorded the appropriate military courtesy. No verbal abuse, no yelling. The school's commanding officer, Col. Terry J. Ebbert, had one lung; the other had been removed after a VC round had pierced his chest during the battle for Hue City in 1968. The executive officer was the ever-colorful Lt. Col. Gerry "Bear" Berry, the CH-46 helicopter pilot who had flown the most hours during the evacuation of Saigon. He could be depended on to motivate the aviation-bound officers with his exciting war stories. Flashing us his Rolex watch, he patently exclaimed, "You can never be too rich, too thin, or have too many medals!"

The new officers sat through hours of lectures on military history and tradition, and infantry tactics at the squad and platoon level. We fired practically every weapon in the Corps inventory: squad automatic weapon, M203 grenade launcher, M19 40mm (multiple) grenade launcher. I had never shot anything before except a friend's pellet handgun and a dozen rounds with the M16A1 at OCS. After two weeks at the pistol and rifle ranges, I had qualified with the Beretta 9mm pistol and M16A2 rifle. Marine marksmanship training was simply amazing. I was not a "gun freak" like many of my fellow officers, but from 500 yards, in the prone position and using a sling to tighten my grip on the M16, I fired nine out of ten rounds into a human silhouette.

Later in the training program, I threw hand grenades and called in artillery and air support. The company also went on long humps, culminating with a 25-miler. We took buses down to Norfolk, Virginia, and participated in a mock amphibious landing. I wasn't particularly fond of being on a ship or sitting in a steel amphibious assault vehicle that sank the moment it hit the water. But I told no one of my fears then and just sucked it up.

Midway through TBS, the aviation-bound officers were notified of their reporting date to flight school, which excited all of us. Our flying dreams were now only months away.

I met a Vietnamese tailor named Dinh at the uniform shop. He was a friendly man and always gave me extra time in fitting my uniforms. A month after starting TBS, the sister of a friend of mine invited a group of us lieutenants to a dance at nearby Mount Vernon College, then an all-women's school. We single lieutenants wanted to impress the coeds, so we decided to wear our dress blues. The only problem was that the uniforms would not be ready for two weeks. I walked over and spoke to Dinh. The next day, he fitted all nine of us and we were off to the Capitol Hilton.

To our surprise, the socialite women were not impressed with our form-fitting uniforms or our near-bald heads. And a couple of us got kicked out of the dance for rowdy behavior. We retreated to the bar and listened to the hotel pianist keying the "Marine Corps Hymn." (Before I left TBS, I stopped by to say goodbye to Dinh. It had been nice to know a fellow Vietnamese amid strangers. I would run into several more during my stints in Florida and Texas. Not all were clustered in ethnic enclaves.)

The first fake Vietnam veteran I met was one of my TBS classmates. He arrived as a member of the Navy Judge Advocate General (JAG) section and wore three rows of ribbons, including the Vietnam Service Ribbon. He was in his thirties and claimed to have taken part in the evacuation of Saigon. I was immediately impressed when I met him at the Hawkins Room (the TBS Bar), but then I did some quick arithmetic in my head and found that something did not jibe. A few years later, I read a piece in a military newspaper that the so-called JAG officer had been court-martialed for lying about his career. A former sailor, he had duped the Marine Corps and submitted phony records, and all legal cases involving this officer had to be overturned.

After six terrific months at TBS I was sad to leave Quantico. (I had graduated in the middle of my TBS class.) As much as I had hated the place two years earlier, I felt as though I finally "understood" what it meant to be a Marine officer. Even if I hadn't been guaranteed flight training in Pensacola, I would have remained in the Corps for at least a three-year stint. I flew back to California to see my mother and to participate as a "swordsman" in a wedding; this would be the first of dozens of sword arches I would form with my fellow Marines.

If I could sum up TBS in a one-sentence lesson, it would be: "Right or wrong lieutenant, make a fucking decision!"

I finally checked into Pensacola, the home of naval aviation, in August 1988, nearly thirty years after my father was one of the first fifteen VNAF pilots to receive pilot's wings in this country. Six weeks of aviation indoctrination awaited me, and I was eager to start.

Navy and Marine pilots often operated off aircraft carriers and flew over open ocean. If we crashed or ditched our aircraft, our lives depended on our ability to swim and survive at sea. For me swimming qualification posed the greatest obstacle to getting my wings. I shuddered at the thought of swimming a mile in a flight suit, treading water for ten minutes encumbered with helmet and flight gear, or exiting a helicopter underwater in what was called the "helo dunker" finale.

The government wanted one final assurance before it gave us its $1 million flight training. My second potential obstacle came as a surprise. Student pilots were randomly selected for an in-depth quality assurance flight physical by the Naval Aerospace Medical Institute (NAMI). Students could be disqualified by NAMI for weak eyesight (less than uncorrected 20/20), sinusitis, or other discovered disabilities. Luckily I wasn't picked; I needed my "anthro" measurements done.

An ancient machine measured the distances between my feet and knees, my knees to my hips, my fingers to my elbows, and my shoulders to fingertips. The Navy wanted to make sure that I could fit into tight jet cockpits and safely eject, without tearing off a leg.

No problem there, but then the Navy wanted to make sure I could reach all the switches while my safety harnesses were locked. That was the closest

I came to washing out of flight school, and it happened before I even climbed into a cockpit.

My arms are short. When the examining medical corpsman locked my harness and asked me to touch a certain switch, I could not reach it. I was at least 2 inches away. I was squirming in my seat, sliding back and forth to loosen myself from the harnesses. The corpsman and a flight surgeon observed silently. They could see I was struggling and sweating.

Miraculously, just before the corpsman gave up, I pulled a "Houdini." Somehow, between squirming and struggling in my seat, I came up with an extra 2 inches in reach and touched the wooden switch. The doctor signed my "up chit" and I ran out of the NAMI building as fast as I could.

I had a few weeks off after training so I frequented the area's pristine white beaches and nightlife. The legendary Trader Jon's was an old, run-down warehouse in downtown Pensacola. Martin Weismann, its owner, had turned it into an aviators' bar. On its walls were memorabilia and pictures of a who's who in naval aviation going back decades. Photographs of aces, astronauts, senators, and various naval aviators (now admirals and generals) hung from its ceilings and walls. The bar was a fire hazard, but nobody cared: the beer was cheap and the music raunchy. Hardly any women frequented the bar in the late 1980s when I was there, although the Blue Angels, based in Pensacola, had made the place their off-duty hangout. (Weismann once asked me to mail him a picture of me and the airplane that I would fly. I never did, knowing that some drunken patrons would laugh and tear it down.)

An F-14 guarded the front entrance of the nearby Naval Aviation Museum. A U.S. Navy A-1 Skyraider sat on the floor with its wings folded. I wandered through, admiring the planes I had only seen in books and on film. But among the grounded war birds a tiny plane suspended from the ceiling caught my eyes. Freshly painted, it had the familiar red and yellow VNAF insignia on its fuselage and the flag of the Republic of Vietnam on its rudder. The plane was VNAF Maj. Bung Ly's observation plane that had landed on the USS *Midway* during the fall of Saigon. A relic from my father's military service had found its way into my branch's museum.

I left and went for a drive along the beach. The sense of karma was overpowering. The VNAF will fly again!

About a fourth of the students opted for primary flight training in Corpus Christi, and I was one of them. I wanted to visit as many states in the nation as I could. (I also acted on the rumor that the Corpus-based flight instructors there were more relaxed; some were called "Santas" for doling out plenty of good evaluations, which meant it was easier to get jet-flight grades.) On the other hand, "Corpus" had its share of high winds that made crosswind landings for new pilots more challenging.

After a short T-34 ground school I was ready for my first flight in February 1989. There was a backlog of students, meaning a month's wait, so two other students and I set out for Mardi Gras in New Orleans. We drove straight from Texas and stayed with some female friends who were attending Tulane University.

After a few days of intoxication, I called the squadron duty officer to check on the duty schedule. "Lieutenant Pham, you are scheduled for 8 a.m. tomorrow for FAM-0 with Captain Close, flight three." I almost shit in my pants. "Ensign Smith, are you sure. Pham. P.H.A.M. Is this a joke? I'm not supposed to start for another month. I'm in New Orleans."

He didn't even pause.

"Then I'd get your ass in that car and start driving now."

The three of us frantically packed our bags. We took turns driving through an ice storm in eastern Texas. I spun out a couple of times so Rob, an ensign from Pennsylvania, took control of his Ford. "You California idiot. Don't you know how to drive in bad weather?" I just laid in the backseat and went to sleep trying to eliminate a monumental hangover from the Big Easy's finest "Hurricanes."

We three arrived back in Corpus Christi after midnight, and my first meeting with Captain Close (my primary flight instructor) was at 7 a.m. I woke up at 4 a.m. and went over the syllabus. FAM-0 involved a forty-five-minute briefing on the ground and a walk around the T-34. Close was to quiz me on systems knowledge and basic procedures. Flight school preparation meant memorization of statistics and flight procedures learned by rote. Students used three-by-five index cards to study—just like in college. I hadn't even prepared mine.

(I found Captain Close's picture hanging on the hangar wall. "Instructor Pilot of the Year, 1988. Captain Guy M. Close, USMC." Captain Close looked like a badass. Marines don't smile in their official photographs until they make general. He had two rows of ribbons consisting of an Air Medal, a Navy Achievement Medal, and decorations from a deployment to Beirut. One thought went through my fevered brain: "You are fucked, Lieutenant Pham. A 'down' in FAM-0, unheard of for a Marine flight student.")

If a student flunked an oral or written test, executed an unsafe procedure, or flew poorly, he would get a "down." Three downs and you were sent packing to find another military occupation specialty. Most flight students got at least one down during flight school, but I certainly could not afford one on my first event.

I walked into the ready room right before 7 a.m. There were two other instructors and Captain Close. No other student was there. "Hey, look who is here. Lieutenant Pham is showing up for . . . FAM-0. Pham for FAM," Captain Close joked as he extended his hand.

"Hey, you look tired. Where have you been?" he asked.

"Sir, we were in New Orleans and we just got back. I wasn't supposed to . . ."

"You guys drove back from Mardi Gras in this weather?" The other instructors broke into laughter. The ice storm had stopped, but light rain was falling that morning and the temperature dipped below forty degrees. "OK, let's get started, Pham. Tell me how to do a 'level speed change.'" I hadn't had the slightest clue about that maneuver. "What's the maximum airspeed of the T-34?" he continued. Silence. I was preparing to get a "ready-room down."

Close also decided he had enough. He started laughing and said, "Let's go get some breakfast. The scheduler made a mistake." I took a deep breath and followed him to the snack bar. I noticed that no one else was in the squadron area, the bad weather canceling the entire flight schedule. The joke was on me.

Three weeks later, I officially began my primary flight training. My goal was to fly F/A-18 Hornet or AV-8 Harrier jets, so I had to qualify for that kind of plane. Helicopters were second, and the C-130, my father's last assigned plane in 1975, was dead last for me. Each flight maneuver was graded as below average, average, and above average. Unsafe performance or poor "headwork" (in-flight decision making) led to a "down." To fly jets, a student needed at least thirty or so net "aboves" or a minimum grade of 3.045. The jokes were that forty "aboves" meant a good chance of getting jets; fifty resulted in a very good chance, and those with seventy or more would automatically become astronauts.

My first flight in the T-34 with Captain Close was close to perfect. He had allowed me to fly in the backseat while he flew a maintenance hop (a freebie exposure). He was thorough with his briefing and asked many questions. He then bought me lunch before we took off (I actually thought he wanted me to get sick and throw up). He turned out to be an extremely patient flight instructor and a great pilot. I was very comfortable in the cockpit and handled the radio calls without much difficulty. The flying itself was not demanding.

I came to believe that all students would graduate from flight school if they were provided extra training the way private students were who paid for lessons. In naval flight training, students had to achieve a certain proficiency within a limited number of flights. The challenges came in handling emergencies, such as simulated engine fire, engine failure, or "chip light" (ferrous material in the oil pan possibly indicating imminent engine or transmission failure). The students were judged on their "monkey" skills, keeping altitude, airspeed, and directional heading, and how they performed emergency procedures under stress. After two flights I had earned four "aboves," well on my way to achieving my goal of earning a ten for the familiarization (basic flying and landing) portion of the syllabus.

On May 2, 1989, I took off on my first solo flight in a T-34 over Corpus Christi Bay. Scattered clouds covered the southern Texas skies. I couldn't actually believe I was piloting a military aircraft by myself. I zoomed back and forth along the coastline before making five touch-and-go landings at an auxiliary field.

The local nightlife had a variety of venues, from country music–only bars to open-air gatherings near downtown, a fifteen-minute drive from the base. The first time I went to a country music bar with my buddies from Texas A&M University was actually fun.

I managed to strike out two weeks in a row in getting a girl to dance the two-step with me. I didn't own any cowboy boots or hats, nor did I wear a huge silver belt buckle, the outfits worn by many locals. But I didn't care. Finally a young lady said "Yes." A minute later I managed to step on her feet and knock her to the floor. *Marine Lt. "Q" wasn't quite as smooth as his VNAF father Lt. Crazy Hoa.* Hank Williams's voice will always remind me of my days in Texas:

There's a tear in my beer
'cause I'm cryin' for you, dear

Another time a group of us were drinking outdoors and listening to a live rock band at Elizabeth's in downtown Corpus Christi. Commander Phil Smith, a reserve Navy pilot and laid-off Eastern Airlines first officer, was in town to do his drills as a flight instructor. As a reservist, Smith was definitely more laid-back than his active-duty counterparts. He bought students drinks and prophesied about his uncertain flying career. I'll never forget his smile and his sunburned red head as he raised a toast to me, "Long live the South. May the South rise again . . . South Vietnam!"

Growing up in California, the ultimate melting pot, I had heard many generalizations about the South. A relative repeatedly warned me before I departed for Quantico, "Don't go anywhere by yourself at night. The East Coast and the South are not like here. They don't like foreigners." Another colleague cryptically wondered, "Don't they still lynch people down there?" During my two years of living and training in Virginia, Florida, and Texas (and on my visits to Alabama, Georgia, and Louisiana), luckily, I never encountered anything to support those stereotypes, on base or off. Despite the good intentions of my California clan, I learned to judge people and regions myself, at firsthand if possible.

After some basic instrument training in the simulator and two additional flights, I was qualified to do acrobatic maneuvers. I could not help but be impressed with the training syllabus that in less than three months took a student with one hour in a Cessna to one qualified to fly basic dog fight maneuvers.

I flew with several female Navy pilots (Marines didn't have any until 1995) who were as good, if not better, than their male counterparts. A good-looking female flight instructor teased me in front of several male colleagues with, "So Q., I heard that you've got a good stick." I didn't know what to say so I kept quiet.

She was not in my flight, but I knew of her reputation as a Jekyll and Hyde: she could flip and turn into a nasty screamer once airborne. And I didn't need to show her my "stick." I could see her trying to fit in with the boys, flying and talking tough. I empathized with that.

I completed primary flight training in July 1989, with a jet grade slightly above the minimum and, miraculously, zero "downs." Captain Close had prepared me well. He used to tell me in the cockpit, "Quang, when you're flying a Hornet in California, don't forget us CH-46 bubbas in New River [in North Carolina]." That motivated me, and like Doug Hamlin, Close would serve as a mentor to me throughout my Marine career.

I did not get my first choice of jets. Due to the "needs of the service," our entire class in Corpus, consisting of Navy, Marines, and Coast Guard personnel, received helicopter assignments that week. Confident of my abilities, I wrote a letter to the commanding officer requesting a "pipeline" change to jets. He promptly denied my overture.

(I returned to Pensacola and completed another six months of training in the H-57 Jet Ranger helicopter.)

On March 30, 1990, I received my gold naval aviator wings and orders to California, along with my buddies Joe Heneghan and Keith Scholfield, formerly from Orange County. My assignment was to fly the CH-46 Sea Knight, also known as the "Mighty Battle Phrogs." I would not be "killing" or "shooting" anyone except in self-defense: the CH-46's mission was to ferry cargo and troops. The jet guys called us "trash haulers"—at least until they had to be medevaced or rescued.

A week later, I reported to Marine Helicopter Training Squadron 301 in Tustin, California, for basic training with the CH-46 helicopter before reporting to my regular squadron. The giant wooden hangar, once used to house World War II blimps, looked empty. A few CH-46s Sea Knight helicopters circled overhead, their pilots attempting a few more practice landings before the airfield closed. My heart was pounding. I had waited for more than two years to get to the mystical Fleet Marine Force (FMF). I got out of my car and tugged on my trousers, making sure I looked sharp. I wanted to make a good first impression and was ready to stand duty in case the squadron scheduled me that first weekend. I had heard of an unofficial rule in the military. *Give it to the FNG (Fucking New Guy).*

A tall, young-looking captain wearing a hydraulic fluid-stained flight suit walked out of the ready room. Gripping my orders with my left hand, I came to attention and saluted him as he walked by. He looked at me as if I had just come from Mars. He had a sympathetic grin on his face, then put out his hand. "I'm Drew. Call me Junior. Check in on Monday. Let's go to the club!"

Welcome to the Fleet Marine Force Lieutenant Q.X. Pham. Relax!

I could not have been more fortunate. I figured I could tolerate helicopters, as long as I was stationed in California. As a single guy, having Huntington Beach, Laguna Beach, and Newport Beach nearby almost guaranteed a social life.

My focus on flying helicopters wasn't as sharp as flying the T-34, and my performance showed it. My grades were average; I was just getting by. At that time, I saw no thrill in flying the CH-46, and knowing that some 5,000 U.S. helicopters had been shot down in Vietnam didn't help matters. (Nothing could be worse than a lackadaisical attitude confronted by an asshole.)

On my sixth flight in the CH-46, I encountered trouble for the first time in my short military career. My instructor was Capt. Kevin Cash, who had a thick moustache and was married to the daughter of a retired general. He had good flight credentials, and hung out with his favorite students. But I was not among them. Captain Cash would not call me by my name or rank. "Phlegm, Flam, that's your new call sign." One of my peers, a son of a retired colonel, was one of his favorites, and he added fuel to the fire by suggesting I be called "Donger" (the Asian exchange student character in the movie *Sixteen Candles*) or better yet, the "Khe Sanh bomber." I just ignored Cash, hoping the call sign would not stick. In two months, I would be on my way to my deploying unit anyway.

After a laborious premission briefing, Cash and I took off and flew down the beach toward Camp Pendleton. He threw emergency after emergency at me, cursing and screaming. "What the fuck are you doing, Phlegm? Watch the airspeed! Jesus Christ, I've got the controls." The abuse went on for ninety minutes, from takeoff to landing. There was a crew chief in the back, a senior corporal, who said nothing.

I had never been treated so badly. In flight school, I had flown with instructors with the worst reputation as "screamers," but Cash easily outdid them. I didn't think I had flown poorly; I was definitely prepared. I was soaked in sweat but kept my cool. We flew back to Tustin and he quickly left the helicopter.

"Sir, that was the worst treatment I have ever seen in my career," the crew chief told me as I angrily grabbed my helmet bag and jumped off the helicopter. I sensed a reprieve; someone had witnessed the atrocious verbal abuse. I also felt a bond with the corporal, a connection that existed in multicrew aircraft. There would be no more tears like those I'd shed in OCS. I had become a Marine officer and a qualified naval aviator, so court-martial or not, I was going to confront Cash about his behavior and settle it. Maybe mano a mano.

I could not find him on the flight line so I returned to the ready room to look for him there. I found my training evaluation that he must have quickly written before he bolted from the squadron. (We were supposed to debrief after each flight, but he was nowhere to be found.) I looked over my evaluation. Surprisingly, he gave me no below-average remarks; all averages. But why did he act like an idiot?

When Saddam Hussein's Iraqi forces invaded Kuwait on August 2, 1990, I had no clue where those places were. Half of Tustin base was leaving for the

Persian Gulf, including my buddy Joe Heneghan with his CH-53 squadron. Marine Medium Helicopter Squadron 161, or HMM-161, a CH-46 unit, shipped out within two weeks. Before HMM-161 left Tustin, its CO and the group commander handpicked pilots to fill its roster from other units, including two instructors from HMT-301: John D. ("J.D.") Harrigan and David ("Guido") Giannetta.

Three months had passed since U.S. forces began assembling in the Persian Gulf. No one was certain that war would take place. On base, rumors ranged from "everyone will be going" to "they'll be back after six months." By November, my chances to join Operation Desert Shield units would rise exponentially. I had successfully completed my CH-46 training despite Cash's continual harassment.

A request came down from our parent unit, Marine Aircraft Group 16 (Rear). HMM-161 needed a pilot to replace a captain who had to return home to be with his sick wife. I volunteered for the slot. And it's not that I was thirsty for war, but as a Marine, I felt that if there was going to be a war, then I needed to be there. I wanted to see if I could actually perform in combat, because there was no real test during peacetime. I figured that a combat record would shield me from potential detractors like Captain Cash. My run-in with him had caused me to temporarily doubt myself again, second-guessing my flying abilities. The only way to try myself was in a combat zone.

I didn't think I would be sent. I was so junior that HMM-161 would have had to spend many flight hours to train me once I got into the operational zone. There were so many other more qualified pilots on base. I thought, too, that Cash might pick up the phone or write a letter to keep me out. But I also discovered that in aviation at least, your flying reputation preceded you, not your other officer skills, your appearance, or how you are perceived by others. You may not make colonel but you could get away with being a fat Marine if you were a great pilot. A squadron CO could easily prevent a poor pilot from joining his squadron. He could also jettison a weak performer already in the squadron—or as Marines called it, "shit canning" someone.

I finally got my wish and my orders for Operation Desert Shield. To my surprise, no one else had "put up his hand" to go. I had also violated another military truism: never volunteer for anything.

I spent the next several days getting my immunization shots and writing a will. I gathered my flight gear, packed my belongings, and visited my mother in Los Angeles. She cried as I showed up for the last Vietnamese meal I would have for a while. I never told her that I had volunteered to go overseas.

My father waiting in Saigon to immigrate, 1990. (Author's Collection)

(I would have missed the war had I remained with my peers in my first unit, HMM-166. Incidentally, Cash transferred to HMM-166 and stayed home.) I did my best to assure my mother that I was going to a combat zone with the best military force there was. I was going with the U.S. Marine Corps. She just shook her head, not able to understand my absolute blind faith in the Corps. She confessed that the night we left Saigon, she never would have guessed that her only son would go off to war for this country. Neither had I.

Top: *"Highway of Death," Kuwait City, 1992. (Author's Collection)*
Second from top: *Jay Leno visits Marines in Saudi Arabia, Thanksgiving, 1990. (Author's Collection)*
Bottom: *Kuwait International Airport with my CH-46 crew on final day of the war, 2/27/91. From left to right, pilot Captain John D. Harrigan, Lance Corporal Kennedy (aerial gunner, kneeling), crew chief Lance Corporal Jesse Wills, me, and Sergeant Smith (aerial gunner, kneeling). (Author's Collection)*

CHAPTER 18

PAYBACK

MILITARY BUSES DROVE OUR CONTINGENT OF MARINES from El Toro to Norton Air Force Base, an hour away in River-side County. I didn't know anyone. At Norton we straggled onto a C-5 Galaxy that would take us to our theater of war. About sixty Marines sat facing backward inside the giant cargo plane, which had only a handful of tiny windows. Flanking me were two sergeants major, both Vietnam veterans heading to a war zone once again. During the long flight, we shared Vietnam stories over the reverberating engine noise and foam-rubber earplugs. After twenty-four hours and stops in Westover, Massachusetts, and Rhein-Main in Frankfurt, Germany, the C-5 landed at Al Jubayl Airfield in Saudi Arabia, 120 miles south of the Kuwaiti border. Adrenaline rushed through my body. I felt as I had when I entered my first varsity basketball game, but the feeling was ten times as strong. Since I had left Tan Son Nhut, I'd never seen this many military aircraft in one place. Row after row of helicopters were parked tightly next to one another: AH-1W Cobra gunships, UH-1N Hueys, CH-53Ds, and CH-53E "Shitters" (they left trails of smoke), and my helo, the CH-46E "Phrogs." Several TWA and Tower Air 747s sat at one end of the runway; fuel trucks were filling C-141 and C-130 cargo planes. Al Jubayl was rocking.

One-fourth of the Corps entire rotary-wing force was in-country and another quarter was aboard ships in the Persian Gulf. Still more were coming from the Second Marine Aircraft Wing in North Carolina. As I left the giant cargo plane, a dry heat blew dust and sand into my face. One of the sergeants major bade me farewell: "Lieutenant, we're not going to lose this one!"

It was mid-November, but the Arabian sun was unforgiving, heating the tarmac to 105 degrees. Two of the HMM-161 junior pilots greeted me at the taxiway as I dragged my bulky flight and sea bags. I had met these guys at the Tustin officers' club, and I was glad they had come out to meet me. Captain Don Buczynski, or "Buzz," eighteen months senior to me, grabbed the heavier bag and smiled. "Welcome to the sandbox, Q.X." Later that night, the other pilot, Capt. Roy Santa Maria, asked me, "Dude, why the fuck did you volunteer to come here?"

"This country has been good to me. I need to pay back my citizenship." It may have sounded corny to some. Not to me. Not to Roy.

The U.S. Army had arrived in Saudi Arabia first, with the 82d Airborne Division jumping into Saudi Arabia just days after Iraq's invasion of Kuwait in early August. HMM-161 was part of the first Marine contingent that followed, and was the first transport helicopter unit to arrive in-theater. Its helicopters had been disassembled and stuffed into C-5s, three per plane. Activated in 1951 during the Korean War, the HMM-161 "Greyhawks" (or "The First") composed the oldest tactical helicopter unit in the Marine Corps. The squadron patch had a winged horse over a three-bladed rotor and the Latin words *Equitatus Caeli* ("Cavalry of the Sky") across its top. Black letters "YR" were painted on the rear pylon of every helicopter. ("Yankee Romeo" was used to identify the squadron.)

When the orders came down for deployment to Saudi Arabia, some squadron pilots were surprised that HMM-161 was the first to go. Two other units at Tustin, HMM-163 and HMM-268, had better in-house reputations and HMM-161 had been the destination for pilots soon to be rotated, or were, for various reasons, undeployable. According to pilots interviewed for this book, it took a lot of effort and last-minute addition of three Marine Aviation Weapons and Tactics instructors and five senior pilots to complete the HMM-161 team.

All twelve HMM-161 helos sported a fresh Earl Scheib desert camouflage paint scheme over their traditional green coats. Like every new guy who ever walked before me, my first squadron became "the best squadron in the Marine Corps." No aviator ever forgets his first squadron, especially if it's a combat outfit.

"Tent City" was only a few hundred feet from the flight line. Marine Corps tent cities looked the same in every war. It didn't matter if it was Vietnam, refugee camps set up by the Corps, or the Persian Gulf. Except I did notice that jungle green did not blend well with the brown desert. I lugged my belongings next to Buzz's cot on the sand floor; every flat surface in the tent was covered with a fine layer of dust. Flight suits, green T-shirts, and clean underwear hung from parachute cords strung together along the insides of our hootch. Some of the pilots had posted photographs of their wives and kids above their cots.

A mosque stood on the southeast corner of our city. Prayers droned from its speakers every few hours, according to Islamic doctrine. In the Vietnam War movies, I remember seeing U.S. troops blaring Jimmy Hendrix or The Doors. In Saudi Arabia, Marines listened to their favorite music on headsets connected to their portable cassette players. Several crew chiefs rigged their portables to the helicopter's communication system and blasted away during flight.

I grabbed several designer-water bottles from the squadron supply (S-4) tent and strolled through my new home away from home. Handwritten cardboard signs pointed to each squadron's living area in the compound, and I passed several rows of tents before I saw the sign for HMM-462, "Dude" Heneghan's CH-53 unit. As I poked my head into one of the tents, a familiar voice hollered. "Q! What the fuck are you doing here?" Joe Heneghan looked as if he had dropped ten pounds. Dirt covered his steel-toed black flight boots. He was wearing a filthy, sweat-salty flight suit with a pistol holster slung across his chest, and a light-brown gas mask cover on his left hip. Like everybody else at Jubayl, he no longer resembled a garrison Marine, with a spit shine and a "high and tight." He was ready for war, sir!

"This place blows, man." Before he'd received his orders, he was living a bachelor's dream in Laguna Beach, his hometown, surfing every weekend: he planned on only playing Marine for a living. As we sweated in the Saudi heat, he gave me a quick lowdown on food: one meal ready to eat (MRE) each day and hot chow for breakfast and dinner; water (drink lots of it); and which of our TBS classmates had made it to Jubayl. Joe was also nice enough to cover the frequently asked stupid new-guy questions.

I met most of the other squadron pilots at chow that night. The XO, call sign "Dawg," was a college football nut and a cool guy. A graduate of Florida State University, "Dawg" would post betting lines every Saturday and accepted wagers against his team. He tried to give me another call sign that night. "Pham, you're now Mongo." Mongo for Mongolian? Or Mongo for Mongoloid? Or for the Alex Karras character in Mel Brooks's *Blazing Saddles*?

The enlisted members of the squadron hung out at night in an area away from "officer country." I also noticed that they worked harder and had longer hours than the pilots. We pilots were the prima donnas who needed crew rest and a good night's sleep so we could fly safely. *Standard operating procedures (SOP)*.

The black enlisted Marines had decided to share one tent, which pissed off one of the more senior white officers. "Those 'dark greens,' they're making it a 'black' thing. We ought to make them move in with others." *Dark* green Marines? I'd been taught there was only one shade of Marine. And that was green.

The next day I checked out my "dry" flight vest with a survival kit and emergency radio, but no life preserver unit. Nearly all of our flying was over desert, so there was no need to add more baggage. We had to leave room on our body for the "chicken plates" or "bullet bouncers," body armor left over from the Vietnam era. The S-4 issued me my personal 9mm Beretta and a box of twenty-five rounds. I stuck it in the standard-issue black holster, strapped it on my hip, and, Shazaam! I was a gunslinger from the east.

I then strolled to the flight line to see the squadron's helos up close. Captain John D. Harrigan, the flight line officer, gave me a quick tour and introduced me to his right-hand man, flight line chief SSgt. Joe Robinson. Several crew chiefs were on duty, working on their respective helos: Sergeant Kelley, Corporal Oakley, and Lance Corporal Wills. They all looked so young but they had a comforting "edge" about them. They had been in-country for three months and they were salty.

I had noticed that the birds had extra electronic countermeasure equipment, "disco lights," on their rear pylons, designed to deflect incoming missiles. Two empty pods, normally loaded with chaff and flares, sat atop fuel stubs on both sides of the helo. The CH-46s had been somewhat improved since the Vietnam War. Beefier engines, tougher rotor heads, higher torque transmissions, off-the-shelf LORAN navigational devices, and makeshift Trimble GPS units essentially separated the Persian Gulf CH-46s from their early years in Vietnam.

Patches on bullet holes from Vietnam were still visible on most every fuselage. It was hard to believe these ancient helos were still flying. Still, the crew chiefs and mechanics worked around the clock to keep 161's fleet in "up" status. When the squadron had first arrived in August, the crew chiefs immediately noticed the fine sand's corrosive effect: the sand ate away the helo's turbine engine compressor blades and leading edges of the rotors. With the help of civilian contractors and technical representatives, the Marines devised a clear tape to cover the blades and filters for the intake manifolds.

It was amazing to watch the young Marines quickly adapt to the harsh flying, living, and working environments (on some days, the temperature rose to over 130 degrees on the flight line). The young ones still went at it, on top of their helos, checking hydraulic fluid gauges on the rotors. Words of wisdom: "If they're leaking, they've still got fluid in them."

It was obvious by 1990 that the Marine Corps needed to find creative ways of keeping the CH-46s in the air. The assembly line had been closed since the early 1970s, and no replacement model appeared on the horizon as the venerable helos surpassed their twenty-fifth anniversary (the first ones had rolled off the line in 1964). After more than $2 billion of research and development, Secretary of Defense Dick Cheney in 1989 tried to cancel the CH-46's replacement, the V-22 Osprey, a hybrid aircraft that flies at airplane speed but can stop on a dime and land vertically like a helicopter. Today, Marines are still waiting for the Osprey, and still flying the "Phrogs" in the meantime.

The "Phrogs" had been the backbone of the Corps vertical-envelopment tactic, developed by U.S. forces in Korea and then honed by the French in Algeria. The ability to lift combat Marines over a wide area and bypass the enemy gave commanders the flexibility to employ subordinate units to meet any mission.

Helicopter tactics mastered in Vietnam were not completely transferable to the Persian Gulf. Small-arms fire was the biggest threat to helicopters in Southeast Asia, but in the desert, the defensive tactic of spiraling down from 3,000 feet over an LZ didn't make sense. There was no terrain to hide behind. In the desert, the enemy could hear and see the helos from miles away. That meant pilots had to fly faster and lower, using terrain flight and nap-of-the-earth maneuvers. And we needed to be proficient at flying at night. Marine aircrews had been training for years in the California desert base of Twenty-nine Palms and at Arizona's Yuma ranges, but there were no mountains in the Arabian Peninsula or in Kuwait.

When you're flying in a cockpit with others, the other pilot can either save you or kill you (the crew chief in the back will usually save both asses up front). It didn't matter if I flew with Captain "Brick" or if I flew with a weapons and tactics instructor (WTI), I paid attention to their flying. At first, I did not take anyone's word or reputation for granted. I said something if the other pilot made me nervous or tried to show off by pushing the ancient CH-46 to its performance limit. Aviation is an unforgiving business; one mistake can result in many deaths, and it doesn't matter if there is a war or if it is peacetime training. Our mission was to safely get from A to B on time, then back to A.

HMM-161 needed all the training it could handle. The squadron had no pilots with combat experience. Only a staff sergeant wore combat aircrew wings, and I could not remember if he had earned them in Lebanon or Vietnam.

Our CO had been with the Marine units off the coast of South Vietnam during the 1975 evacuation, but he didn't fly in that big mission. So it would be on-the-job combat training for just about everyone. On the first day of the war combat time mattered little; our squadron had none.

My first flight in Saudi Arabia was a troop-lift mission inserting Marines into a facility fifty miles north of Jubayl. There were no bodies of water like lakes and streams to be seen anywhere. *Sabkhas* were the most visible features used for navigation. Red markers dominated the maps—tall electrical wires and their stanchions. A huge cement plant that could be seen from miles away was there. Pilots referred to the giant plant as "Oz." A dirty gray haze covered the horizon, and fire and smoke billowed from black pipes marring the scenery. The reason our forces were deployed was made abundantly clear to me in that flight. I could feel it, see it, and smell it: oil, oil, and oil.

For most of December 1990, I flew training missions to increase my combat readiness percentage. Most flights involved one other aircraft. We would do low-level navigation and landings in the desert. I managed to fly one NVG hop bumping my total NVG time to 4.7 hours, hardly close to the twenty-five minimum hours to carry troops while wearing NVGs. At night, flying at 100 feet or below, the stanchions, poor landings, and vertigo became our biggest threats on training runs. Maybe I was destined to be a day-only combat helo pilot. An occasional chow and mail run to the forward areas where the grunts were dug in gave me a hint of the battle that lay ahead.

A host of celebrities visited the Marines during the Thanksgiving and Christmas holidays. The cast from "Major Dad" and Jay Leno were clearly HMM-161's favorites. The "Greyhawks" flew Leno from base to base to visit Marines scattered across the Arabian Peninsula. Arnold Schwarzenegger (President Bush's Physical Fitness Council chairman) sent the Marines weight-lifting sets—and we put them to good use. (Well, OK, I lifted weights twice while in Saudi.)

The celebrities came to see us, but there was no R&R or liberty. We were restricted to the airfield. No babes, no boob books, no booze, and no bullshit. We were focused on the mission at hand. Aircraft spare parts and flight hours were plentiful. There was no doubt in our mission. The United Nations was behind us, and so were the American people.

I had absolute trust in our president and our senior military leaders, especially, all of whom had experienced the debacle of Vietnam: Walter Boomer (a Marine three-star general who led all Marine aviation, infantry, and supporting units and one army brigade), H. Norman Schwarzkopf, and Colin Powell. They had remained in the military despite the difficult years following Vietnam. And the men and women under their command needed their leadership. Desert Storm would be the first time the United States had ever sent an all-volunteer military force into harm's way since before World War II.

However, each night, I noticed that the air force ground crews boarded a truck to leave the airfield. While Marines walked back to Tent City, the airmen headed somewhere else. "Sir, we're staying off-base at barracks with mattresses and air-conditioning," was the response. That blew my mind. (Go Air Force. Aim high. Sleep nice and cool.)

The January 17 deadline for Saddam Hussein to withdraw his troops from Kuwait quickly approached. My inbound mail volume increased twofold. Everyone was writing me—my mother, my sisters, the boys in Oxnard, my college buddies, and women to whom my college buddies had passed on my military mailing address. After a month in-country, I began generating form letters because I couldn't keep up with responses. Postage was free, so I mailed dozens of one-page synopses once a week. One thing was certain. Although I had wanted someone to write me love letters, I was damn glad I was single. War is a young man's game, and love during wartime is a liability. There was already enough stress on my mother and my sisters; I didn't need a girlfriend or a spouse to worry about me. I could tell married pilots from aircrew members in my squadron. The former were writing letters late at night to their wives and children.

If I die in a combat zone
Box me up and send me home
Pin my medals on my chest
Tell my mama that I did my best

When you're twenty-six years old, have no wife and kids, and you're doing what you've been dreaming all your life, death was for the other guy.

On the night of January 16, 1991, Joe stopped by my hootch around 10 p.m. "Q. It's starting tonight. I just overheard our CO." Several of us had thought there would be no shooting: Saddam Hussein would withdraw at the last minute and we'd all go home. I didn't want to take any chances, so I told Buzz and the pilots in my tent what Joe had told me. I had my flak jacket, my helmet, my gas mask, and chemical suit by my side. Ready for anything, I hit the rack.

The air raid siren shrieking through the cold Arabian night sounded like the ones I had heard in Saigon. (Must be the same manufacturer.) I sat up on my rack and looked at my watch. It was 3:00 in the morning. (Fucking A! The war is starting!) I slipped on my flight suit, grabbed my mask and the rest of my gear, and did a 40-yard dash to the bunker in back of our tent. Everyone else was awake and doing the same thing. I took a deep breath and donned my gas mask just outside the bunker. Within two minutes everyone was inside the sandbagged bunker. I heard no explosions.

My mind drifted back to 1973 when I had freaked out in the bunker with my mother and my sisters. I felt helpless back then; I was just a little boy. I just wanted the rocket attack to end. Now the sirens in Saudi Arabia continued whining. Ten minutes went by, then thirty. My bladder was full, but I wasn't about to go outside the bunker. We sat there in the dark peering at one another through gas mask lenses, looking like space aliens holed up in a cave. My breathing got heavy and my lens fogged. The "all clear" order finally sounded over the compound's loudspeakers. We had just survived our first Scud missile attack of the war.

Morning came fast that day. I grabbed a quick shave and headed to the operations area with all my military gear. The message board with all-important announcements was sitting on top of the operations officer's desk. I picked it up and flipped open the binder to the first message:

Z 170001Z JAN 91 ZFF-1

FM USCINCENT

TO ALL DESERT SHIELD FORCES

SUBJ: DESERT STORM MESSAGE TO OUR TROOPS

PLEASE GIVE THIS MESSAGE FROM USCINCENT WIDEST DISSEM-
INATION POSSIBLE

SOLDIERS, SAILORS, AIRMEN, AND MARINES OF THE UNITED STATES
CENTRAL COMMAND. THIS MORNING AT 0300C WE LAUNCHED OP-
ERATION DESERT STORM, AN OFFENSIVE OPERATION THAT WILL
ENFORCE UNITED NATIONS RESOLUTIONS THAT IRAQ MUST CEASE
ITS RAPE AND PILLAGE OF ITS WEAKER NEIGHBOR AND WITH-
DRAW ITS FORCES FROM KUWAIT. THE PRESIDENT, THE CONGRESS,
THE AMERICAN PEOPLE AND INDEED THE WORLD STAND UNITED
IN THEIR SUPPORT FOR YOUR ACTIONS. YOU ARE A MEMBER OF THE
MOST POWERFUL FORCE OUR COUNTRY, IN COALITION WITH OUR
ALLIES, HAS EVER ASSEMBLED IN A SINGLE THEATER TO FACE
SUCH AN AGGRESSOR. YOU HAVE TRAINED HARD FOR THIS BATTLE
AND YOU ARE READY. DURING MY VISITS WITH YOU, I HAVE SEEN
IN YOUR EYES A FIRE OF DETERMINATION TO GET THIS JOB DONE
AND DONE QUICKLY SO THAT WE ALL MAY RETURN TO THE
SHORES OF OUR GREAT NATION. MY CONFIDENCE IN YOU IS TOTAL.
OUR CAUSE IS JUST! NOW YOU MUST BE THE THUNDER AND LIGHT-
NING OF DESERT STORM. MAY GOD BE WITH YOU, YOUR LOVED
ONES AT HOME, AND OUR COUNTRY—

H. NORMAN SCHWARZKOPF, COMMANDER IN CHIEF,
U.S. CENTRAL COMMAND.

I made a copy of the message to keep for myself. I still couldn't believe the
shooting had started. Our six months in the sand had failed to dislodge Saddam Hussein. Now it would be our turn. The I Marine Expeditionary Force
would take the lead into Kuwait.

Almost immediately proof of the violence of war visited itself upon us.

A French Jaguar bomber made an emergency landing at Al Jubayl shortly
after sunrise. Marines rushed out to the flight line to see the damaged jet. The
pilot had limped back to Saudi Arabia after a night bombing mission in Iraq.
One of the bomber's tailpipes was damaged. The aviator stood on the tarmac,
resplendent in a flowing white scarf and wowed Marine aircrew members as
he re-created his harrowing run-in with a guided missile with his hands. The
French were with us.

A flight schedule was hastily written, and I made the first cut. Sweat
curled down my neck during the preflight briefing. My wet hands, underneath flight gloves, shook from the cold air, further amplifying the vibrations
on the stick. My voice cracked on the radio while I fumbled to turn on the

electronic countermeasure equipment in our cockpit. After about fifteen minutes, my initial adrenaline rush leveled off as we reached 130 knots at 100 feet. Our section of two CH-46s had taken off in case we were needed to pick up downed jet pilots near the Saudi Arabia-Kuwait border. We flew for ninety minutes and returned to base without incident. That was my first logbook entry denoting flight time in a combat zone, and it was nothing to write home about.

In Los Angeles, my mother was a nervous wreck, constantly watching CNN for reports of choppers going down. (A dozen or so had already crashed during training missions leading up to the war.) She could not focus on her accounting job. In Saigon, my father was waiting for the paperwork that would allow him to go to the United States. No one had told him that I was in a war.

My mother was afraid the Communists would not permit my father to leave if they knew of my Marine Corps affiliation.

I could not believe it. Sixteen years after the war ended, the Commies still affected our lives. The Vietnam War certainly hadn't ended for my family.

On January 29, 1991, three Iraqi armored divisions attacked the small coastal town of Khafji and held it for thirty-six hours. To untested U.S. troops, and thanks to overblown Pentagon and media assessments, the Iraqi military loomed larger than life.

News quickly filtered down to Jubayl, 100 miles south. Buzz and I convinced ourselves that Iraqi tanks were rolling toward our position. Deterrence would have been minimal all the way to Bahrain.

Fortunately, understrength Marine reconnaissance units fought back. Along with Marine F/A-18s and air force A-10s, Jubayl-based Cobra gunships destroyed many enemy tanks.* One A-10 pilot, however, had mistaken a Marine light armored vehicle for an enemy rig and fired a Maverick missile, instantly killing eleven Marines—and that would not be the last incident from "friendly fire" in the "new technology" war. USAF 11 USMC 0.

In mid-February, Marine helicopter units leapfrogged some 80 miles north closer to the action to Tanajib. HMM-161 parked its helos at the small airport that had also served oil camps of the Arabian-American Oil Company in Saudi Arabia. We were 35 miles from the Kuwaiti border.

*Marine Capt. Randy "Spanky" Hammond destroyed twenty Iraqi vehicles of the war, including the first tank.

When the ground war finally arrived on February 24, 1991, I was on the schedule for a test flight. This was also the day of the biggest Marine helicopter lift since the Vietnam War. Over fifty helos from nine squadrons from three different wings including reservists took part in the operation, all without a rehearsal. The goal was to insert a company-sized antitank blocking force to the east of the 1st Marine Division. As the flight lifted off and the dust cloud settled, a CH-46 from HMM-161 remained on the ground, rolled on its side. Luckily no one was hurt. All Marines had safely gotten out and run from the crash site, taking no chances in case the machine gun rounds or the TOW missiles would explode. The helo was being piloted by two of our best pilots, one of them a WTI. News of the downed craft filtered through the squadron.

On the fourth day of the ground war I was posted on the flight schedule. My HAC, J.D., and I grabbed our NVGs, filled up our canteens, and flew with our section leader to Lonesome Dove, an expeditionary base near the "elbow" of Kuwait. We shut down and topped off our gas tanks and waited for our mission. Then the skies above us turned dark, ash sprinkled down on us from above, and oil residue and fine black dust crept into our eyes, our noses, and our ears. The fleeing Iraqis had set the oil fields ablaze.

An hour later we got the call. The 1st Marine Division had reached its final objective, Kuwait International Airport, and a medevac was needed. We immediately took off and radioed our Direct Air Support Center. No Cobra gunships were available to escort us; those guys were still busy killing Iraqi tanks. We were on our own.

In the flight to Kuwait International Airport, the smoke was so thick that the ceiling had dropped to 150 feet with less than a quarter-mile visibility. We dropped to 50 feet, slowing to fifty knots. Giant electrical-power stanchions loomed above us. We bumped up our altitude. Our door gunners were jittery. In the haze and smoke, flashes could be seen on both sides. We couldn't tell if they were vehicle headlights or muzzle flashes in the distance.

After about twenty-five minutes the haze began to clear a bit and there before me was the most magnificent sight I had ever seen. At 100 feet, our CH-46s roared over a column of hundreds of tanks, armored personnel carriers, and supply trucks converging on the airport, still 10 miles ahead. It was like a scene out of *Patton*. Victory was within reach. My helmet visor was down, so J.D. could not see my wet eyes. I was overwhelmed for a moment.

(Why couldn't we have done this in Vietnam?) I was about to enter Kuwait City airspace and experience the "other side" of liberation.

We approached the airport from the south keeping an eye out for any remnants of the Iraqi Army. A forward air controller (FAC) had cleared the LZ. On our second pass over the airport, J.D. shot a steep approach into a taxiway near the base of the tower. I looked over my right shoulder to make sure there was no communications antenna that we might hit. The enemy was nowhere to be found. Barrels of unmanned antiaircraft artillery stared silently at the skies a few hundred feet from our landing spot; their gunners had probably fled north the night before. Loose papers blew along the empty runways, which were pockmarked by coalition force air strikes. The terminal buildings looked as though they had been through an earthquake— collapsed walls, cracked windows, and open roofs.

As J.D. and I began to shut down our CH-46, two filthy men in green camouflage began running from one of the buildings toward our helo. They were too big to be the enemy, plus I recognized the jarhead hairdos.

I looked at J.D. as he took off his helmet. "Who the hell are those guys?" Gas masks and 9mm pistols dangling from their sides, I could see their white teeth and eyeballs peeking out through blackened faces. There lay the difference between aviators and grunts. J.D. and I were wearing our white crewneck undershirts designed for use with our "charcoal" protective suits. We looked like two skiers about to go on our first run, still clean and fresh.

But these Marines *were* aviators.

J.D. finally chuckled, "Fuckin' Hofley and a 'Shitter' guy!" The Marines were Drew Hofley and Jack McElroy, two captains serving as FACs with the 1st Marine Division. The night before Drew and Jack had earned their combat pay. They were directing air strikes to repel an attack on the 1st Division combat operations center with the division commander in it. Cobra gunships directed by Lt. Col. Mike "Spot" Kurth destroyed the Iraqi column. Kurth would win the Navy Cross, the highest personal award given to Marines during Desert Storm. Captain Ed Ray won the other; McElroy was given the Bronze Star for these actions.

Two more CH-46s from HMM-161 landed a few minutes after we had shut down. "Guido" Giannetta strolled up with a huge grin on his face. Two Hueys soon followed. Everyone was joining the party even though the war wasn't officially over yet. In the distance smoke billowed on the outskirts of Kuwait City, floating toward Basra, in Iraq. The smoky skies had cleared somewhat, yet the haze, the brown Persian Gulf miasma, still covered the late-morning Arabian sun. My section leader took the wounded Marine we'd come for, and I took three Iraqi enemy prisoners of war. I saw their gaunt faces; I looked into their hopeless eyes. They had given up.

We took off for a field hospital in Saudi Arabia, and landed with just drops of fuel remaining in our tanks.

That night the cease-fire took effect. Two days later I flew over the "highway of death," the road leading from Kuwait City to Iraq. A traffic jam of fleeing Iraqi soldiers had been discovered by Marine attack pilots and promptly destroyed. The mile-long column of charred vehicles looked like a junkyard; no human remains could be seen. War was brutal. Kill, overkill, or be killed.

Two weeks later HMM-161 left Saudi Arabia. Our brief war had ended, and it was time to fly home. Our Delta airliner touched down at El Toro after dark; a large crowd awaited us as we left the plane. I saw the face of the one I had missed. Half of her hair had gone gray, she was noticeably thinner, and she looked as if she had aged ten years in just four months. Tears rolled from her eyes. Her husband had been released, and now her only son was coming home from war, alive and well.

God was with our family.

CHAPTER 19

COMING AND GOING

A FTER THE LIBERATION OF KUWAIT, THE HOMECOMING parades and the victory celebrations in the United States did not stop for six months. No one had expected the war to end so abruptly or the overrated Iraqi Army to be destroyed by the coalition forces in such a convincing manner. The country had its first major clear-cut victory since 1945. Besides the local revelries, there was a ticker-tape parade in Manhattan and a victory march in Washington, D.C. Yellow ribbons were festooned on trees, outside houses, and on streetlights for months after the war ended.

While returning veterans were relishing the homecoming, many Marines were still abroad, participating in the relief of displaced Kurdish refugees in northern Iraq (Saddam Hussein was already reasserting his rule over his people). And on the way home to bases in Hawaii and California, Marines participated in a humanitarian operation in the Indian Ocean, helping Bangladesh recover from a major tropical cyclone. A Bangladeshi had spotted the amphibious task force off the coast and nicknamed it "angels from the sea," so the effort became known as Operation Sea Angel. Navy and Marine warriors were suddenly transformed into saviors.

For the Corps participants in Desert Storm, the rotation policy had been "first in, first home." What the brass didn't tell us was the second part: "first home, first back out."

The timing of HMM-161's next deployment became a lively topic in the ready room and among spouses of the Marines in our squadron. The destination of our deployment was no secret—a return trip to the Persian Gulf. Marines like to refer to deploying as going on a "cruise," going to "the boat" or "pumping" overseas. That meant a minimum of six months on the high seas, starting in San Diego, then steaming to the Persian Gulf and back, hopefully with a few exotic ports of call along the way.

It's not just another job, it's an adventure. See the world, meet interesting people . . . and kill them.

The U.S. force in readiness or "911 force" was the U.S. Marine Corps, and we had proven this once again. But in the annals of Corps history, Desert Storm had been the exception, an anomaly of force on force, open desert warfare, with unlimited air and armor unleashed on an unconcealed enemy. As convincing as the outcome in Kuwait was, no one could have guessed then the long-term effects of not going all the way to Baghdad.

But the victory was enough for this nation to finally purge itself of the guilt over the despicable homecoming it had given Vietnam War veterans two decades earlier. In its reception of Desert Storm veterans perhaps our country overcompensated, but as the beneficiary of this gesture, I loved every minute of it. So did Hollywood and the celebrities who had visited the troops in "the sandbox."

And so my Hollywood dreams abandoned long ago were about to finally happen.

Mark Adams had been working as a personal trainer (long before it was chic to have one) in Los Angeles, and one of his clients was a writer on *The Tonight Show*. At that time Jay Leno was subbing for Johnny Carson on Friday nights. During his visit to Saudi Arabia, Leno had literally "jumped" into a picture with me. Soon after, I mailed Mark a copy of that photograph as proof of my only cameo shot with a celebrity. Mark then gave it to his client (along with my home number) who mentioned it to Leno.

A week after I got home, Leno called my apartment. My roommate, Joe Heneghan, answered the phone. (Joe had returned to California at the same time I did, and the two of us immediately rented a pad in Newport Beach, ready to resume our normal lives again.)

"Hello, is this Quang?"

"No, this is Joe, his roommate. Let me get him on the phone."

"Hello Joe, this is Jay Leno from *The Tonight Show*."

"Yeah, right. And I'm John Wayne. Hey, Q, some dude calling himself Jay Leno wants to talk to you."

Leno could not have been any nicer on the phone or in person.

"Hi, Quang. I saw that photo of us together overseas. Welcome home. I'm hosting the show this Friday and would like to have you come down to the [show's] taping. Bring your girlfriend, and I'll have you onstage after my monologue."

I had only been in my squadron for four months but I knew better than to blindly accept that invitation as it was presented. Going on the show by myself, as if I had single-handedly won the war, would have meant never-ending ridicule for the rest of my career. I spoke with Leno and his staff and arranged for eight Marines from HMM-161 to attend the taping in uniform: four officers and four enlisted Marines. No one bothered to check with the brass. *Woops.*

I had a blast. Leno jokingly introduced us to his audience and they cheered. He then showed some pictures taken during his visit, thanked us for our service, and expressed his happiness at our safe return. He treated us with first-class hospitality, and I felt his sincerity behind the jokes and laughs. Sure, it was a superb publicity stunt for Leno, but he had been well on his way to taking over for Carson. He didn't need to do what he did.

(Hollywood is not so bad after all. It's showtime . . . and it's not about Vietnam!)

My fifteen minutes of fame quickly ended and my Marine Corps reality returned like a boomerang. We were given a week off upon returning to the States and then we were back at work, flying our helos over Southern California. We had little time to reflect on our fast and furious war.

I read through our squadron's record. HMM-161 lost no lives during the war, even a crashed helicopter was being shipped to North Carolina to be fixed and would return to flying status as part of another squadron. The Marine Corps could not afford to lose any more CH-46s—there were no replacements on the horizon.

In contrast to the war in Vietnam, where the Corps suffered the highest number of casualties in its history, twenty-three Marines died in combat (out of 121 Americans) in our 100-hour war, Desert Storm. Eighty-one Americans perished in accidents, and twenty-three more were listed as MIA.

In quiet moments, I would recall a briefing from our CO a few weeks before about the impending assault by Marines into Kuwait. Casualties were expected to be high; the ground campaign was expected to last sixty days or more. The Pentagon had ordered thousands of body bags—just in case. My squadron was prepared for mass casualty evacuations from the battlefield. When not ferrying troops or resupplying the grunts, our helicopters were configured to carry twelve canvas stretchers, plus a navy medical corpsman in the back. He would have provided first aid en route to a nuclear, biological, and chemical decontamination area or to the USS *Comfort* and USS *Mercy,* hospital ships stationed in the Persian Gulf.

None of the nightmare scenarios ever materialized.

Still, the public wanted to hear about the fighting from the troops themselves, so many speaking invitations came to the base and to my squadron. I gladly accepted a handful. I gave oral presentations combined with a color slideshow about my experiences in the war to local Rotary Clubs and at company meetings. I told the HMM-161 story as best as I could from the perspective of the secondmost junior pilot in the squadron, one not even privy to the big picture. A month after I got home, the Marine public affairs officer called me about a "unique" community relations event.

The Vietnamese American Community in nearby Little Saigon was requesting a Desert Storm veteran to appear at their annual ceremony to mourn the fall of Saigon. He chuckled. "I told the representative that the Marine Corps would do better than that. I said I will send him one of his own."

"Of course," I said. "Yes."

I pulled my service "A" uniforms out of storage: green polyester jacket and trousers, silver lieutenant bars, rifle and pistol shooting badges, gold aviator wings, and one token red and yellow ribbon awarded to everyone in the military during the Gulf War. That was the National Defense Service Ribbon, or more popularly referred to as the "fire watch ribbon." Personal and unit decorations were still awaiting approval from the brass.

In 1991, Little Saigon was the new official name for a 1-square-mile block of small restaurants and immigrant-owned businesses located in the city of Westminster (such Vietnamese concentrations would later take root in neighboring Garden Grove and Santa Ana). This area catered to the largest Vietnamese population outside Vietnam. Many of its residents had migrated from the refugee camps at Camp Pendleton 70 miles to the south, and others moved there from other parts of California and the rest of the country to be closer to their own, to be connected to their native community. I had no idea I had been living so close to so many old friends of my parents in their immigrant community only twenty minutes from my military base.

Every year since the mid-1980s, residents of Little Saigon gathered for a commemorative ceremony near the April 30 anniversary to remember loved ones and mourn the day they lost South Vietnam in 1975. Flags of the former Republic of Vietnam adorned the stage, hastily constructed in the middle of a shopping center parking lot. Red and yellow balloons swayed with the wind. The crowd swelled to over a thousand; radio and television reporters from local Vietnamese-language stations covered the event. Politicians gave patriotic speeches laced with fervent anticommunist rhetoric, even though only one of the dozen elected officials present that night had actually served in the military. None had been in Vietnam. In my mind, much of it was chickenhawk bullshit, obviously seeking to capitalize on the raw emotions of former refugees for future votes.

Forty-five minutes later, after long-winded speeches, the master of ceremonies, a former VNAF pilot, invited me onto the stage. Two young Vietnamese-American women wearing the traditional *ao dai* silk dresses greeted me with smiles and leis of flowers. I felt as if I were a U.S. Marine landing in Vietnam. *Déjà vu.*

The emcee said a few words in English and Vietnamese and told everyone about my academic and military background. I had not informed him of my father's predicament or about my family. He then asked, "Now that the lieutenant has returned from victory in Desert Storm, is he ready to fight and win back South Vietnam?"

I couldn't believe he asked that question.

With the microphone in my face, I could feel the hush in the audience, made up of mostly Vietnamese Americans. I imagined they wanted to hear a feverish *Da Dao Cong San!* Down with communism!

I temporarily froze, my reaction muted by the unrehearsed rhetorical challenge. I finally replied, "No comment," and stepped off the stage. At that moment, I realized that, just as for me, the war had not ended for many of my fellow refugees.

After my public appearance in Little Saigon, I began to wonder about my father's immigration status. I had not spoken to him directly, as my aunt's house in Saigon did not have a phone. My family was getting mail sent via France from Vietnam. A year earlier, the first group of former prison camp detainees had arrived in the United States under a special program called the Humanitarian Operation, better known as H.O. It had been over three years since my father was released from the prison camps, yet he was "still on the waiting list."

But I didn't realize that my parents had had a falling out and that my angry father never bothered to continue with the necessary paperwork. He could have left Vietnam at least a year earlier than he did. My mother had al-legedly written a "dear John" letter to my father that was supposed to be hand-delivered by an aunt in Paris. Somewhere in the family loop communications broke down, accidentally or on purpose, with regard to my mother's feelings about my father. My aunt had torn up the letter and tried to explain to my father, but to no avail.

Just two months after returning from Saudi Arabia, we Marines of HMM-161 were notified that we would be returning to the Persian Gulf in May 1992 as part of the 11th Marine Expeditionary Unit (MEU), capable of conducting special operations. In the Marine Corps, the MEU was considered its crown jewel, the "tip of the spear."

My squadron would spend the next twelve months preparing for its overseas deployment. Our unit had to quickly transition from operating in a desert environment to flying from amphibious ships. We needed hundreds of hours of flight training, especially experience with NVGs, but our CH-46s were tired, their spare parts limited. The CH-46's rotors required intensive inspection for invisible cracks after every ten hours of flight time. The other deploying units had priority, so my squadron did not fly much in the months after the war.

For me, life as a Marine pilot stationed in Southern California in the early 1990s could not have been more perfect.

The Tustin base sat in the middle of Orange County, a bustling suburb with a population of 2.5 million. Booming high technology, tourism (Disneyland), and real estate industries bordered our base, the built-up area inching its way to our front gate and perimeter fences. The locals welcomed the Marines, except for a few residents who lived beneath our noisy flight paths and would call the base duty officer daily to complain.

Orange County was also "Republican country," home to John Wayne, the John Birch Society, and Congressman "B-1" Bob Dornan. It made a perfect fit for the anticommunist residents of Little Saigon.

As the training officer for the squadron, I decided to send myself to POW survival training before I sent the other pilots. I drove down to San Diego for my two-week training at Survival, Evade, Resistance & Escape (SERE) School. SERE staffers trained pilots and aircrew in techniques to avoid capture and to survive imprisonment as a POW. Most of the training took place in a classroom environment on beautiful Coronado Island, but the graduation finale was a three-day survival romp in a mock POW camp located in a mountainous area north of San Diego.

We arrived at the "prison" greeted by singsong Arabic music blasting through loudspeakers. The staff placed sandbags over our heads and forced us to crawl on our knees to our prison cells, a cement area that looked like a dog kennel. A navy chief knelt next to me and whispered a few words in my ears. "You're not an American pilot. What are you doing here?" I was stunned at his command of Vietnamese. I figured he was a Vietnam veteran and had recognized my name. I answered in English, in accordance with the classroom training I had just received. "I am an American."

"No, you are not. You're an impostor!" the chief shrieked, again in my ancient tongue. He pulled me by my elbows, stood me on my feet and pinned me against a corrugated-steel wall. I was slammed against the wall, which swayed as I leaned back on it. It was not rigid, intentionally designed to be flexible and absorb the full effect of a body slam.

My first instinct was to strike back, to pummel the chief, and . . . flunk. But students had been warned that flunking out of SERE School meant losing flight status. "Students must resist and not react to training techniques." Simply stated, the staff could beat the crap out of me as much as they wanted, but I could not fight back, or else I would be grounded.

I had figured the chief was merely "training" me how to survive my first interrogation. Then something happened for the first time in my military career.

He slapped me with his open hand at least six times, until stars appeared in my vision. I bit my gums and my mouth was quickly filling with blood. The chief proceeded with his simulated interrogation. "You're a fucking liar. You're not an American pilot. You're an impostor and we're going to kill you."

I still figured he was just doing his job, and after a few more slaps, the chief sent me back to my cubbyhole, my dark prison cell, and I sat there for hours, hunched over a bowl of drinking water and feeling miserable as the temperature began to fall.

I had wanted to get the full training experience so I decided to escape, consistent with the fourth letter in the SERE acronym. Around midnight of our first night in captivity, I poked my head out of my cell to look for a place to run and hide. The gated prison was illuminated with bright spotlights. A watchtower, surrounded by barbed wire, stood in the middle of the camp. Before I could turn my head, two staffers pulled me out of my cell and took me to another part of the camp for additional "training." They laid me on my back and tied me up on a wooden board, securing my ankles and wrists with shackles so that I couldn't wriggle loose. A group of interrogators stood over me, but I could not see their faces as one of them was shining a bright flashlight into my eyes.

One of the men placed a small wet towel over my face. I could still breathe so I guessed the "torture" was just beginning. The men then tilted the end of the board where my head rested until my head was below the level of my feet. The men then asked me questions about my unit and my operating base. I gave them some bogus answers and repeated the textbook robotic reply: "Pham, Quang X., first lieutenant, U.S. Marine Corps, 123-45-6789."

Then someone began pouring water into my mouth and nose. I felt like I was drowning. The men allowed me to quickly catch my breath then continued the procedure for what seemed like two or three minutes. More questions were screamed but I could hardly make out the words. My chest tightened as I struggled to free myself. My heart was pounding so hard I felt as if I was going to have a heart attack. I then blurted out "HMM-161, Tustin, California."

The prison guards had "broken" me. My physical limitations had been exceeded by the infamous "waterboard" torture, allegedly invented by the North Vietnamese. The staffers stopped the drill, allowed me to sit upright, unbuckled my ankle and wrist restraints, and escorted me back to my cell. I was soaking wet and cold; and to add insult to insult, I had accidentally kicked over my urine bowl and had to spend the rest of the evening drenched in my own piss.

At the graduation ceremony, the navy chief who spoke Vietnamese came up and shook my hand. "No hard feelings, Lieutenant. I married a Vietnamese woman during the war." He smiled then moved on to congratulate the next student. I left SERE school a few pounds lighter, with a swollen mouth and an incredible fear of being captured by the enemy.

The SERE training was the most physically abusive experience I have ever faced, and that includes OCS, but I thought it had prepared me well to do my job. As I thought of the POWs in the Hanoi Hilton and about my father's twelve years in the prison camps, another thought shook me: "I would not have survived in captivity for as long as they did."

Right after SERE training ended, I drove from San Diego to Twentynine Palms, a vast desert training base near Palm Springs. Our squadron had deployed there to gain NVG experience. There was no better place to do it than in Twentynine Palms or the "Stumps." Marine units from all over the country rotated through the Stumps to conduct combined-armed exercises where they would get live-fire training around the clock.

Under the starry skies and sometime moonless nights, our squadron flew in formations of two, four, and six helicopters, practicing our land navigation techniques, shooting our machine guns, and landing on the dry and dusty desert floor. Green-tinted views became a way of life at night. We never flew anywhere at night without the NVGs on top of our helmets. Flying at night unaided (without NVGs) was frightening, like driving at 100 miles per hour without the ability to see anything on the road. I don't know how the Vietnam-era chopper pilots flew at night in the jungles amid tall mountains and in bad weather. But they did it.

Our CO, Lt. Col. Tom Rollins, or "Tank," simply repeated our mission, "To be in the right [landing] zone, on time." I thought he had brilliantly and succinctly summed up our training objectives.

During a flight to Northern California to resupply a detachment on a training mission, one of our CH-46s crashed into the Pacific off Oxnard. Lance Corporal Johns, a twenty-year-old avionics technician, was killed in the mishap. (Naval aircraft accidents are referred to as mishaps.)

I had run into Johns two weeks earlier in the squadron spaces. He was always helpful in answering my questions about radios and was full of energy. News of the crash was sketchy. The crew had experienced a single engine failure (the CH-46s had two engines and could fly on one if proper emergency procedures were implemented), but continued the flight for a few minutes before the helicopter crashed into the ocean with three crewmen, six passengers, and 2,000 pounds of gear. Everyone who managed to exit from the sinking helicopter was rescued by a navy search-and-rescue helicopter, except Johns who went down to the bottom of the ocean inside the craft.

That would be the second crash in HMM-161 within a year, and both accidents would be blamed on pilot error. The mishaps reminded me of the ever-dangerous nature of my profession. Unlike fighter pilots who had ejection seats to save their butts or who usually killed only themselves when they made fatal mistakes, helicopter pilots who screwed up usually killed many people.

After the crash off Oxnard, the pilot who was the HAC departed the squadron, pending a mishap investigation and a Judge Advocate General (JAG) Manual investigation. The pilot had also been the squadron's legal officer, acting as a military paralegal. As a result of his departure, the XO summoned me to his office and asked me if I would like to move from my training officer job to become the legal officer. I had begun to think about my post–Marine Corps career and one of the options that caught my interest had been law school.

I gladly accepted my new assignment and spent several weeks at the Naval Justice School in San Diego to learn the nuances of my new job. I had no idea how busy I would be (when not flying) the next nine months in coordinating the administrative requirements of various nonjudicial punishment proceedings and more aircraft mishap JAG Manual investigations.

Our squadron kept pressing on with the training syllabus because we needed to be ready. Our training, no matter how dangerous, would continue. I could sense an increase in safety awareness after yet another CH-46 from a sister squadron crashed into the ocean off the coast of Africa. I certainly was extremely aware of my limitations and began nurturing a humble respect for my ancient helicopter. Or as one of my grunt lieutenant friends darkly reminded me, "The '46 is God's machine. That helo has sent more Marines to God than anything else I know."

In April 1992, HMM-161 flew aboard the USS *Tarawa* for the 11th MEU's final evaluation called fleet exercise (FleetEx). The squadron's full complement of aviation assets included six AV-8B Harrier "jump jets," four AH-1W Cobras, four UH-1N Hueys acting as gunships and as command-and-control helos, four CH-53E Super Stallions, and twelve CH-46E Sea Knights. Some of our fellow infantry mates from the 1st Battalion, 4th Marine Regiment (one-four or BLT 1/4) joined, as did our service support component. The MEU was a small army in its own right, with 2,200 Marines equipped to fight a seven-day war without resupply.

I was copiloting the second helicopter in a flight of four CH-46s as we approached the *Tarawa* for landing. The amphibious assault ship/helicopter carrier USS *Tarawa* was nicknamed "Eagle of the Sea" and it spanned the length of three football fields, rose over 20 stories with a flight deck 70 feet above the waterline. It served as a floating airport, barracks to house the combat Marine force, and could also launch surface amphibious assault vehicles (AAVs) from its well deck.

"Proud Eagle, Greyhawk 11 and flight 1 mile initial for the break," our CO radioed the ship's tower. The gray-painted CH-46's were close together in parade formation, within one rotor's arc from each other (25 feet). The four-ship armada was a beautiful sight to see as I prepared the landing checklist.

"Roger, Greyhawk flight. Winds 15 degree starboard at 15 knots. Clear to land spots two, four, five, and six."

The 11th MEU was evaluated on its ability to conduct a set of twenty-seven missions, with six hours from notification to execution—three hours to plan, three hours to rehearse. The staff was critiqued on its mission planning and briefing as well as its execution. The missions ranged from a full-scale war to an *in extremis* hostage rescue to noncombatant evacuations and humanitarian operations.

With the staff from our sister squadrons and higher headquarters acting as evaluators, HMM-161 managed to pass its required milestones, but the feat was not accomplished without another close call. After taking off from the *Tarawa,* a flight of six CH-46s had to rendezvous on a windy night before proceeding to their LZ. The aircrews were wearing NVGs but, somehow, two of the helos nearly collided in the air, further shaking the confidence of some of our pilots, especially the new ones. And me.

Ten days after operating off the Southern California coast, the 11th MEU was declared "mission ready" to deploy. I felt that the squadron had "barely" passed its required readiness tests, although no one would publicly admit to it and neither did I. Unit loyalty was among the most important traits of Marines (sometimes to their detriment).

HMM-161 flew home to Tustin as squadron members finalized their personal plans with their families, updating their wills and enjoying their waning days on land.

A week after our squadron flew off the *Tarawa,* a major sociological event happened in Los Angeles. The Rodney King trial resulted in the acquittal of four Los Angeles Police Department officers. Within hours of the court's decision, the "City of Angels" erupted into riots unseen since the 1960s. Stores were looted, buildings were set afire, and some 10,000 people were arrested. Korean-American liquor store owners (some had fought in Vietnam with the South Korean Marines) brandished sawed-off shotguns and semi-automatic rifles. They stood together on rooftops, vowing to defend their livelihood as looters approached their stores. Fires could be seen for miles as the rioting spread.

National Guardsmen, U.S. Army regulars, and U.S. Marines were mobilized to assist in quelling the riots. For a few days I thought that HMM-161, the most mission-ready transport helicopter squadron on the West Coast, might be summoned to fly resupply or run reconnaissance missions over the city. The thought of flying combat missions over my former college town had never crossed my mind since the day I signed up for the Corps.

Thankfully, our squadron never did receive a call to help, and the riots quieted after several days. Millions of dollars in damage had been done and race relations in Los Angeles had taken a step backward. The rest of the country watched in despair, quietly hoping the melee would not spread to their communities.

Captains Don "Buzz" Buczynski and Roy Santa Maria, the two pilots who welcomed me to Saudi Arabia, had taken on increased responsibilities in HMM-161. Buzz became the CH-46 check pilot and Roy the assistant logistics officer. One of Buzz's assignments was to give recommendations to the CO on the progress of copilots in their training syllabus to become HACs.

After three check flights with other senior pilots in the squadron, I flew a three-hour evaluation flight with Buzz. Upon landing, he debriefed me on my performance.

"Q.X. Pham. You're not the ace of the base but you're a safe pilot, well qualified to be a HAC in this squadron. Congratulations!"

"Welcome Home Dad." Our family reunion at LAX seventeen years after we left Vietnam, 1992. (Author's Collection)

I was extremely proud to earn my HAC papers. Now, I would be in charge of a multimillion-dollar helicopter. Along with the helo, I would be charged with the safety of a copilot, one or more enlisted crewmen in the back and, at times, a squad of Marine grunts. My turn to lead had arrived.

Two weeks before our scheduled departure date, my family finally received the news we had been awaiting for two decades to receive. My father's immigration paperwork was approved by the Vietnamese government and he would soon be joining my mother in Los Angeles. I could see the fear in my mother's eyes at that prospect. I could sense her nervousness, her body shaking at times when she spoke about my father. She was panicking, unsure about the long-awaited reunion with her husband. He was going to "live" with her, the two of them alone, since my sisters had moved to other cities and I was on my way to a six-month "pleasure" cruise. After all these years she wasn't sure that's what she wanted.

"Weaseling" my way out of the deployment would not be an option for me even though my unique family situation might have allowed me to stay home. Certainly, there were plenty more capable pilots at Tustin to take my spot if I were to decide to spend time with my father. I would have been allowed to join the next deploying squadron six months later. But, I didn't want special treatment; I didn't want to whine. I had to fulfill my destiny. The reunion with my father was going to have to wait at least another six months.

A week later, I drove to Monterey, California, to take part in my roommate Joe Heneghan's wedding to his fiancée Cindy. At the reception, I met the father of one of the bridesmaids who was a retired Navy SEAL captain and a Vietnam veteran. When he learned of my postponed reunion with my father, he became visibly angry. "Those goddamn Marines, don't they have any heart? They should give you some time off to see your father, for Christ's sake."

I didn't need *another* special favor, especially from a stranger, and a sailor. "I'm going to make some calls to San Diego tomorrow."

He kept his word. When I showed up at my squadron for work the next week, the XO summoned me into his office again. "Q, how come you didn't tell us about your father?"

"Sir, I didn't want any distraction. We're leaving in five days, plus I am not sure he will actually be here by then."

"OK, I talked to the CO. Just get your trash aboard the boat and meet us in Pearl Harbor. Go see the S-1 [administration] for orders and airline tickets."

I was elated. The Corps (and the navy) had taken care of me and my $300 American Airlines ticket to Honolulu where the *Tarawa* would be berthed at Pearl Harbor. And they gave me the rest of the week off to boot.

Two days before the USS *Tarawa* was scheduled to sail out of San Diego, my father finally arrived from Vietnam. As hundreds of passengers departed the Air Thai 747, my mother, my sisters, and I huddled near the international terminal at LAX. Mostly Asians, the passengers all looked weary from the eleven-hour trans-Pacific flight. Then, I noticed a thin, gray-haired, and slightly hunched man. He looked much older than the dominating and cocky pilot I had remembered. He appeared lost—an aging man in a strange land. Yet this would be his third time in this country.

The older man looked around, paused, and stared right at my mother, my sisters, and me. A huge smile creased his face and his wrinkled eyes sparkled with joy. The Communists had not broken his spirit. *My father was finally a free man.* We frantically rushed toward him. For the first time in seventeen years, the Pham family was united. We had absolutely no clue of the difficulties that still lay ahead for my father. It took nearly two decades, but apparently, the United States had not forgotten its duty and moral obligation toward its former allies.

CHAPTER 20

FROM THE SEA

OMINATING THE ROW OF GRAY-HULLED WARSHIPS WAS my new home. I hurried up the gangplank, one bag in each hand, admiring the gigantic vessel towering above me. A "1" was painted on the departure end of its flight deck and on its superstructure (island tower). I dropped the bags at my sides, faced the ship's stern, came to attention, and saluted the national ensign (flag). The boarding procedure was the first in a long list of naval customs and traditions and lingo that jarheads would have to learn.

(Bow is front, stern refers to the rear end of the ship; port is left, starboard means right. Showers must be short. Water is precious and don't drop the soap. A captain in the navy outranks a captain in the Marines. Sailors are squids and so on.)

"Lieutenant Pham requesting permission to come aboard." I sounded off to the duty officer, a navy lieutenant junior grade, the equivalent of a Marine first lieutenant. He smiled and shook my hand. "Glad you made it. We pull out at eight a.m. tomorrow. Liberty is secured at midnight."

I fought my way up several flights of narrow stairs, passing sailors and Marines rushing off the ship for a few hours of precious downtime in Waikiki Beach. Walking through tight corridors crammed with cables and tubes overhead, I entered a section with "Officer Country" inscribed on a wooden board and secured above an oval hatch. My stateroom was located down the hall, one deck beneath the flight deck on the port side of the ship, (under landing spot 4 to be exact).

The *Tarawa* was a mammoth vessel, and for the first few weeks, rookie seagoing Marines like me would get lost finding our way around the ship. Compartments, decks, and frames were categorically numbered but still didn't make sense to me at first. I needed a personal guide but at my pay grade I didn't rate one.

Along with most of the pilots in HMM-161, my three roommates, a Harrier pilot and two Phrog drivers had left for liberty. I stuffed my bags atop a yellow metal locker and lay down on the left top rack, my twin-sized bed with a worn-out mattress to serve me for the next six months. Dozens of officers had slept on this rack since 1976, when the *Tarawa* was commissioned, so I made sure I had clean sheets.

My mind wandered back to the previous week's reunion with my father. He had finally come, then I was gone. He had reached freedom in America; I was off defending freedom (and oil) for America. After all the crying and hugging at the terminal, my father turned to me and asked the question only an aviator father would ask first. "So, Quang, what do you fly?"

"Helicopters, Dad. U.S. Marine CH-46s."

"Helicopters?" He looked in dismay. I later learned that in the VNAF, the best pilots flew A-1 Skyraiders and transports. Pilots with less ability got assigned to OV-1 Bird Dogs and helicopters.

By the look on my father's face as I was driving him from LAX to my mother's apartment forty-five minutes away, I could tell he was overwhelmed. He asked me to slow down, and I was only doing sixty. He had gotten dizzy looking outside as cars, billboards, and the Los Angeles skyline rushed by. At the age of fifty-six, he looked older than he was as he slouched in the back of my Jetta, falling asleep.

My mother did not talk either. She sat in the front passenger seat. Awkwardness filled the car, two separated lovers reunited and a son who could not decide whether to speak English or Vietnamese to his father.

We arrived at my mother's place just before dinnertime. Retreating to her kitchen, my mother cooked a Vietnamese meal later that night. Stewed pork in *nuoc mam, rau muong xao* (fried spinach), vegetable soup, and steamed rice filled our table. I couldn't even recall the last meal we had together as a family. While the meal would be my father's first supper with his family here, I was merely looking forward to stuffing my face. The dinner would be my last Vietnamese home-cooked food for a long time.

My mother stared at my father. He sat on the floor and watched television with his hands and his legs crossed. There was not much talking in the room by anyone. (What the hell were we supposed to do after all this time apart? My family needed a guidebook on family reunions.) My mother motioned me into her bedroom and whispered: "Look at him. He's sitting on the floor the way Communists taught him. He won't sit in a chair like normal people. I am scared, Quang."

(For Christ's sake, Mom. Give him a break. He just got here today!)

I felt like scolding my mother but I figured her babbling was her way of dealing with the uncomfortable situation. In a few weeks, when my sisters would leave, I'd be floating somewhere in the Pacific, and she would be all alone with my father in her apartment. And she was extremely anxious about that prospect.

My youngest sister Thu, not quite twenty, could not speak Vietnamese fluently, so she and my father conversed in English, to my mother's dismay. My two other sisters occasionally chimed in, both looking happy as ever.

My sisters and I slept in the living room for a few days, and my father slept in the second bedroom. In preparation for his arrival, my mother had neatly arranged the room, including a small desk, a chair, and a television. It was clear to everyone that my parents would have separate rooms, for the foreseeable future. I don't know what my father had in his mind but I knew that universal soldierly dream of Mary Jane Rottencrotch (fictional girlfriend) and the Great Homecoming Fantasy were not going to happen!

For the next few days, I drove my father around Los Angeles, helping him buy necessary items for men like aftershave, deodorant, razors, and cognac. We also stopped by a sporting goods store where my father selected an oversized Wilson tennis racquet and several cans of balls. He tried on some shorts and tennis shoes as I followed him clutching shopping bags full of athletic clothing and sweatpants. He was ready to pick up life where he had left off in 1975.

(Game, set, match. Hoa!)

"Captain Phillips, arriving." Four loud bell gongs over the 1-MC loudspeaker brought me back to the present. Thoughts of my father vanished as I rose from my rack, nearly hitting my head on the overhead (ceiling). The U.S. Navy spoke a strange language, crafted 217 years earlier like the Marine Corps.

Navy Capt. Braden Phillips was the commander of the amphibious task force. He was a member of the 1968 Naval Academy class, which included Oliver North, former secretary of the navy and decorated U.S. Marine James Webb, and Marine Col. Mike Hagee, his counterpart on the *Tarawa*. Colonel

Hagee commanded the 11th MEU and had the title of commander of the landing force. He led all Marines in the task force.*

Phillips and Hagee hadn't crossed paths since their days at Annapolis taking German-language classes together.

The morning after I boarded the *Tarawa,* we were on our way. Marines and sailors stood at attention on the flight deck to pay tribute to our fallen comrades as our ship passed by the USS *Arizona* Memorial. I could not help but feel a deep sense of pride, a sense of camaraderie, standing next to my naval brethren.

During the first few days, getting my "sea legs" was top priority as the *Tarawa* headed for Okinawa in the Western Pacific, where the high seas could get rough in a hurry. During the week we sailed for FleetEx off the California coast, I had felt slightly queasy and had to sneak topside several times for fresh air. Miraculously, I struggled through it and also fought back my longtime fear of drowning. I forced myself to walk to the edge of the flight deck while the *Tarawa* was anchored and looked down at the sea 70 feet below. For me, confronting fear was always better than avoiding another phobia. Once the ship got under way there was no getting off the "boat." Seasickness was no excuse.

Before the Persian Gulf War, marines and sailors stationed on the West Coast deployed to WestPac (Western Pacific) and conducted exercises with our allies in Australia, the Philippines, Japan, South Korea, and Thailand. Their counterparts on the East Coast sailed on Mediterranean (Med) Cruises. After the war with Saddam Hussein's military, deployments became "Gulf-Pac" cruises, combining the Persian Gulf and the Western Pacific. That meant less time spent in Eastern Asia—and, less fun.

As the *Tarawa* and her three sister ships sailed westward, Marine Corps history lessons from OCS and TBS came to light. We passed within miles of the once volcanic island of Iwo Jima. I stood on an upper deck of the *Tarawa* and stared at Mount Suribachi, site of the iconic flag-raising where "uncommon valor was a common virtue."

Within 100 miles of Okinawa, the site of another famous World War II Marine battle, HMM-161 prepared to launch aircraft for Exercise Valiant Usher 92, a simulated assault on the island.

As I sat in the left seat of the third CH-46 in a flight of six preparing to en-

*In 2003 General Hagee would become the thirty-third Commandant of the Marine Corps.

gage rotors, the sun rose brilliantly to the stern of the ship. The *Tarawa* was turning into the wind while keeping her point of intended movement (PIM) as far westward as possible. I was still flying as a copilot while awaiting my "cherry" or initial flight as a HAC.

"Tower, say winds." Somebody in the flight queried to make sure the winds were within limit to turn our rotors. Out of limit winds (above thirty knots and more than 30 degrees port or starboard of base recovery course) could cause rotors to droop and strike the helicopters.

"BRC two-nine-zero. Winds at 10 degrees port, twenty-five knots." BRC stood for base recovery course. Since the ship was always moving, a BRC was necessary so pilots could properly align their approaches, and along with the PIM, calculate the approximate location of the ship after a long flight without the ship in sight.

Upon hearing the flight leader's countdown for a simultaneous rotor engagement, I released the rotor brake, along with all the others in my flight. Every little item in our mission checklist had to be in sync. Two rotors resembling giant eggbeaters slowly whirled above me like Hula hoops, slightly flapping in the wind then spooling up to full speed. Loud rotor thump and steady vibrations shook the helicopter on its three wheels, bouncing it up and down on its hydraulic shocks.

Lines of grunts briskly walked toward the helicopters, the tips of their M16s covered with red blank-firing attachments. This was not a live-fire exercise, just a heliborne raid. Flight deck crews in colored vests crisscrossed the busy flight deck: brown (plane captain), green (landing signal enlisted, or LSE), purple (fuel), red (crash and ordnance), yellow (aircraft handlers), and white (medical personnel and visitors).

"Proud Eagle, Greyhawk 14 and flight for takeoff. Dash 1, 2+00 [of fuel], 16 souls aboard. Dash 2, 2+00, 17 souls. Dash 3. . . ." The calls rippled through the radio waves.

"Winds at fifteen degrees port, twenty knots. Greyhawk flight cleared for takeoff."

I finished the takeoff checklist and placed my right hand on the power management system (PMS) switch, ready to turn it off in case our helicopter lost an engine. That was second nature for CH-46 pilots. Turning off the PMS enabled the good engine to obtain maximum power to resume level flight. The possibility of losing an engine on takeoff, with a full load of grunts, and fuel, made this a very dangerous part of the flight.

With a heavy load in the back, sometimes the CH-46 would temporarily "sink" below the flight deck as it flew out over the ocean and lost its lift over the flight deck.

After seeing the takeoff hand signals from the LSE, my HAC slid left, picked up airspeed, and followed Dash 2, the second helo in the flight, which had taken off fifteen seconds earlier from the spot in front of us. Soon, the entire flight rendezvoused at 300 feet and eighty knots on the starboard side of the *Tarawa*.

Two Cobras and two Hueys flew in the overhead delta (holding pattern). Their pilots were among a select group of fliers from Light Attack Squadron 367 based at Camp Pendleton, nicknamed "Scarface."

Two CH-53s had been circling a few miles away. The Shitters always took off first since they carried the most fuel, flew the fastest, and, most important, carried the most weight, including the 105mm howitzers. The helos came from Heavy Helicopter Squadron 466, or "Wolfpack," based at Tustin like HMM-161.

As the last CH-46 was taking off, the flight deck crew towed two AV-8 Harriers (from Attack Squadron 211 known as the "Wake Island Avengers," based in Yuma, Arizona) into their takeoff spots at the 300-foot line on the flight deck, their pilots ready to launch to join the helo flight for the insert into Okinawa.* At full throttle and without external fuel tanks or aerial refueling, Harriers often had an endurance of less than one hour. Thus they took off last and landed first.

The two Harriers roared off the *Tarawa* and screamed toward Okinawa to simulate an attack on the LZ ahead of the assault force's arrival. Two Cobras sped ahead of the six CH-46s and one Huey flew the mission commander while the other acted as a gunship. The CH-53s carried whatever the CH-46s couldn't.

Upon reaching a predetermined checkpoint, the flight leader called out a code word over the radio. My adrenaline was pumping through my veins. Flying in a big formation was a thrill unmatched in any other helicopter training, something I hadn't done much Stateside or during the war.

I turned to my right, flipped up my tinted sun visors, and looked back into the cabin. Our crew chief stood over the machine gun on the right side, while

---

*The Harrier is a fixed-wing attack jet that can take off and land vertically. It was originally designed and first used by British forces.

another crewman manned a similar gun on the left. Two rows of six green-and-black-camouflaged young Marines sat on red canvas seats, the white of their eyes staring at each other across the aisle. I guessed none of them was more than twenty, except for the sergeant.

One of the grunts smiled at me and gave me the thumbs-up sign. I returned his gesture and flashed him five fingers, signaling five minutes from the LZ. He looked motivated; grunts enjoyed flying in the back of helicopters, even though many of them have heard horror "sea stories" of heavily weighed-down Marines drowning, trapped in the back of fast-sinking helos. For CH-46 pilots, we had escape hatches located right next to our seats. Our crew chiefs could egress through their side openings. *The grunts were screwed.*

The flight slowed down to 100 knots at the initial point (IP). I reset the stopwatch on the dashboard. From the IP it would be less than three minutes to the LZ, a large clearing in the Northern Training Area on Okinawa.

The Cobra flight leader cleared the zone for landing. Six gray CH-46s landed 60 feet from each other, their rear ramps lowered to the ground. Grunts sprinted out the back of the helos, most likely screaming "Oohraahh" and "Get some!" They lay on the ground in the prone position with their M16s at the ready and formed a half-circle perimeter facing toward the area of anticipated enemy contact. They had been instructed to make sure they had been well cleared of the helos in case one had to land again. No one wanted the wheels of a twelve-ton helicopter on his back.

"You've got the controls, Q." My HAC relinquished the flight controls and allowed me to fly back to the ship. Helicopter pilots traded off flying; the HAC always made the decision to fly certain parts of the mission. My HAC raised the rear ramp, signaling to the flight leader's crew chief that we were ready for takeoff. Two clicks chimed over the radio, a signal that the last aircraft was ready to depart the LZ, its ramp's status not easily seen. The flight lifted off and safely flew back to the *Tarawa*. In a few hours we would return to the same LZ to pick up the grunts, ready for a ride back to the boat for a hot shower and greasy chow.

After leaving Okinawa, the *Tarawa* ARG sailed to Hong Kong for three days of liberty. A year earlier, the navy would have pulled into Subic Bay in the Philippines ("the P.I.") and emptied its ships of wound-up, horny Marines and sailors into the raunchy neighborhoods of Olangapo City. I had seen bawdy homemade movies shot by pilots during their R&R in the P.I. As in

Vietnam, there were thousands of unclaimed Amerasians there waiting for their fathers to return.

It didn't matter anyway. Earlier in 1992 the Filipino government decided to kick the U.S. military out of its country. Many had missed visiting the P.I., where $10 would get a young American a full night of pleasure, his laundry cleaned, plus a neck massage in the morning, but I would have taken a pass. I was not the "virtuous officer." I just decided to have fun by other means. I rebuked no one for their behavior. (What happens overseas stays overseas . . . until the divorce proceeding.)

The leg from Hong Kong to Singapore created some excitement for our Harrier pilots, especially through the Straits of Formosa. Tensions between China and Taiwan were high; Chinese-made Silkworm missiles posed a credible threat to the four-ship ARG. Two fully loaded Harriers were placed on five-minute alert with pilots in their seats. They took off once to intercept a simulated "Bear attack" flown by a U.S. Navy P-3 antisubmarine aircraft training nearby. (Bear was the code name for a Soviet-made long-range bomber that often shadowed U.S. Navy ships.)

En route to Singapore, someone announced that the *Tarawa* was 100 miles off the coast at Hue City in central Vietnam. It was nighttime, just after evening chow. I left my stateroom and climbed the stairs to three decks above the flight deck. There was no flying, so the flight deck was quiet. Only the watch officer and several Marines were there, checking the chains and tie-downs on the Harriers and helos. (A plane or helicopter blown into the ocean was a big no-no, second only to a man overboard.)

Ocean breezes cooled the sticky air. I stood next to thick chain railings, bracing myself as the giant 40,000-ton ship pitched and rolled in the dark seas sprinkled with white foam. A mile-long wake trailed the *Tarawa,* the ocean churned by its twin screws moving the ship along at twenty-two knots. A quarter-moon rose halfway up the horizon, casting a bright streak across the ocean. I glanced at the dark vastness, to the starboard side, but saw nothing. In the distance was my birthplace, so close yet so far away.

I didn't realize until much later that I wasn't the first Vietnamese to board the mighty *Tarawa.* In 1979, during the *Tarawa*'s first WestPac deployment, its crew had rescued 400 Vietnamese drifting at sea in fishing boats and brought them to safety.

A Vietnam veteran once told me of a South China Sea superstition. Travelers would hear faint cries for help, voices of drowning boat people. Offerings and incense were thrown into the sea to honor the dead. I heard no such cries that night and I had nothing to throw into the sea. I had seen the hallowed grounds of the U.S. Marine Corps, the islands of valor in the South Pacific. Now I had traversed sacred waters, where some 300,000 of my fellow South Vietnamese had lost their lives trying to reach freedom in the years following the fall of Saigon.

I could feel a lump in my throat and tightness in my chest, but I could no longer shed a tear. I was a U.S. Marine, deployed at sea, merely sailing by my past and steaming toward my future. But I still wanted to pray for the dead. I finally went below.

While traveling between ports of call life on a navy ship was memorable. While sailors worked around the clock and aircraft mechanics turned wrenches through the night, some Marines got to work out, train on fast ropes, dry-fire weapons, and sleep. One officer even joked that "if you sleep twelve hours a day, the cruise would only be three months." Pilots laughed about their respite (MORP, for Marine officer rest period). Then there was chow, four times a day, as much as you could eat.

Junior Marines and sailors took turns working the officers' mess and doing our laundry. At first, I was not comfortable with the service so I decided to do my own late at night. Letting someone else wash my dirty clothes and flight suits was not the way I was taught but I had to live by the navy's way. *It's their ship!*

Fortunately for its "guests," the *Tarawa* did not have a stale odor like the other ships I've been on. It was by far the cleanest ship I've ever seen, its quarterdeck always shiny, its brass polished. Sailors chipped paint, mopped floors, swabbed decks, and stood watch. Besides the harmless and tireless jokes about the navy, I quickly grew to admire the "black shoes," a fond reference to those sailors who worked on ships for a living. But I saw theirs as a life of endless, confined toil. I could never be a sailor.

While in port in Singapore, I was promoted to captain along with six other peers. In a squadron full of lieutenants, the promotion meant I would not be too busy assigned duty as integrity watch officer while the ship was in port. I had ten new guys in tow, and half had families back home, so I wouldn't expect too much trouble from them. In addition to keeping an eye on my flock, another damper on my liberty plans was the ongoing investigation of the 1991 annual Tailhook Convention in Las Vegas, where drunken navy and Marine pilots had groped young female attendees.

(I had to coordinate with the MEU's JAG to schedule sexual harassment and "sensitivity" training. All pilots on the ship were asked whether they had attended Tailhook. I hadn't gone but I had been invited to attend as a guest of fighter pilot friends.)

After a month under way, I wrote my father to update him on our deployment and I got a letter back from him three weeks later.

Van Nuys, Calif., 7/22/92
Hi Quang,

Your mother and Thu are getting ready to send you letters and gifts. I want to drop you a few quick lines to say hello. Last week I went to San Jose and ran into many VNAF friends. There was a big reunion.

My friend Bao took care of me and helped me get my driver's license. Thu moved home from college for the summer, so I will not be alone while your mother is at work. I am waiting to hear back from a potential employer. I am hopeful that I will get the job.

I ran into former VNAF commander, Brigadier General Minh. He knows about your Kuwait Liberation Medal. If I don't brag nobody will know. Hope you enjoy your tour and see you soon.

Your Dad Hoa.

It sounded to me as if my father was adapting to his new life rather well, until I got letters from my mother indicating otherwise. She wrote to complain about my father's weekend bachelor-like escapades with his friends in Little Saigon. I felt helpless, floating on the open sea 12,000 miles away. I was glad my sister Thu was home for the summer to help bridge the gap between my parents as well as to spend some time with my father.

My mental distractions evaporated the moment the *Tarawa* entered a severe tempest in the Indian Ocean. Flight operations were canceled for three days. The giant ship was tossed in the ocean like a small leaf tumbling down a whitewater river. Marines walking in the corridors leaned forward and backward, struggling to brace themselves as the ship rolled and pitched. Inside the officers' mess, paper cups and plates flew off the dining table, spilling their contents all over the deck. In the ready room, a large television broke loose from its straps and nearly landed on one of the pilots sitting in the front row of leather chairs.

Between squalls flight deck personnel performed maintenance, since HMM-161 was expected to fly as soon as we reached the Persian Gulf. One morning, the ship ran into a powerful storm cell that could have easily blown people and aircraft (and our helos) overboard. My friend Roy was standing watch and he immediately sounded the storm alarm and cleared the flight deck. Fortunately everyone ran to safety in time thanks to Roy.

When the ship cleared the squall damage was glaringly visible. One of the CH-46s had not been properly secured, its rotors not being tied down. As a result, the rotor blades had rotated and flapped in the wind, striking the aft fuselage, causing significant damage to the helo, its blades, and transmission. Metal-shop mechanics fixed the fuselage damage; all other parts had to be replaced. Roy would later be blamed for the accident; somebody had to take the hit.

When the *Tarawa* finally reached the top of the Persian Gulf off Kuwait, the helicopter contingent flew into the army post, Camp Doha, erected after the Gulf War to host U.S. military personnel operating in the region. There was a huge parking lot at Doha that had been converted into a helicopter LZ with plenty of room for at least fifty helos. The Harrier detachment flew to Kuwait International Airport where it would fly training missions over the Kuwaiti desert and drop bombs on the Udari Range in northwestern Kuwait.

We were to participate in the joint exercises Operation Eager Mace and Operation Nautical Mantis with Kuwaiti and Saudi Arabian forces. The maneuvers should have been named Hotter than Hell.

It was August and the temperature, coupled with the high humidity from the Persian Gulf, was nearly unbearable. Sand flies and the occasional scorpion would scatter from underneath metal trash cans every time the bins were moved. It became obvious to me why Desert Storm (and the 2003 invasion of Iraq) took place in spring. Heat casualties would have decimated the ranks.

The next day a flight of four CH-46s flew from Doha to Al Jaber Airfield in southern Kuwait. We were to brief and fly a mission with the revamped Kuwaiti Air Force flying French Gazelle and Puma helicopters. Two senior pilots from our squadron were supposed to act as "liaisons" to the Kuwaiti pilots, teaching them briefing techniques, flight maneuvers, and tactics. A joint briefing was conducted between U.S. Marine and Kuwaiti pilots, interweaving English and hand signals over a large map spread across the sandy floor. After thirty minutes, it was clear to every U.S. participant in the briefing that the joint training was not going to be "Marine-perfect."

On the night of August 9, 1992, tragedy again struck HMM-161. A Cobra crashed into the Kuwaiti desert, killing Capt. John "Beav" Beving and 1st Lt. David "Davey" Jones. Both had taken off on an NVG navigational route; their wingmen had mechanical problems and had to cancel.

I flew a recovery crew to the crash site, which had already been visited by a medevac helicopter a few hours after the accident. The hop happened to be my first flight as a HAC. As I circled to land, I could see a black smoke trail about 100 yards long scorched against the dun desert floor and leading to small burned pieces of what once had been a helicopter gunship.

Beav had been a Desert Storm veteran, and Davey was on his first overseas tour. I hardly knew the two fallen aviators but I felt a great sense of loss, just as I had felt for Lance Corporal Johns in the CH-46 crash. Peacetime training missions were killing Marines—just as they have done throughout our history. *Train as you fight.*

After dropping off the recovery crew at Doha, my flight was a routine navigation training mission over the desert floor, interspersed with practice landings in various LZs. The terrain was familiar to me, since I had seen Kuwait from the air fifteen months earlier. The smoke had disappeared, the Iraqi Army defeated. But remnants of the war could still be seen, with the "highway of death" still littered with charred vehicles.

After two weeks ashore, the helicopter party departed Camp Doha and flew back to the *Tarawa* on August 16. The Harriers were scheduled to arrive the next morning before the ARG sailed southward.

Then tragedy struck again; our run of bad luck seemed unbreakable. A Harrier had gone down while on a night training run in Kuwait. Captain Mike "Rip" Vansickle died without attempting to eject. Like Davey, Rip left behind a wife and a young son. The news traveled to the *Tarawa* shortly after I hit the rack. Two CH-46s immediately launched and attempted to find the wreckage on the dark desert floor.

The Harrier crash was the fourth noncombat aviation class "A" mishap in HMM-161 within fifteen months. Eighteen months before Desert Shield, HMM-161 had lost another CH-46 in South Korea during its last WestPac deployment, killing all four Marines aboard. That made a total of five major crashes in four years, making HMM-161 the most accident-prone squadron in the Marine Corps—maybe in the entire U.S. military during that period.

I couldn't come up with a rationale; no one could explain the reasons for the tragedies. Inquiries were begun, hours of interviews and aircraft component engineering investigations were conducted. Except in one of the crashes, all the pilots had been excellent aviators, well experienced and well regarded.

Even so, naval aviation was and has always been an inherently dangerous and unforgiving business.

I sat down and wrote to the families of the deceased Marines and received wrenching letters from Beav's girlfriend and his parents.

Two days later, Marines and sailors stood on the *Tarawa*'s flight deck in a memorial service for the three fallen Marines. Then the ARG pulled into Bahrain, where another major announcement was made in the ready room.

HMM-161's top three officers, the CO, the XO, and the operations officer (OPSO), were relieved of their duties, effective immediately. No reasons were given, but we could figure this out on our own. The high accident rate had been unacceptable, aircraft losses and fatalities too many. The departing officers' replacements would arrive from stateside within ten days; until then the squadron would undergo a mandatory safety stand-down.

Morale bottomed. In the ready room the mood grew somber. We weren't flying. We were stuck in the Persian Gulf and there was nowhere to go, no war to fight, no one to kill except ourselves.

I saw my CO as he was packing his bags to go home. I never saw the XO and OPSO leave the ship. Tank looked devastated, his career finished. I had heard from many Marines that he would someday make general and I didn't doubt it. I saw him lead Marines and flew with him on several occasions; he was even better than his reputation. I felt the squadron had let him down, especially the senior officers on his staff, who should have worked harder to prevent the mishaps. But what did I know? I could only speculate until the information from eventual JAG Manual investigations was released.

In the Corps the leader, the CO, the commander, was always responsible, and Tank took his lumps like a professional, even at the nadir of his career.

As I handed him some last-minute legal paperwork requiring his signature, I managed to mumble, "Sir, I am really sorry about what's happening to you."

Tank looked at me and I thought he was going to break down. But there was no way in hell the salty, likable lieutenant colonel was going to melt. "Don't worry about me, Q. I'm through. You guys still have half a cruise to go, so you better get back at it. I'll be fine."

Listening to Tank at that moment, I had never felt prouder to be a Marine Corps officer. We didn't hug each other or shake hands; he must have felt my respect by the way I looked at him. He grabbed his belongings and left his stateroom; I saw him walk down the gangplank with his head held high.

Two lieutenant colonels and a major joined HMM-161, and the *Tarawa* finally set sail again. The new commanding officer, Lt. Col. John "BOFA" Lemoine, and new operations officer, Maj. Bruce "B.D." Coleman came from HMM-268; the new XO was a Huey pilot from Camp Pendleton. As the ship neared the mouth of the Strait of Hormuz, every pilot in the ready room cheered to the announcement over the 1-MC. We were ready to get out of the "Gulf of Gloom" and the "Desert of Despair" that took the lives of three of our buddies. The *Tarawa* was headed to Perth, Australia, and the 11th MEU was to conduct a joint exercise with the Australian military.

An hour later, I sensed a sharp right turn and had to grab a bulkhead to keep myself from falling over. When an 820-foot ship kicks in right full rudder, you feel it! The ship's captain came back onto the 1-MC and shared the latest news. "Attention, this is the captain. You are probably wondering why we took a right turn. Australia is not that way. [Laughter.] We have received a new mission from CentCom [Central Command]. We are headed for Mogadishu, Somalia."

I had no clue why we were heading to Somalia, although I had read that the U.S. Embassy there had been evacuated just before the Gulf War.

While crawling along the African coast, I received a second letter from my father.

Van Nuys, Calif., 8/30/92
Hi Quang,

Glad to hear from you. Congratulations on your new bars and on becoming aircraft commander. I flew A-1s low-level with no [night vision] goggles over water with only moonlight; the only difference was a lot of nose-up trim.

Last Friday night, Thu, her boyfriend, and I went to dinner at Bob's Big Boy—all you can eat. I felt like I was back in a USAF mess hall. Then we went bowling. Haven't played since 1966. I got 100, Thu 125, and her boyfriend 135. My VNAF buddies say "it's too late for me to start" 'cause I'm seventeen years behind. I try anyway.

It's sure sad when you lose a friend in the same squadron. I lost many of them. I either had to make a speech at the funeral or bring the bad news to their families in class A uniform with black ties. Stood honor guard too.

Haven't played much tennis lately. The U.S. Open's early matches have already started. Both [political] parties' national conventions are over. No one knows until November.

A quarter million people are homeless because of Hurricane Andrew in

Florida. Troops are sent down there for rescue, C-130s are flying all of sort of supplies, food, and tents. If you're here, you'd probably be down there too.

Well done Quang . . . I meant "Captain Quang."

Your Dad, Hoa.

For the first time in my military career, I felt as if my father, the first member in my family, had fully understood what I was going through. He had been there, done that.

The 11th MEU had been assigned to assist with transporting 3,000 UN troops from Pakistan to Somalia to provide security and to protect the famine-relief food supply. HMM-161's CH-53s flew Captain Phillips, Colonel Hagee, and their staffs to Nairobi, Kenya, to meet with U.S. diplomats and military officers in the region.

As flight operations resumed, the mood in the squadron improved. HMM-161 was a deployed Marine squadron with combat experience; with a contingency on the horizon, pilots weren't about to quit in the middle of a deployment. There would be no union-led airline strike or a boycott.

Still, I couldn't get the crashes completely out of my mind.

The newly arrived CO and OPSO had been to Desert Storm with HMM-268, one of the best CH-46 squadrons in the Marine Corps. They rallied the squadron; we pilots rallied ourselves to continue our mission.

The new CO, whose call sign of BOFA stood for "breath of fresh air," allowed me to continue flying as a HAC, which made me feel more confident about my contributions to the squadron. As I expected, given our recent high accident rate, he brought a conservative approach to our routine. In order for two helicopter pilots to fly together, there had to be a minimum of 1,000 total flight hours in the cockpit between the HAC and the copilot. At that time, I had just passed the 700-flight-hour mark, and most of the ten copilots had less than 400. (On some of the missions my helo crew barely met the minimum.)

A Marine wisecrack ran through my mind: "If the minimum wasn't good enough, it wouldn't be the minimum."

With two CH-46s and two Cobras aboard, the USS *Ogden* and the USS *Schenectady* steamed toward Mombasa, Kenya, to support the MEU staff, while the USS *Tarawa* and USS *Fort Fisher* trailed behind. The former U.S. ambassador to Somalia, Robert Oakley, was named special envoy for Somalia and he flew in and out of African countries to coordinate with U.S. personnel in charge of Operation Provide Relief, a food-relief effort flown by C-130s.

The S-2 department (intelligence) briefed the pilots on anticipated threats in Mogadishu, which were minimal in September 1992, a full year before Task Force Ranger would lose sixteen soldiers in a fierce firefight depicted in *Black Hawk Down*. A civil war was taking place in Somalia amid a famine. Warlords ruled Mogadishu; Mohammad Aideed was one clan leader, his son, ironically, being a Marine reservist studying in California. Early daylight flights were preferred because it was believed that the Somalis slept late into the morning, still high from chewing *khat* (or *qat*), leafy amphetamine-laced leaves from a local plant.

A few days after the hard right, the *Tarawa* arrived 25 miles off the Somali coast, remaining beyond the horizon, unseen by Mogadishu inhabitants.

Our first mission was to fly Colonel Hagee, Captain Phillips, their staffs, and UN personnel into Mogadishu. Hagee was scheduled to meet with warlord Aideed, but I didn't know when he would actually do so.

The rules of engagement (ROE) were shaky; we could not mount our machine guns on our side doors because some bureaucrat didn't want Marine helicopters to show a "threatening" profile. Our crew took machine gun rounds on the flight, but it would have been impossible to mount the guns while in flight and fire back at the enemy effectively in time. Each Marine packed a Beretta 9mm pistol and twenty-five rounds. *If the threat was minimal, why are we taking personal weapons and preparing to defend ourselves?*

Two Harriers were being towed into their takeoff positions. Unlike conventional jets that are hurled off aircraft carriers, the Harriers only need a couple hundred feet and no catapult to get airborne. Ordnance personnel had loaded the Harriers with 20mm cannon rounds, cluster bombs, and a pair of MK-82 (500-pound) bombs. The Harriers' job was to escort the CH-46s from high above, yet not cross the Somali coastline. If the CH-46s took hostile fire, the Harriers would roll in as part of a tactical recovery of aircraft and personnel package. And an international incident would have made CNN.

No Cobra helicopters were allowed to escort our flight into Mogadishu; they circled off the coast. *Something didn't smell right.*

As the rotors began to turn, a salty mist splashed the front windows of my CH-46. The scent of the sea and the leaky hydraulic fluid hoses and the oily stench combined to heighten the senses of a combat-ready Marine helicopter crew. There was no other smell like it anywhere except on amphibious ships, in the "gator" navy. The sun rose behind a hazy sky, the horizon obscured by dirty brown clouds with sporadic black smoke rising from the ground.

Colonel Hagee and his staff boarded my helo and I radioed Brick, my section leader, "Dash 2 is set for liftoff."

I maneuvered the CH-46 into a hover and slid to the left, pointing the cyclic slightly down to pick up airspeed. Brick was a quarter-mile ahead, but I didn't need to fly too close to him. The flight would take less than twenty minutes; our directions were crystal clear: Fly a straight line to the southern end of the Mogadishu Airport; do not fly over the built-up area to the south.

Two miles from the coastline, Brick suddenly veered to the left and swung wide of our flight path. He did not make a radio call to me so I proceeded on course and did not follow him. I remained on course as confirmed by my copilot. He double-checked his map coordinates against our GPS heading indicator. The distance between the two helos widened. I had chosen to follow the S-2 briefer and not my section leader, an act that usually led to a nasty postflight debriefing. Plus I didn't want to fly over the small buildings just south of the airport.

Nothing unusual took place. The Harriers remained on our radio channel, circling high overhead. I could not see them but I knew they were just a quick call away from unleashing bombs on any Somalis who threatened us. As I touched down at the Mogadishu airport, I could see what appeared like "technicals" moving slowly on the ground, their guns pointed skyward. "Technicals" were makeshift combat vehicles such as Toyota Land Cruisers, Mercedes trucks, and flatbed pickups with sizable weapons manned by several Somalis. I also saw trucks with "UN" painted on their sides. I instructed my crew chief to keep an eye on one technical, sitting about 200 yards from our helos, its occupants observing our every move. If the technical had started firing, we would have taken hits. The best I could have done was to immediately take off from my position, exposing my helo to more fire.

I was very edgy during the forty-five-minute wait while the colonel was at his meeting. We kept both our CH-46s' engines on line, rotors turning. *Never shut down a helo in the field unless you absolutely have to. There is always a chance you will not be able to restart it.*

Our flight made several round-trips into Mogadishu that day, for over seven hours of flight time, all without incident. When we landed back on the ship both aircrews were summoned to see our CO.

"Who fucking broke off the flight path?" the CO demanded. Brick readily admitted that they had done so and tried to blame his copilot for getting him "lost." Later, he got a private ass-chewing from the CO. The HAC (and section leader) was in charge, not his copilot.

I informed the CO about the technicals and asked him about our sketchy ROE. "Sir, what is it going to take for us to mount the .50-cals? Does one of us have to be shot down?" The CO gave me his best reply. "I don't know, Q. But I will find out and let you know." He didn't try to bullshit me.

Our Mogadishu Miscellaneous Operational Details, Local Operations, ended after three weeks and the *Tarawa* ARG sailed toward Perth, Australia. En route, the ships dipped below the equator and their crews took part in a "Wog Day" initiation, a long-standing half-sadomasochistic naval tradition consisting of a bizarre combination of *Rocky Horror Picture Show* antics and a college fraternity pledge initiation. Participation was voluntary, but like most traditions in the military peer pressure ruled the day. Even though I felt ridiculous crawling on my knees for hours while getting spanked with canvas fire hoses by "trusty shellbacks" (those who have already gone through initiation), then, finally having to suck a cherry out of a fat navy chief's hairy belly button full of lard, I too succumbed.

A few years later, the navy would ban Wog Day. Carrier deployments would then include female sailors and Marines and ships would have access to the Internet, e-mail, and telephones. *Welcome to the new navy! And for the better.*

After forty-five days at sea, the *Tarawa* ARG finally pulled into Perth for seven days of R&R. Pepe, Torch, and I and the rest of the squadron roamed Perth and its surrounding areas. Everyone agreed that Perth had been our best port visit by far for three reasons: the natives spoke English, the women were beautiful (OK, a few) and overly friendly, and Foster's beer was cheap and abundant. When the *Tarawa* left Australia, several sailors and Marines were left behind. "Missing movement" was a major offense, punishable under Article 87 of the Uniform Code of Military Justice. But I was sure the guilty men had had a great time—and didn't plan on making the military a career anyway.

(On November 3, 1992, I overheard the news of Bill Clinton's surprising presidential election victory over George H. W. Bush. There was a silence in the ready room—the majority of Marines I knew were Republicans. I was an independent, like several officers in my squadron, and had voted for Bush again by absentee ballot. I only had a slight impression of Clinton, and mostly about his hanky-panky and avoidance of military service during the Vietnam War.)

The ARG stopped at Guam for thirty-six hours, enough to refuel and to get mail. I walked off the ship and flagged down a taxi. I told the driver to drive me by Camp Asan, site of a former refugee camp. I had torn a picture of the camp out of a Marine history book. The taxi driver recognized the location and drove me to it. The large yellow Quonset huts were no longer there; the camp was now a giant empty field next to beaches with ankle-deep surf. I stood outside the taxi for a few minutes, staring at what once had been a temporary home for me and my family seventeen years earlier.

I could remember the old camp filled with tormented refugees and friendly Marines. A little boy stood in line for chow with his friends, oblivious to why he had been taken there with his mother and sisters. I saw my youthful but frightened mother scanning the bulletin board, looking for a message about my father. I again felt the pain in my right leg, when something in the water had bitten me.

I shook myself out of my daze. My father was in California with my mother. *Life had turned out all right for the Pham family.*

As we sailed from Guam to Hawaii, I realized that some Marines were as superstitious as the Vietnamese. On Friday, November the 13, the *Tarawa* crossed the International Date Line. *Bingo, it was Friday the 13th again,* and no flight operations for two days due to a convenient "maintenance stand-down."

Mike "Vegas" Jones, a Harrier pilot, and his five detachment mates celebrated this bizarre circumstance by donning Jason Voorhees hockey masks (the character from the *Friday The 13th* movies) and watched the taped series on the television in our ready room.

Now, a dozen years after GulfPac 2-92, I remember how proud I was to be a part of HMM-161. We'd had a tough deployment, but according to retired Capt. Braden Phillips, "You guys made one helluva comeback!"

I also remember sleepless nights, tossing over nightmares of losing an engine on takeoff and having to ditch at sea, fighting my way out of a dark sinking helicopter filled with freezing ocean water. I'd imagined pushing on my emergency hatch to no avail, the water pressure on the outside preventing me from exiting. I would sink 2,000 feet to the bottom of the Pacific, maybe deeper into the Marianas Trench. I remember the night I flew an actual instrument approach through a storm to 200 feet above water but still could not see the ship. I had to fly another approach as we finally landed with low-fuel lights lit during the last fifteen minutes of the flight.

I don't know if anyone else in my squadron was as scared as I was after the series of accidents. If they were, they didn't show it or talk about it. I too could not lose my cool, display any weaknesses, in front of other Marines. I had made some off-the-cuff remarks but I kept most of it to myself. In reality I barely survived that deployment. If the *Tarawa* had turned around and returned to Somalia, as scuttlebutt had it, I don't know how I would have managed to keep flying. As it was, the only thing that kept me going was that I didn't want to let my fellow Marines down. I was part of them, part of HMM-161, and part of the 11th MEU—a United States Marine.

But I didn't want to die for them. I wanted to see my father again.

Two days before Thanksgiving 1992, the *Tarawa* arrived off the coast by Camp Pendleton. The Harriers flew on to Yuma, the Cobras and Hueys returned to Pendleton. The gung-ho grunts went ashore on AAVs and landing crafts; they would've swum if they had to.

HMM-161's twelve CH-46s and four CH-53s rumbled through the skies of southern Orange County, approaching Tustin with its two landmark wooden blimp hangars almost 200 feet tall. Sixteen helicopters broke overhead, landed on the runway, and taxied toward our squadron's flight line.

I could see my father wearing a suit standing in a crowd of family and friends gathering near the base of the tower. His smile was wider than I had ever seen. He must have seen our flight arrive.

Pilots and crew chiefs promptly shut down their helicopters. We exited our helos and stood in formation with the rest of the Marines of HMM-161. Our CO made some brief remarks and dismissed the squadron.

As the formation broke, I ran toward my father, elated to see him again. He was there to welcome me home just as my mother had when I returned from Desert Storm. (To my father, the "YR" identifier on my helicopter may have appeared similar to the "YK" on his rescuer's chopper in Do Xa.) My new friend journalist Mike Tharp stood nearby and watched the moment, having no idea how long I had waited to come home—the longest six months of my life.

CHAPTER 21

TRANSITION

A LOW MARINE LAYER (FOGGY OVERCAST) HUNG OVER THE
Southern California coast, keeping the late afternoon spring temperature cool. A flock of seagulls trailed the 65-foot fishing charter
boat, diving for dead bait slung overboard, as it slowly plowed its way into
the Newport Beach harbor. Two giant brown pelicans, their wings fully
spread, took off from the nearby rock-lined jetty covered white with guano
to join the feast, scattering the frenzied smaller birds. On board, dozens of
men and some women were packing their rods and reels after a fun day at
sea, with lots of bites but not many fish worth keeping.

It had been nearly twenty years since I last cast a rod with my father, when
we used to fish from the banks of the Saigon River. After his release from the
prison camps, I never learned if he had ever fished again in Vietnam. Growing up without him in Oxnard, I had learned to tie my own hooks with the
knots he taught me.

After returning from my USS *Tarawa* deployment, I tried to relive the
past, to reconnect with him through the threads that once bound us as father
and son. I looked at my father standing at the rear of the boat, puffing a
Salem. He didn't say much during the trip but he appeared content just to be
hanging out with me. The way he was slouching made me wonder whether
he actually had enjoyed a breezy Sunday bobbing at sea. Perhaps I saw an ap-
preciative smile on his face, thankful of my gesture.

Once we were both living in Southern California, I only saw my father
sparingly, every other weekend at most. He lived with two other Vietnamese
latecomers, an hour away in the San Fernando Valley north of Los Angeles,
hopping from one hourly wage job to another, trying to make ends meet with
some help from his children. Only three months after landing in this country,

he had found part-time work at a senior center. I was extremely proud of my father: his once oversized ego was still there but he was not angry at the world.

At age fifty-eight, he applied for a five-dollar-an-hour job as a gas attendant at nearby Van Nuys Airport. In his résumé, he did not list his VNAF pilot career with its over 7,000 flight hours, probably more than any aviator then operating at Van Nuys.

He didn't get the job pumping gas into corporate jets and private planes. I truly don't know how he got by, but he managed.

As I had envisioned during my deployment, my parents' marriage lasted only one year after my father arrived in the United States, with their divorce finalized in early 1994. My hopes for a *Brady Bunch*–like family union had been dashed; my expectations were unrealistic for a couple who had grown apart after seventeen years. My father was hungry for life, to regain the prime years that had been taken away. My mother had become fiercely independent; my sisters grew to be equally autonomous, each achieving her own personal and professional successes, totally contradicting Hollywood's depictions of Vietnamese women. A line from a rap song and a scene from Stanley Kubrick's *Full Metal Jacket,* one of the most popular movies among Marines then, came to mind. *Well, baby . . . me so horny . . . me so horny . . . me love you long time.*

I took my father, my uncle, and some of their friends to the annual Marine Corps El Toro Airshow, one of the largest of its kind in the world. I believed my father would enjoy that day more than our fishing expedition. For the first time since he had swept the runways at Tan Son Nhut (the initial days of reeducation), my father was walking on the tarmac of a military airfield, on Tustin's sister base. Rows of planes lined the taxiways; biplanes flew overhead, warming up the crowd for the Marine Corps Air Ground Task Force demonstration, and then came the Blue Angels.

We stopped by my helicopter and entered the cockpit of a static CH-46. I pointed to the ancient pressure gauges similar to those in aircraft he once flew. I wanted to show him the GPS system, but the crew had removed the expensive green box to keep stray military buffs from "borrowing" it.

We walked past row after row of helicopters and planes, from a Huey to a B-52, each filled with curious spectators, mostly fathers and young boys. Then he saw a four-engine, gray, propeller-driven airplane with a black flag ornamented with a skull and crossbones sticking out of the top opening. His eyes opened wide, his finger pointed toward the familiar bird. The aircraft was a KC-130 from Marine Aerial Refueler Transport Squadron 352, nicknamed the "Raiders."

A Marine captain from 352 took my father into the cockpit of the aircraft he last flew for the VNAF, the same type of plane that had unloaded 15,000-pound "daisy-cutter" bombs on advancing NVA troops in 1975. A CBU-55B fuel/air explosive asphyxiation bomb had also been pushed out the back of a VNAF C-130 on top of an advancing NVA Regiment. I don't know if my father actually flew these missions, but he later told me about these flights. He had been the XO of one of two VNAF C-130 squadrons and one of the first instructor pilots trained in the transporting of that deadly cargo.

As I watched from the middle console, my father quickly slipped into the left seat where aircraft commanders and instructors usually sat. He touched several knobs, reached above to feel the engine control levers, looking as comfortable as I had ever seen him since he'd come to this country. I only wished that the friendly Marine captain could have jumped into the right seat, fired up the engines, and flown around the El Toro landing pattern once for my old man's sake.

We left the C-130 elated and then lined up behind a large crowd to watch the Marine air-ground team conduct a simulated assault. AV-8 Harriers and F/A-18 Hornets rolled in on a mock objective a few hundred yards in front of the crowd. Marines set off loud faux explosions and set fuel drums ablaze to add verisimilitude to action. Then CH-46 helicopters inserted troops followed by CH-53s with howitzers dangling beneath them. Cobra gunships circled overhead; grunts rushed out of the back of CH-46s and fired blank rounds as they rushed toward the objective.

My father watched stoically. At that moment, amid the explosions, fires, and helicopter rotor noises, I looked at him and wondered if he was having a flashback to the war, a PTSD moment. Five minutes later, a civilian pilot took off in a Korean War–era F-86 jet to demonstrate the aerial maneuverability of the famed warbird. The Blue Angels were getting ready to follow the F-86. On the third pass in front of the crowd and over the El Toro runways, the F-86 pilot attempted a tight loop. As he rolled inverted, I thought to myself, "This doesn't look right. He's too low." A few seconds later, the F-86 leveled on the downside of his loop but pancaked into the ground, exploding in a fireball and killing the pilot.

As firetrucks and rescue crews rushed toward the crash site, my father stared at the runway and shook his head. I grabbed my backpack and with my father quickly headed for the parking lot trying to beat 500,000 other departing attendees.

(The airshow had been a bad idea. Go fishing, less trauma!)

Like most squadrons after an overseas deployment, some Marines leave the unit and others join. I had fulfilled my unspoken obligation—two deployments in my first two years in the Fleet Marine Force. I was due for further orders but I didn't want to leave Southern California because life was comfortable and I wanted to live near my father. I opted to fulfill a staff position at Marine Aircraft Group 16 as the "frag" officer, responsible for the coordination of helicopter support requests from the 1st Marine Division and other military and civilian organizations on the West Coast.

I was still an unmarried officer, "deployable" in the eyes of the Corps. After SERE School and Desert Shield and Desert Storm, I had learned never to volunteer again. Sure enough, a call came my way five months after I returned home. Major Roger Baty, the operations officer from HMM-268, the "Sea Dragons" and the next squadron to deploy, telephoned me one day at my office.

"Hey, Q. Roger here. How would you like to pump with us as our S-2?"

I was flattered, my pride swelled. HMM-268 was one of the best CH-46 squadrons on base; its former CO and operations officer had brought HMM-161 safely home from the *Tarawa* deployment. I quickly imagined myself briefing "Sea Dragon" pilots and leading a flight into Mogadishu, where Marines and army soldiers were taking part in Operation Restore Hope. And then within seconds, I shuddered at the thought, as I remembered my father and my new girlfriend, whom I had met through Buzz.

Let someone else go. I've done my time.

"Sir, I appreciate the call but I've got some family matters to take care of . . . you're not going to send me orders, are you?"

"Don't worry about it, Q. We'll find someone else." Major Baty was sympathetic and didn't try to lay a guilt trip or spout off a loyalty speech on me.

The next month, a request for nominees to interview for the aide-de-camp position for the new commanding general of the 3d Marine Aircraft Wing was posted on a message board. I jumped at the opportunity, not to further my career in the Corps, but to ensure that I would be able to remain in Orange County, to spend more time with my father. I would not have to deploy unless there was a big war like Desert Storm, when the entire wing and its general and his aide would have to go. I would remain in Southern California for at least a year, the standard tour for aides, before the next set of orders arrived.

After a quick lesson on etiquette and duties as an aide by my group commander, a colonel who had been an aide to the Commandant of the Marine Corps, I was ready to proceed to my interview. The colonel looked over my uniform and gave me one last assurance. "General Frat is tough. He can be mean and nasty. Do your best and don't make us helo bubbas look bad. He's not going to pick a helo driver as his aide; he's a fighter jock."

I drove to the general's headquarters, a new two-story building with a Marine Corps flag and a major general's red flag with two stars flying in front. The secretary asked me to wait in the lobby; I was the third candidate to interview for the position, jokingly referred to by squadron pilots as the general's "butt boy" or "coffee boy."

Major General Paul A. Fratarangelo finally called me into his office, shook my hand, and sat me down. He then put on his gold-rimmed glasses and scanned my short "military" résumé.

General Frat had just finished a tour as the second in command of the I Marine Expeditionary Force, the same parent unit of all Marines in Desert Storm (and Iraq in 2003). He also led Operation Provide Relief in Somalia. Before that he had served as a one-star inspector general on General Schwarzkopf's CentCom staff during the Gulf War and in Somalia. A former F-4 fighter pilot by trade, he had reached the pinnacle of a Marine pilot's career after twenty-nine years of service. He was about to take command of one of the three air wings in the Corps.

When I first saw General Frat, I was caught off guard. He didn't look or act like my notion of a general officer. He was my height, about five feet, eight inches, stocky, and losing his hair. And he smiled and called me by my first name and pronounced it correctly, much to my surprise. I had been told that in order to make general, officers had to be tall, act mean, and look tough and sharp in uniform. I remember briefly meeting Gen. Al Gray in 1988, a former commandant of the Marine Corps (CMC), during his visit to Corpus Christi while I was a flight student. Gray was short and had the same gregarious, approachable demeanor as General Frat. He was also responsible, along with former secretary of the Navy James Webb, for taking the Corps back to its warrior roots in the 1980s.

After six years as a Marine, my interview was the first time I had spoken to a general officer privately. In the Marine Corps, generals numbered only seventy or so in a body of 180,000, and they were worshipped. All general officers indirectly reported to the CMC, a four-star posted in Washington, D.C. All Marines knew the name of their current CMC and those of the first three, that being instilled in us since the first week of boot camp or OCS. Only the sergeant major of the Marine Corps, the highest enlisted rank, had equal name recognition.

Following my self-introduction, I told General Frat about the helicopter community and that some of the helo pilots had felt neglected, flying thirty-year-old whirlybirds while the jet jocks flew new Harriers and Hornets. I also joked about how some of the officers had been talking about the general's arrival at El Toro. He suddenly interrupted me in mid-sentence and became serious. "So, Quang, what do the [helo] guys around there think about me?"

This may sound like a self-defeating answer but I automatically responded without one second of hesitation.

"Sir, they think you're an asshole."

General Frat looked at me and I thought he was going to give me the old OCS boot and orders to Kuwait. My interview was over, my prospect for the aide's job and another year in California flew out of the general's office like an F/A-18 catapulted off a carrier.

I drove back to Tustin, parked my car, and walked up the steps of Marine Aircraft Group 16 Headquarters. A fellow captain came rushing toward me. "Go see the group commander, Q. General Frat picked you and you're to report to the wing headquarters on Monday."

Voilà. Easy as that.

But then after a few days as aide-de-camp, I thought I was going to be fired.

The general's staff was setting up his new office, including his personal computer and files. One afternoon, after the general had left the building, two Marines and a civilian government worker entered my office and asked for my help. They had wanted access to the general's PC to set up his password. The general had told me his call sign, BOZO, and for me to use it as his password. (That's a funny call sign, Bozo the Clown. I wondered how General Frat got that call sign.) I relayed the item to the information technology Marines.

The next morning General Frat attempted to use his PC for the first time. As he sat in his leather chair and entered his call sign, he was unable to gain access. "Quang, my computer is not working. What password did you use?"

"General, enter your call sign," I replied from my new desk, in a cubicle just outside his corner suite.

"It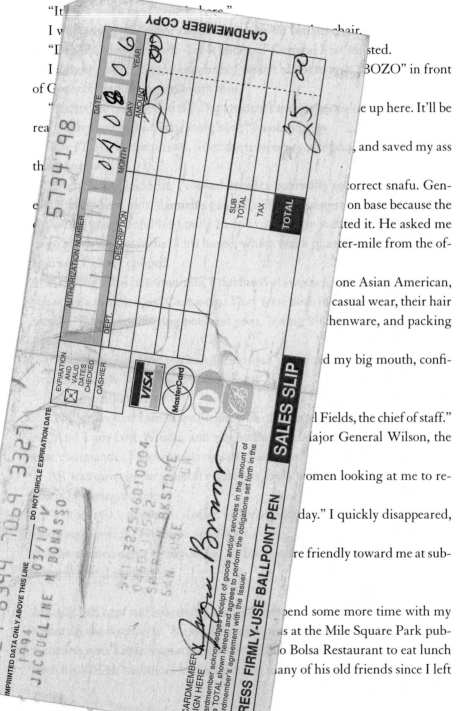

I

"D

I BOZO" in front of G

e up here. It'll be

rea , and saved my ass

th correct snafu. Gen-

e on base because the

ted it. He asked me

ter-mile from the of-

one Asian American,

casual wear, their hair

henware, and packing

d my big mouth, confi-

l Fields, the chief of staff."

lajor General Wilson, the

omen looking at me to re-

day." I quickly disappeared,

re friendly toward me at sub-

oend some more time with my

s at the Mile Square Park pub-

o Bolsa Restaurant to eat lunch

any of his old friends since I left

Vietnam. Their children were now thirty-year-old adults like me living in this country.

My father and I would play doubles against other partners, either two men or a couple about his age. I had to restrain myself from smashing overheads at the seniors while at the net; I was always a serve-and-volley player, too impatient to exchange baseline forehands or backhands. My father, on the other hand, was smooth and consistent, covering shots behind me, running back and forth from sideline to sideline, though not quite as fast as he was at Le Cercle Sportif in Saigon.

On one occasion after playing, we met up with a group of thirty VNAF veterans at a small Vietnamese restaurant. We had been sitting around sipping tea waiting for the arrival of a former general, someone important. I was getting hungry and a little pissed off. I was an aide-de-camp, and, by God, everybody should be on a time line, preferably one that I had drawn up. I was wasting my precious Saturday, not with my father, but at a goddamn restaurant waiting for an ex-general.

As the general entered the restaurant with his former aide, Ho Dang Tri (a close friend of my father's as I was later informed), both in their sixties and in civilian clothes, everyone in the restaurant hurriedly stood up. Except for my father. Someone belched out in Vietnamese, "Attention! Air Marshal Ky has arrived."

I immediately recognized the Clark Gable mustache, the flair in his walk, the cockiness in his face. General Nguyen Cao Ky, the former head of the VNAF and vice-president of South Vietnam. Even though I had lived across the street from his house at Tan Son Nhut, I had seen him only in photographs, in American textbooks. I was excited; I once thought of Ky as a hero, along with all the other VNAF fliers during the war.

My father slowly got to his feet and so did I.

Another veteran handed General Ky a beer. Ky then made a brief speech, commenting that he had just returned from a business trip to Hong Kong. He walked toward my father and they awkwardly shook hands. Then the former general turned to me and asked me what I flew.

"General, I fly 46s in the Marine Corps."

"Marine Corps huh . . . hmm . . . hmm." Ky shook his head. I wasn't sure what his body language meant but I was excited about meeting a former head of state and the top officer in the VNAF. He chatted with the other veterans, then strutted out of the restaurant, disappearing after a token appearance.

For the next hour across the luncheon tables, I listened to VNAF veterans exchange their thoughts on President Clinton and his impending normalization of trade and investment with Vietnam. I heard them talk about abandonment by the United States during the rout of 1975; I overheard others discuss their lives here; not all former fliers had stories to brag about.

The end of the Vietnam War had brought these veterans to the States, and, like my father, they all had to start life over. Their social status and their military rank no longer mattered; salutes were left in Saigon. Everyone began at the same starting point when they got here, the same as millions of immigrants before them. The earlier they had arrived after the war, the better off they had become.

As I eavesdropped on the animated conversations, my mind wandered back to an earlier social event for General Frat, in the privacy of the El Toro officers' club, swarming with servers and waiters and aides-de-camp. The crowd that night was also mostly Vietnam veterans, American Vietnam veterans, and they were reminiscing about their days of flying in the war. Most had retired as lieutenant colonels or colonels; some were now flying for major airlines or were filling corporate executive positions. They had served their country honorably and were about to enjoy the fruits of retirement after long successful careers. They had earned everything they were getting.

Back to what was going on around me in the Vietnamese restaurant, my father was having a ball, drifting from table to table, joking with everyone. The men in this small linoleum-floored eating place had also served their country, South Vietnam, with honor, but they were a long way from a comfortable retirement. Even so, the VNAF veterans eating three-dollar bowls of spicy noodles were as honorable as the Marine brass sipping merlot at the O' club.

I felt blessed that I could be a part of both worlds. I was built from both— my roots and my new country.

Another time, I went with my father to a crowded VNAF reunion in Anaheim, near Disneyland. The festivities were held at a giant hotel, a favorite of convention attendees. Red and yellow balloons, yellow flags with red stripes, and VNAF logos covered tables and walls inside the ballroom.

I came alone; my father brought his new girlfriend, some fifteen years his junior. The music was Vietnamese, the conversations were in Vietnamese, and I wasn't dating a Vietnamese woman at the time. It would have been too cumbersome to bring a non-Vietnamese to roam the ballroom, meeting my father's old friends.

Half of the veterans, men in their fifties, sixties, and seventies, wore makeshift VNAF uniforms or flight suits with their old VNAF squadron patches. My father wore a sports coat and tie, and so did I. Although I was repeatedly encouraged by my father's friends or the organizers of this and similar functions, I never once strutted in with my Marine Corps dress blues and medals at a VNAF event. It didn't feel right. I didn't want to appear as if I was trying to one-up the VNAF veterans, and, most important, my father. My war experience was *ti ti* (tiny) compared to his.

Most of my father's friends were cordial to me at the reunions, several expressing their envy of my access to military aircraft and the bases. A few made pointed remarks like, "So, Quang, you're flying for the Americans huh? How do they treat you? Better than they treated us?"

The old officers frequently encouraged me as my Marine career progressed. "Stay in for at least twenty. You'll get all those retirement benefits and get to go to the PX. I am proud of you. Make at least colonel. Your daddy was a lieutenant colonel. Show them [Americans] that we can do it too!"

At one reunion, my father was dancing the night away and, at age fifty-nine, still looked like a Vietnamese Fred Astaire doing the tango. He was having a blast, and I enjoyed watching his moves, knowing full well that I could not match his grace. He then returned to my table and grabbed me by the hand. "Come on, Quang, I want to introduce you to somebody." I instinctively followed him.

We pushed our way through the crowd, finally reaching the opposite side of the dance floor, away from all the hoopla. A circle of VNAF veterans crowded around a table, looking up watchfully as my father and I approached. The ballroom was dark, and it was late. I had to strain to look but I recognized him right away from the famous photograph.

There he was, sitting with a few older men, all slightly hunched over their drinks. He appeared shrunken, his shirt collar floating around his scrawny neck. He seemed diminished, not the same vigorous man who had stood erect wearing a flak jacket, helmetless, on the streets of Saigon's Cho Lon District in 1968. The man who had ignored American cameras and pulled the trigger of the pistol inches away from a Viet Cong officer's head—an image that forever changed the war.

Major General Nguyen Ngoc Loan, South Vietnamese National Police chief and ex-VNAF pilot. When he saw my father, he flashed a huge smile, then looked at me.

"General Loan. This is my son Quang. Pham Xuan Quang. He's also a pilot like us. He flies for the U.S. Marines." My father proudly introduced me in Vietnamese, acting with a respectful military protocol I had never seen before.

I bowed my head and extended my arm. *Chau xin chao bac.* I was trying to express my introduction in Vietnamese but wasn't sure I had greeted the general with the appropriate courtesy. *It's an honor to meet you, General.* He kept his seat and shook my hand, mumbling something too soft for me to hear. My father and I then returned to our table.

The strange meeting stuck in my mind but I never asked my father why he had introduced me to one of the most despicable South Vietnamese, according to many Americans of the Vietnam generation. My father never bothered to tell me either.*

Back at El Toro, I received some good news and bad news in early August 1993, a month after I began my aide tour. When I got to my office on a summer morning at 6:30 a.m., the phone on my desk rang. Usually early phone calls, coming from Washington, D.C., went directly to General Frat's unlisted number, available only to other generals and their aides.

I noticed the "I MEF" telephone number on the caller identification.

"Good morning, 3d Marine Aircraft Wing Headquarters, this is Captain Pham."

"Q! This is Rifle."

I hesitated for a moment.

Who the fuck is "Rifle" and why is he calling me at 6:30?

Then I realized it was Brig. Gen. Mike "Rifle" Delong, the deputy commander of the I Marine Expeditionary Force, and a hotshot Vietnam veteran and CH-46 pilot. General Delong had also commanded the prestigious MAWTS-1 "Top Gun" Squadron.

---

*In 2004, I visited Eddie Adams in his New York City studio a few months before he died from Lou Gehrig's disease. The Pulitzer-prize winning photojournalist, who had snapped the Viet Cong execution picture, was debilitated from the disease. He had to use a voice communication box to express his admiration for General Loan and his regrets for taking the photograph. His assistant then showed me a pictorial called "The Boat with No Smiles," a collage of pictures Adams had taken in 1977 as he boarded a Vietnamese boat that had been pushed back to sea by the Thai government. Adams relayed to me that the photos had been his proudest work, and which later were presented to Congress and helped persuade President Carter to pursue legislation to help the refugees. After an hour, as I got up to leave, Adams motioned me to look at his left shoulder. He then rolled up the sleeve of his polo shirt, revealing a large faded blue tattoo depicting an eagle, globe, and anchor, the Marine Corps emblem. I gave him the best compliment I could give a fellow Marine. "Semper fi, Eddie." He could still hear and a huge smile lit up his face.

Shit. Why is General Delong calling me? Who did I piss off now?

I had only met General Delong once, and he seemed to be happy to see a young CH-46 captain as General Frat's aide.

"Congratulations. Have you seen the message board this morning?" General Delong continued. "You were selected for augmentation."* He then jumped off the phone. I thought it had been nice of the general to personally call me.

I put the receiver down and ran down the hallway, where the administrative gunnery sergeant had hung the message board, basically daily announcements from different Marine commands around the world but predominantly from headquarters. I flipped through the first several pages, finally coming across a message with "RESULTS OF THE ORB 2-93 BOARD." I quickly scanned for familiar names, saw mine, but didn't recognize any others on the list except one: "GRATHWOL, PHILIP. 7562. MAG-36."

I had known about Phil's achievements in the Corps so I was not surprised that he was also selected. He was my roommate in flight school and one of my closest friends. The number 7562 was the military occupational specialty designation for CH-46 pilots. Only two had been selected from California- and Hawaii-based units. The selection rate was 6 percent for my specialty's year group.

I was surprised and honored. I knew that my old CO, Tank, had written outstanding officer fitness reports for me, ranking me third out of eighteen lieutenants in HMM-161 competing for augmentation. Tank had relied on his department heads to rank us, as well as a peer evaluation system where the lieutenants were asked to rank the top three among themselves. Back then, only ROTC, Annapolis graduates, and a few honors graduates of TBS received regular commissions. I had also received "A MUST FOR AUGMENTATION" on three other fitness reports. A board of four colonels had ranked me as the top candidate out of fifty-one officers in Marine Aircraft Group 16 during the interview portion of the process. Another major had commented on my performance as "clearly in the top 5 percent and functions at an advanced level."

Congratulatory phone calls and e-mails arrived sporadically throughout the day; the augmentation board's results had been highly anticipated be-

---

*Augmentation is the process used to manage the regular-officer population through time in service and occupational categories. Officer retention boards (ORBs) meet to select reserve commissioned officers for retention.

cause most of my peers had less than two years remaining on their tour. The economy was sagging; airlines were slow to hire helo pilots. The next day I began to sense a shift in the tone of best wishes.

One peer exaggerated the gossip. "Everyone in the squadron [my old unit] thinks you got 'augmented' because you're a minority and you're the general's 'coffee boy!' "

(How would they know? Did they sit on the board? Have they seen my fitness reports?)

I knew that the board had reached its conclusions before I even took the aide job but I wanted to make sure. I walked right into General Frat's office and asked him point-blank. "Sir, did you make a call to the augmentation board for me?"

"Quang, I did not do that and would not do that for anyone," General Frat tonelessly answered.

I tried to see the skeptics' point of view. There weren't many minority officers in the Marine Corps at that time, and even fewer were pilots. I wondered if the Corps had picked me because of my race.

I pushed the second-guessing aside and proceeded to assist General Frat with the demands of his official schedule. I accompanied him to many meetings, including the secretary of the navy's war games in Quantico, live-fire exercises, high-level aviation leadership boards, and community relations events in Orange County where I met dozens of elected officials and private citizens. I researched and wrote his speeches because he trusted me with helping him.

By far the best perk of being General Frat's aide was the opportunity to fly in the back of an F/A-18D Hornet, fresh off the McDonnell-Douglas assembly line in St. Louis. (OK, my dream as a fighter pilot didn't materialize but a supersonic backseat flight would beat any "E" ticket ride at Disneyland.) I pushed hard to fly as often as I could with General Frat, who was qualified to fly the Hornet and had to meet his annual flight-time requirement. I made sure the general *needed* me to accompany him everywhere, especially to meetings across the country when he would occasionally commandeer a Hornet.

I rushed through a week's worth of abbreviated training. I spent two hours in the F/A-18 simulator, went through the ejection seat qualification, and got my G-suit fitted perfectly to my body. I wanted to make sure that if something bad happened, I'd be able to land the jet or eject myself.

The big day finally came. The Marines of All-Weather Fighter/Attack Squadron 242 gave me their best support, well aware that I was only an opportunistic helo bubba looking for a fast joy ride. I never hid my motives. I could still remember, as a fourteen-year-old, seeing the sleek Hornet prototype coming in for a landing at the Point Mugu airshow. Fifteen years later, I was about to climb aboard a Hornet with only five flight hours in its life.

The leather on the rear ejection seat headrest smelled like a brand-new car, the avionics were state-of-the art technology. The plane captain handed me a pair of clear plastic booties so I would not "scuff" up his new jet. I had to laugh at myself; in my CH-46 squadron, the helos were filthy. (We would have had to wear the booties to keep our boots clean!)

General Frat took Runway 7 at El Toro.

"Bat 03, switch Departure, cleared for takeoff." The tower gave us our instructions.

He then slowly pushed the throttles forward with his left hand, then informed me over the cockpit communication system. The jet began its takeoff roll.

"OK, Q, I'm lighting the ABs [afterburners]."

I braced myself against the ejection seat, my straps pinning me to the cushion. I could hear a loud screaming noise at my back, where two General Electric engines, each with 18,000 pounds of thrust, rocketed down the runway, pulling me to the back of my seat. *Oohhrahhh.* The acceleration was unbelievable, the hangars blurred by me as the Hornet became airborne en route to Yuma, Arizona. *I could not keep up with the radio calls.* A minute later, we were at 18,000 feet. In a CH-46, I'd be lucky to get to 3,000 feet.

Fifteen minutes later, we were over Yuma's firing ranges. General Frat switched to "range control" for entry into the Restricted Area 2507 (bombing range requiring permission to enter). He looked around his left and right and I followed his head movement, thinking he was keeping an eye out for traffic. Suddenly, my head snapped, my vision blackened at the edges, the forces of gravity slamming me against my seat. I glanced at the dashboard and saw *only* 6.5 on the G-meter. I then recognized the maneuver from my days of flying the T-34 in flight school. We were in a tight loop. (Geez, my fifty-one-year-old general is trying to get me sick on my first jet hop. No chance in hell, sir!)

On October 31, 1993, Marine Corps Commandant Gen. Carl E. Mundy Jr., appeared on "60 Minutes" with Leslie Stahl and commented on minority officers:

"In the military skills, we find that the minority officers do not shoot as well as the nonminorities. Now how do you rationalize? I don't know. I can't explain that to you but we're going to find out. . . . They don't swim as well. And when you give them a compass and send them across the terrain at night in a land navigation exercise, they don't do as well at that sort of thing."

I had known about the show, having been informed by one of the show's participants, a black captain and former CH-46 pilot who had been accepted at Harvard Law School the previous spring. He alleged that he was called a "boy" by white officers in his squadron before he was "boarded," his flight status revoked.

I notified General Frat since several black officers appearing on the "60 Minutes" were serving in his command, the 3d Marine Aircraft Wing. He and I were attending a live-fire exercise in Twentynine Palms. The general appeared disgusted at the news, stating, "I can't believe we still have that shit in the Marine Corps! Those goddam rednecks!"

In 1993, a discomforting undercurrent began to flow within the Marine Corps about diversity and equal-opportunity programs. Marine minority-officer issues boiled to the top amid military downsizing, the Tailhook scandal, "Don't ask, don't tell," and the "women in combat" controversies.

As an aide-de-camp I had access to the "Early Bird," a daily headline news summary faxed to our offices daily, and other documents. I saw official data for minority personnel in the Corps, by rank. As of October 1992, out of 19,000 active duty officers, 90 percent were whites, 5 percent blacks, 3 percent Hispanic, and 2 percent "Other." The U.S. Army had 10,000 black officers in its ranks. I guess I was counted in the "Other." (Maybe that's why the Corps had stamped "MINORITY CANDIDATE" across my OCS application back in 1986.)

I watched the entire "60 Minutes" segment and recognized another black officer on it, a classmate from TBS. I tried to dispel the commandant's perception of minority officers' orienteering and marksmanship skills, even though I realized that he was referring to blacks versus whites in the interview. I compared my performance to the comments made by the Commandant. I did so because I had believed in the Marine Corps as well as in our commandant.

"Minority officers do not shoot as well as the nonminorities." I had qualified as a sharpshooter (the middle ratings) with the 9mm pistol and the

M16A2, missing a rifle expert badge by one point. I had also requalified several times since TBS.

"They don't swim as well." Despite my fear of water, I had been designated as water survival qualified, or WSQ, the highest rating a Marine could get. I had successfully graduated from water survival during flight training (and three subsequent times), a feat much more difficult than becoming WSQ.

"When you give them a compass and send them across the terrain at night in a land navigation exercise, they don't do as well at that sort of thing." I had graduated in the top half of my basic school class and in the top 10 percent for military training, which encompassed all training regimens.

So why did the commandant say what he said? What data was he looking at?

I felt disappointed and let down, an outsider constantly having to struggle to fit in, never fully accepted. I took his remarks personally. The rumor mill criticism about my selection for augmentation was still bothering me. (My buddies called me "thin-skinned." I had rejected all racial call signs—they would only have reinforced stereotypes. "Q" was my call sign and I was comfortable with it.)

I still wanted to believe the Commandant had been misquoted, his sixty-second interview extracted for sound bites from a two-hour interview. As many "lifers" jumped to his defense, I desperately hoped that he had been quoted out of context. Marines I knew wanted this racially-tinged episode to disappear, buried under the carpet.

What about Asian Americans in the Corps, grouped under "Other"?

There weren't many in the Corps. I found out that as of 1991, there were six Vietnamese-American Marine officers, according to the *Navy Times*. I had met Van K. Tran,* a Vietnamese American CH-53 pilot from Texas who had received his wings a few months after I got mine. His father had been a VNAF veteran like mine. I also knew of several Asian-American Marine aviators, Roy Santa Maria, a Filipino American, and Roy "Kato" Akana, a Japanese American flying Harriers.

Asians didn't matter in the Marine Corps until the *New York Times, Washington Post, Los Angeles Times, Navy Times,* and *Good Morning America* showcased former officer candidate Bruce Yamashita, a Georgetown-trained

---

*As of this writing, Lt. Col. Van K. Tran is still on active duty in Virginia.

lawyer who charged that he had been racially discriminated against. He got booted from OCS two days before graduation, classified as a "leadership failure." OCS staffers called him racial names and told him to "go back to your own country!" and "during World War II, we whipped your Japanese ass!"

Hey, they called me a Viet Cong!

Yamashita waged a five-year legal battle against the Corps, with the help of civil rights groups, powerful Japanese-American veteran associations, and elected officials. In early 1994, under pressure from the office of the secretary of the navy, the Corps issued an apology and commissioned Yamashita as a captain.

I was livid. I was confused, I was torn. (I am damned if I excel and I am damned if I don't—the double-edged sword of equal-opportunity and minority programs.) I was getting tired of the constant pressure, the "Marine team player" image I had to uphold; my contributions and presence in the officer corps dismissed as token. The Kool-Aid was wearing off. The straw that broke my back took place at the 1993 Marine Corps Birthday Ball, which I had attended with my girlfriend at the time.

As I was heading to the restroom near the end of the evening, I heard something behind me that sent chills down my spine. "Chong. Yang. Fong. Fu." When I turned around, I saw two white Marine officers laughing, drinks in hand, one a first lieutenant, the other a captain and a peer of mine. They were wearing dress blues and so was I. Except I had an obnoxious gold braid called an "aiguillette" around my left shoulder. I guess I had to wear that so my general could spot his "butt boy" in a crowd. To be blunt, I stood out.

I was in no mood to joke around. "What the fuck did you guys just say?" I confronted my fellow officers.

They immediately stopped laughing, their eyes focused on my date who had heard the taunting. "Nothing, man, we didn't say anything."

"I didn't fucking think so." I walked away fuming. My hecklers had backed down, after exhibiting the worst kind of racism, the subtle, deniable type. I was ready to resign my commission and turn in my wings to General Frat that night.

I'm glad I waited. I began thinking about Doug Hamlin, Guy Close, Mark Henderson, Phil Grathwol, Joe Heneghan, Pepe, Torch, General Frat, and all my buddies in the Corps. The assholes were few and far between, no more than a few percent of the Marines I've met. Contrary to another word of warning by a civilian: "You've got to watch out for the enlisted guys, they don't have a lot of education." I had no run-ins with enlisted Marines; all of my hazers were officers. I couldn't possibly indict the whole Corps as Bruce Yamashita had done, taking his legal case to the public and making the Marine Corps look parochial. I still believed in *semper fidelis,* Always Faithful. I decided that I'd had enough.

I could have gone as far as I wanted in the Corps, but it was no longer worth the stress.

An officer recruiter I knew often repeated: "We've been around for over 200 years. Why the hell would we need you?" I agreed with him. No individual could "break" the Marine Corps.

In June 1994, after nearly seven years of service, I officially turned down my regular commission, resigning from my beloved Corps, quitting my profession of arms. I also declined a seat at the upcoming Amphibious Warfare School, a career-level school for 200 captains selected annually. I had made the alternate attendee list, only to be immediately offered orders by my monitor (assignment officer) once I had resigned. He too tried to persuade me, offering me practically every assignment. General Frat did not try to talk me out of my decision. Instead, he ordered me to visit four colonels who attempted to find out my reasons. One even spoke about the prospect of sending me through jet training. I was reminded of my helo affiliation and a popular phrase by rotor heads: Jets are for kids. Thanks but no thanks.

Right after my resignation, a bubbling nuclear crisis in the Korean Peninsula nearly resulted in me packing my bags to accompany General Frat and the 3d Marine Aircraft Wing to South Korea. We waited for our orders—to be prepared for combat operations should the North Koreans maintain their nuclear weapon development posture. The wing headquarters was going to be located at an airfield south of Seoul, its location and parts of OPLAN 5027, the war plans against North Korea, revealed to me by the G-2 in a top secret briefing. I had only a secret clearance. I had tried to apply for a top secret clearance but was told that since I still had relatives in Vietnam, a communist country, there was no way the U.S. government would grant me one.

After ten days, things cooled off and we stood down.

One of the best things I learned from the Marine Corps had remained with me since my days in Quantico: Make a decision. And stick with it.

In early 1995, I went on terminal leave (using my sixty days of paid vacation) from the Marine Corps. I had become a better U.S. citizen, more informed than the twenty-year-old who indifferently took his oath of citizenship a decade earlier. I also had three job offers in hand, one from one of the world's most esteemed pharmaceutical companies. I left the Corps with unquestionably more confidence but also harbored an enormous unresolved anger. For the first time in my life, I had retreated from confrontation. Yet I wanted to show myself and those few bigoted and jealous Marines that I no longer needed the Corps.

Expressing my thanks at the Vietnam Wall with its founder, Jan C. Scruggs, 1998. (Courtesy of Chau Tran)

CHAPTER 22

CAN'T GO BACK

AFTER SEVEN YEARS IN THE MARINE CORPS, I YEARNED TO be rebellious, unstructured, and borderline "unsat" again. I didn't want to have to worry about my trouser center line, my uniform, and my flight hours. I grew my hair long—my head started to look like a "bowl" again. I stopped shaving and tried to grow a goatee, able to showcase only a few whiskers after a week. I peeled off the red Marine Corps sticker on my car bumper. I stopped running, until a fellow drug sales representative challenged me to a jog, mockingly asking if the "Corps had really been that tough?"

(I ran his ass into the ground, leaving him choking in the diesel fumes of a city bus in midtown Los Angeles.) The competitive fires were still burning inside me.

In the midst of all the psychological conflicts, my new marriage was falling apart.

I hadn't spent much time with my father for most of the second half of 1994, too busy looking for a job, too embarrassed to tell him the true reason why I had left the Marines. I didn't want to have to answer his friend who had once asked, "So, Quang, you're flying for the Americans, huh? How do they treat you? Better than they treated us?"

Despite the residual bitterness, deep down inside, I knew the answer was a resounding, "Yes."

During my first several months as a civilian, I was adrift, starting all over again. Money wasn't a problem, but my new job schlepping prescription drugs quickly bored me. My civilian counterparts weren't exactly impressed with my Marine credentials; only a fraction had worn a uniform. I wasn't about to tell them the true reasons why I left the Corps. My new boss assigned me a sales territory in rough neighborhoods because I was an "ex-Marine." It didn't matter anyway; the doctors only wanted free drug samples and pizzas. My sales pitches lasted thirty seconds, eight sales calls a day equaled a day's work, which could be completed within hours.

A recurring headline drew deep interest from me—Vietnam, my birthplace. Talks of normalizing trade relations were rampant, with expatriate entrepreneurs rushing back to their homeland, looking to make the big bucks. I had other compelling reasons to visit, so I convinced my Marine buddy Scott "Goober" Dodson, himself an entrepreneur and ex-pilot, to come along. I really needed Scott to accompany me, since I had heard about human rights abuses in Vietnam and jailed dissidents. I wanted to go with a *real* American—the Vietnamese wouldn't dare touch Scott and maybe stay away from his *Viet kieu* (Vietnamese expatriate) sidekick, Quang the civilian.

Two nights before I left for Vietnam, my father dropped a 50,000-pound bombshell on me. He rang me at home, just before I crawled into my queen-size bed, no longer a twin rack.

"Quang, it's Dad." He hesitated for a minute.

"Yes, Dad?"

"When you get to Saigon, I want you to go see your brother. You have a brother there."

What the fuck, over? I couldn't seem to kick my Marine habits.

"Go see him, Quang. He's your brother."

I was expecting my father to tell me that my "new" brother was my age, someone from his past who had grown up like me.

"His name is An. He's almost three and he looks like you."

I thought to myself. "He's three now? So he must have been born in 1992, the year Dad got to the United States. Huh? What's going on?"

I decided not to interrogate my father, who sounded as depressed as I was. Yet I sensed that he was relieved about no longer having to withhold a family secret. I would meet An soon enough. I jotted down his mother's address and phone number.

"Go back to Vietnam!" The words of the Aleric Street bully rang in my ears. *OK, OK....*

The day after I was officially discharged from the Corps I landed in Saigon. Nobody was waving flags and welcoming me home the way they did for us after Desert Storm. But I was sure glad to see my Aunt Nhang and all my long-lost relatives again.

"Homecoming." At the same Saigon intersection thirty years later with my sister Thi, 1995. (Author's Collection)

It was April 1995. The twentieth anniversary. Reunification. Liberation. Unfinished business . . . and new business.

I was simply visiting my birthplace and, at the last minute, a newly discovered brother made my travel itinerary. I went "home" to see distant relatives before they all died, to stroll the streets of my hometown, to use my native tongue, and possibly to blend in again. I went back to Saigon as a U.S. veteran, a Vietnam vet of a different kind. Was it me, the Vietnamese, clinging to old memories? Or was it me, the American, who grew up with portrayals of my homeland from Hollywood directors, politicians, journalists, and old soldiers—all of them foreigners? Or was it both?

In Vietnam two decades earlier I was not an immigrant, a refugee, or fresh off the boat. Back then I looked like everyone else. Back then no one ever mispronounced my name or made fun of it. Growing up back then, nothing made me stand apart from the other kids—until I came to the United States speaking the only English I knew: "OK, Salem, Coke, GI." Back then, had I remained in Vietnam, I might have had to fight a war as a child soldier in Cambodia or against China.

When my family left Vietnam, I didn't know then that we were leaving forever. Luckily for me, forever lasted only twenty years. I sat next to Goober on the Airbus jet from Hong Kong, and my stomach knotted as we circled through the bumpy skies over Tan Son Nhut Airport. Even while flying helicopters off the USS *Tarawa,* I wasn't this nervous. We began our descent, and images from my childhood flashed through my mind.

My family had lived on the airfield that I was now seeing below me. The plane landed, just as I had taken off in 1975, in darkness. My hopes of blending in didn't last long. The immigration officer stared at me and asked in English, "Is this you first time back from America?" I stammered a "yes" in Vietnamese, but he continued in broken English, as if the language we shared was too hard for me to comprehend. He didn't even bother to look up, pocketing the twenty dollar bill that I had slipped in between my passport pages and moving on to the next expatriate. Glancing at the skinny, hollow-eyed policemen in oversized polyester uniforms, I was glad my Marine Corps ID card and dog tags had been left in California. (The Corps wasn't with me to watch my back.)

When I ventured downtown after leaving the airport, long-forgotten smells washed over me: charcoal smoke, motorcycle exhausts, kerosene fumes, the pungent odor of *nuoc mam.* I was greeted by what seemed like every *cyclo* driver in Saigon. They all spoke to me in piecemeal English, then were surprised that I could pronounce Vietnamese words and that I wasn't a Taiwanese, Japanese, or Hong Kong businessman. My Western clothing and extra twenty-five pounds of weight over them helped differentiate me from the locals. Some drivers in their forties and fifties had served in the ARVN, and pedaling a *cyclo* was the best work they could now find. They spoke fondly of the years before 1975, bitterly about their time in reeducation camps, and enviously about their comrades living the good life in the States. The youngest were college students by day, *cyclo* drivers by night. It was eerie to think that, had I not gotten out of Saigon, I could now be pedaling for a living like one of them.

I went by my elementary school that stood next to the Presidential Palace, now the Reunification Palace. Standing there, I could still feel the phantom concussion from two 500-pound bombs sucking the air from my tiny lungs, dropped by a defecting pilot a few hundred yards from the school. (The VNAF Benedict Arnold later became the chief pilot for Vietnam Airlines.) The only familiar face still in the neighborhood was a nurse who told me most of my teachers had retired or had gone to the United States.

I visited my favorite park, where the old Marine statue with two Vietnamese carrying a machine gun (probably modeled after the famous Iwo Jima Memorial) stood near the Rex Hotel. But it was gone. Around the corner I stared at a statue of Ho Chi Minh holding a child, a reminder of my hometown's current name.

Disappointed, I retreated to the rooftop of the Rex Hotel, once the old U.S. officers' club. Several American veterans hustled in the lounge, back from a day trip shooting AK-47s at the Cu Chi tunnels, playing tourist and exorcising their demons. In the late afternoon sun, we sipped cold drinks together and imagined the view from this high terrace two decades earlier, as Marine choppers clustered like dragonflies over the old U.S. Embassy, extracting as many friends as they could. Strangely enough, of all the esteemed American journalists who had covered Vietnam over the war years, few were still *embedded* in country on that dark day. But they all converged on Saigon that week in 1995, for "Namstalgia" sake.

I finally found my way to my brother's home; his mother's shack was in a crowded section of Saigon, hundreds of Vietnamese squeezed into a square block. Five adults lived at her house, but I didn't know who they were. I looked at the woman's face and I became angry. (Was this the person who derailed my mother's marriage? Does my mother know about this?)

An's mother then left us alone for a few minutes. I didn't know what to say to a three-year-old boy who couldn't understand English. ("Hello? Sorry? How are you? Dad says hello.")

Compared with American children, An appeared sick, his arms and legs as thin as those of a one-year-old. I didn't know if he was undernourished. I wasn't a parent myself. I had to admit he looked like me and my father, resembling my father more than I did.

I had to leave after thirty minutes. My heart was not in the visit; I came only because my father had asked me. I gave An's mother $100 cash (U.S.) and rubbed his head as I quickly left her shack.

The strangest episode occurred later in my visit when I had dinner at my aunt's home with a second cousin in his late thirties. He was only a teenager when the war had ended, but later became a major in the People's Army of Vietnam. My innate U.S. Marines reaction to meeting a communist officer was confrontational at first, but I held back. Wrong reason, wrong place, and wrong time. Later in the evening, it really didn't make any difference in our relationship, since he had never shot at me nor I at him. Even so I couldn't shake his hand when I left.

I also met an aunt from Qui Nhon, my father's sister, who had lost everything after the war, and an uncle who spent nearly $10,000 (the per capita income then was about $400) to get his three sons to the States. He failed, and my cousins went to prison after trying to escape. They're still there.

Everywhere I went, there were signs and billboards announcing the celebration of April 30, marking it the day of "liberation" rather than "evacuation." In Little Saigon in Orange County, former refugees mourn this date every year as "Black April."

On every corner was a *pho* stand, selling hot white noodle soup in beef broth, now chic in the States. There was not much meat in the bowls. Every resident, it seemed, had something to sell. I was looking to buy back my childhood, but I found only a giant void in the black market.

The best salesman in Saigon I met was a tattered little boy offering bootleg, poorly bound copies of Graham Greene's *The Quiet American* near the Hotel Continental. He unloaded three of the novels on our group at $5 each, probably enough money to feed his family for a month. As he ran down the sidewalk, yelling with joy and clutching our greenbacks, I suddenly saw myself. Except for luck and fate twenty years earlier, I would have been hustling on the streets like him, a boy left behind to fend for himself and his family.

I would learn that discrimination against the children of former South Vietnamese officials, and against *Viet kieus* like me, would make my American "prejudice" experiences seem like a picnic.

Later in the week, I felt strong enough to visit the graves of relatives, especially my grandmother on my mother's side. On the road, I passed many marked cemeteries, unaware of many more that had been unearthed by Communists shortly after their "liberation."

I thought of the American Vietnam vets I knew. Some remained bitter; many went on with their lives and became very successful in military or civilian careers or comfortably retired. And quite contrary to the Saigon *cyclo* driver's perception, my father and many of his South Vietnamese colleagues who emigrated late (the H.O. group) worked menial jobs in the United States, facing their "golden years" without a pension or veteran's benefits. Most tragic was to watch their pride slip away. Once their VNAF parties had ended, some in the H.O. group were again *nobodies*.

To lose a war was one thing. To lose your country was another.

My week in Vietnam ended at the same place I had taken off in April 1975. Getting out was much easier the second time. As the Vietnam Airlines jet lifted off and banked left over the Saigon River, I sat by myself in the last row, half-dazed, staring down at the hazy countryside I had now left twice. I was looking at a place where sorrow had struck millions of lives, where policies and policymakers failed miserably, and where brave young Americans and South Vietnamese paid with their lives in a sincere effort to secure freedom for the Republic of Vietnam.

A month earlier, I had visited the Vietnam Wall in Washington, paying my respects again to those who had given everything they had in a futile effort that brought me as a boy to their land. They weren't wrong. Their leaders were wrong. As the tile-roofed houses and the brown rice paddies receded below, and twenty years of memories and feelings came rushing back, I could no longer hold back the tears.

Life goes on. Once again, I was on a plane heading for a place where I had found a chance to live. This time I was really going home, back to America, as an American.

CHAPTER 23

FINAL FLIGHTS

F IVE MONTHS AFTER I RETURNED FROM VIETNAM, AFTER the emotions had cooled, and nearly a year after submitting my resignation, I ran back to the Marine Corps. I no longer *needed* the Corps, but I *wanted* to be a part of it again. And I missed my Marine friends. In the midst of my divorce, it was my buddy "Stinky" Brennan who moved in as my new roommate, providing companionship and support for this grateful former jarhead.

And I wanted to get back into the cockpit again.

By mid-1995, the Pham family had been spread out all over the United States and the world, all of us living our own private lives and in our own homes. It was not what a typical Vietnamese family would do. Two sisters married and moved to Northern California, another to Washington, D.C. My father remained in Los Angeles County, me in Orange County. My mother, my sixty-year-old mother who had become a grandma, had left the States to pursue her own dreams. She too would join the "Corps." I had initially thought she was running away from all of us. I was wrong.

After their divorce, my parents would still see each other, remaining cordial at holiday and family gatherings. They actually seemed as if they got along better than when my father had first emigrated three years earlier. My mother had finally earned her B.A. degree in accounting, not for career advancement, but to qualify for the Peace Corps Program. She landed in the former Soviet Union, in the capital city of Almaty in the Republic of Kazakhstan following the footsteps of my uncle's 1975 American sponsors, Ron and Bonnie Counseller. She had admired them greatly. For two years and two subzero winters, she helped small businesses with her accounting skills.

She sounded happy (and freezing) every time I spoke to her across the globe. Her phone was always scratchy as if her lines had been tapped. My sisters and I jokingly called her a "spy" for the CIA; she would have been their oldest rookie ever and the only "free" Vietnamese in Russia who spoke three languages and knew something about military aviation.

With my family scattered everywhere, and my independent sales job a routine and my divorce a disappointment, I had become depressed and lonely. I found myself sitting in a family therapist's chair, embarrassed at first to enter his office and afraid someone might recognize me.

Marines don't need shrinks.

Fortunately for me, I had another friend besides my roommate Stinky. He was Dean Sawyer, a former undersized linebacker for the University of the Pacific, and my roommate during sales training at my new employer. He took me under his wings, explaining the pharmaceutical trade, and shared his "best practices," especially with the coeds.

By the fall of 1995, I was beginning to pull myself out of a twelve-month funk, and I decided to pursue two endeavors that had been close to my heart—a renewed relationship with my father and with the U.S. Marine Corps. At that juncture I was on good terms with neither.

For weeks after I returned from Vietnam I did not want to see my father. I was angry at him for telling me last, after he had revealed the existence of his second son to my sisters. Perhaps he didn't want me to think less of him; maybe he felt our relationship had only an artificial connection of fishing and flying and nothing more. Even though we enjoyed each other's company at functions and outings, my father and I did little talking one-on-one. I tried several times to ask what had happened in the years that he had been incarcerated. But he only gave a slight hint. After finding out about my half-brother, I wondered what other secrets he might have. I will never forget one sticky afternoon in Los Angeles, where he and I sat in an empty Vietnamese restaurant, calming each other over our marital failures. He did more consoling than me. (Father knew best.)

A year earlier, concurrent with my psychological wrestling match with the Corps, General Frat's second in command, the assistant wing commander, Col. Don "Buff" Beaufait, was also going through his own struggle, albeit with much more at stake than I. "Buff" had been second in command of Marine Hornets during the Gulf War. As a squadron CO, he had also led the 1986 airstrikes against Libya's Muammar Khadafi. He owned the distinction

Finally there with my son. My mother and my father at my promotion to major in the reserve, 1997. (Courtesy of C. Tran)

of being the first Marine to land a Hornet aboard an aircraft carrier and, like General Frat, had flown many F-4 combat missions in Vietnam.

Buff was a bona fide war hero, a nice guy, and an avid mako shark fisherman. He would also take the biggest pummeling by a Marine pilot as a result of the Tailhook scandal fallout.

I must profess to not knowing all the details of Tailhook, and, I don't condone the actions of some of the attendees, but I knew that Buff had been selected for brigadier general and that his promotion had been held up. Only five or six colonels got selected each year for general; their opportunities came after twenty-five years of outstanding service.

I don't know if General Frat would have picked up his third star (he retired as a two-star in 1997), but I knew that he had supported Buff. He wrote two letters requesting the brass to promote Buff to brigadier general, going against the politically correct pendulum.

His efforts were in vain but they were *semper fidelis* at its highest level.

Don Beaufait retired as a colonel and moved on to a successful private-sector career. At the peak of his career he had endured more turmoil than I could ever have imagined. Like my old CO, Tank, who was relieved of command during the 1992 deployment, Buff remained a professional, a true Marine until he took off the uniform. Both took their lumps in stride, never blaming anyone for their misfortunes, dealt with their adversities, and finished their careers.

Both of them gave me hope as I returned to the Corps as a reserve pilot, trying to undo my sour-note departure.

I finally found my niche; I was able to continue my private-sector career in pharmaceutical/biotech sales while taking to the air several times a month, 50 percent at night, sometimes more, sometimes less. I joined the Reserves, the weekend Marine Corps. I became a part of El Toro–based Marine Medium Helicopter Squadron 764, HMM-764, aptly called the "Moonlighters."

One thing I didn't know about HMM-764 was that the squadron could afford to be selective. It was the only reserve CH-46 squadron on the West Coast, and its longtime core members could unofficially blackball crappy aviators and, more important, jerks. By the time I interviewed with HMM-764's CO, Lt. Col. Ray "Weasel" Wersel, his OPSO, Maj. Robert "Hermbo" Hermes, and five other "players" in the squadron, they already knew about my reputation as an officer and as a pilot. After an hour-long semiformal interview, I left the squadron wondering if the Corps would take me back. I hadn't exactly been a pleasant Marine to be around during my last year on active duty, and some pilots in HMM-764 still remembered. (First impression wasn't important as a lasting impression. Don't burn your bridges.) I would finally grow up.

Later that afternoon, "Weasel" called me at home.

"Q, you're in. Congratulations!"

For the next four years, I served in HMM-764, deployed to the Caribbean, and flew NVG missions over Death Valley to insert Drug Enforcement Agency agents. The counter-narcotic efforts were coordinated through Joint Task Force 6 Headquarters, based in El Paso, Texas. The squadron also went to the "boat" and participated in summer live-fire exercises in Twentynine Palms.

Compared with the "1,000-hour" cockpit of my active-duty squadron, HMM-764's paired aircrew usually combined to exceed 3,000 flight hours, not counting the thousands of flight hours that nearly a fourth of the pilots had through their airline careers. I had no close calls; the "Moonlighters" crashed no helicopters and killed no Marines during my stint with the unit. My buddies from HMM-161, Pepe, Roy, Torch, and longtime friends Crash,

Guido, Hondo, and Stinky also joined the unit, and all of us had a blast, flying with each other, training in case we ever got activated for war.*

In October 1997, my father joined my mother and me at a HMM-764 Saturday drill. My CO, "Hermbo," presided over a promotion ceremony and administered the oath of office to four of us captains who were about to become majors. When Hermbo called me front and center, my parents followed. A decade after I became a Marine 2d lieutenant on a bright June day at UCLA, my father had finally witnessed one of my promotions. He pinned the oak leaf clusters onto my collars as I had once wished he could. Just as I had attended my father's VNAF reunions, he would also come to one of our HMM-764's Marine Corps Birthday Balls. We had come to terms with each other, me more so than he, because I had been the one with the issue.

There was no prouder moment for us collectively than in 1999, when I accompanied my father to the Los Angeles Convention Center for his U.S. citizenship ceremony. It was much more special than my lonely and indifferent trek in 1984. My father was thrilled; he had rehearsed his immigration oral interview question bank with me. I knew he wouldn't have any problem. As the two of us stood on the convention floor, a federal judge strolled onto the stage and gave a feverishly short, but patriotic, introduction. I recognized Judge David O. Carter, a Marine veteran who had been seriously wounded in Khe Sanh. I had met Judge Carter at a UCLA football rally; he was also a die-hard Bruin season-ticket holder and active in Marine Corps circles in Orange County. He was gracious to my father and me. He invited us back to his chamber and brought us coffee. We milled around with him for forty-five minutes, interrupting his usual busy day of presiding over serious legal cases.

In 1999 HMM-764 relocated to Edwards Air Force Base in the Mojave Desert. Its former home, and my base El Toro, was closing, victim of military downsizing; Tustin had closed two years earlier. I had begun an entrepreneurial endeavor and decided it was time to hang up my wings and leave the Corps. This time it was my choice again. This time it would be on good terms.

I flew my final flight in May that year. As the one-hour hop came to an end, I could feel the emotional rush of a decade-long association with Tustin,

*In 2004, HMM-764 was activated and sent to war for the first time in its history. During a six-month rotation in Iraq, the squadron flew hundreds of combat missions and returned home intact. Pepe, Torch, and Hondo remained in the unit, which is scheduled to return to Iraq in the spring of 2005.

El Toro, and the Marine Corps. The Corps had taken me on a whirlwind tour, a journey I could have never imagined. The people I had met—only the good ones came to mind—became my supporters, my mentors, my lifelong buddies. Their powerful sense of teamwork, duty, and mission accomplishment had permeated me, enabling me to rise above my problems, to reach down and grab hold when things got difficult, to realize my weaknesses, and to compensate for my shortcomings.

As the CH-46 reached the bottom of its final approach, I added power and pulled back gently on the stick, bringing the ancient chopper to a nose-high hover, then a smooth final touchdown. Mission complete. On that note, my military aviation career came to an end with a goal I had set long ago—to have the same number of landings as takeoffs.

In August of 2000 my father also flew his final hop. He had returned to Vietnam to attempt to bring my brother to the States. Shortly after arriving, he became ill and had to rush back here. He was immediately taken into surgery so physicians could remove a large tumor in his brain. He was also diagnosed with late-stage lung cancer, most likely as a result of a thirty-five-year smoking habit that he had kicked for four years. The damage was done; his remaining quality of life would be determined by the treatment he chose: chemotherapy, radiation, or watch and wait. The prognosis was less than one year.

My old man gave it his all. At age sixty-five, he left the hospital a week after major brain surgery. I picked him up in Los Angeles; he would be moving in with me in Orange County, sleeping in a spare bedroom next to my mother. I had been living with my mother; actually, she moved in with me after she completed her Peace Corps tour. For six weeks, I lived under the same roof as my parents, something I hadn't done in twenty-five years. I was still a single man, although I had fallen head over heels for Shannon Ryan, a Floridian whom I met at a medical industry trade show in Vegas. During my father's sickness, Shannon (now my wife) was able to meet him on two occasions; both times remain dear to me.

As I worked my way through the city traffic, my sick and dying father gave the best praise I could have ever wished for. During the commute, I had to conduct a teleconference with the management team of my fledging Internet pharmaceutical marketing startup called MyDrugRep.com (now Lathian Systems). I was its chairman and CEO. I had neglected some of my corporate duties while tending to my father during his hospitalization. He must have listened attentively to my comments, specifically directed to my chief financial officer and my vice-president of marketing. Like most of the dot-bombs, I had managed to allow our company to burn through most of a $5 million investment from our investors, Hummer Winblad Venture Partners. My company was going bankrupt, my father was dying.

But I couldn't afford to fall apart, my father still needed me.

As I finished the call, my father shook his head in amazement. Tears welled in his eyes. "Oh, I'm so proud . . . so proud of you, Quang."

On Friday, November 10, 2000, at 7:10 p.m., my father took his last breath. He had lapsed into a ten-day-long coma, resulting from a massive stroke amid radiation therapy treatment. Around the world, in every clime and place, Marines celebrated the Corps' 225th birthday. Except me. I was crying. In Vietnam an eight-year-old boy would also grow up—like my sisters and me—without knowing his father.

Full circle. With my father's rescuer, retired Marine Col. John Braddon, 2004. (Author's Collection)

CHAPTER 24

FULL CIRCLE

PEOPLE HAVE TOLD ME THAT WITH DEATH COMES CLOSURE. It was the opposite for me. My father's passing away raised more questions and created a greater void inside me, a burning desire to ask him the $64,000 question. Fortunately, my friend Bernie Edelman had the foresight and the opportunity to get the answer when he interviewed my father in 1999.

More than three years after my father's death I pulled the audiocassettes out, the ones that Bernie had mailed me, slowly rewinding them to the beginning, and listening several times.

"When you think back, were all the fighting and the bloodshed worth the price?" Bernie inquired as only a professional journalist and veteran like him could phrase it. He drew reactions from my father that I never dared to pursue.

My father paused, then answered, "The way I see the war—it needed to end some way or another. When I was fighting the war in Vietnam, I still had many relatives in the north. My wife also had relatives in the north. And my friends had relatives in the north. Both sides had families on the other side. I don't know how the Communists felt.

"But we [in South Vietnam], we knew that we're not going to win the war. We just kept it that way forever until we [would] die. That was it. In 1954 some South Vietnamese went to the north. From the north a million fled south. I could not figure out the war, so let's just end it that way. Yeah, we're the losers. But the war must end somehow. The killing has been going on for quite a long time. And now you don't know who the winner is."

I didn't expect my father to say those words. I thought he would still be gung-ho about how we (the South Vietnamese) could have won, how the

United States had abandoned us and how we need to keep fighting communism today.

I had been wrong all along about my father, and now I know the reasons why. I may still be wrong but I can surmise that my father saw the humanity in his supposed enemy, the Communists. He experienced firsthand kindness from my Great Aunt Phu and Great Uncle Minh, the high-ranking communist official, who brought him food and medicine while he was incarcerated in the north and from the prison camp cadre who fed him rice and sugar that saved him from beriberi.

My father's refusal after imprisonment to blame anyone for the betrayal, his lack of bitterness, his avoidance of hatred were his greatest legacies, affecting me more than his sense of humor and his military service. He somehow managed to move on, until his final days, even calmly telling my sister Thi during one of her visits to the hospital before he went into surgery: "I'm not afraid to die. I've lived a full life, I have no regrets."

There was another person I needed to meet to fulfill my filial duties.

After reading the Do Xa (the battle where my father was shot down in 1964) narrative posted at HMM-364's website, I sent its webmaster an e-mail. The next day, retired Marine Maj. Frank Guttedge, fondly known as Uncle Frank, forwarded former Marine helicopter pilot John Braddon and crew chief Warren Smith's e-mail addresses. I promptly contacted them, and they responded with utter but pleasant surprise.

Smith had missed the April 27, 1964, Do Xa Operation because he had been on liberty. A few days later, he flew into an open field to salvage parts from several helicopters shot down during the operation. My father's VNAF A-1 Skyraider was also there. He walked around wreckage, marveling at the line of bullet holes carved by VC machine guns. He took several photographs of the A-1 and kept them in his Vietnam memorabilia box for over three decades. After several long conversations, he mailed two 8 × 10-inch original photographs of the wrecked plane to me.

After I interviewed retired Marine Col. John Braddon over the phone, I jumped on a commercial flight to Washington, D.C., to meet my father's rescuer. I hailed a cab from the city to Dulles International Airport.

At age seventy-four, John Braddon still sounded like a tough Marine fighter pilot (he only flew helicopters for one tour), proudly volunteering at the new Smithsonian Air and Space Museum (the Steven F. Udvar-Hazy

Center) near Dulles Airport. As I approached the docent desk, I hesitated for a moment to make sure it was him. I glanced at the pages that I had printed from the Internet. Braddon's headshot was taken in 1964, when he was a young major flying H-34 helicopters with HMM-364 in Danang. A shock of gray hair now fell across his forehead, just above steely blue eyes that could still clearly see across the gigantic museum hangar without glasses.

I did not think Braddon would believe me, so I brought along the tape of my father's interview by Bernie as well as his military records and his flight school yearbook. He too brought his Marine cruise book, with photos of his helicopter squadron and their year in Vietnam, in and out of combat. We traded war stories, his much longer than mine.

We had only chatted for a few minutes, when Braddon began introducing himself to fifteen or so visitors for a walking tour. I decided to tag along at the back, already familiar with most of the history of the aircraft on display. Unlike the other senior docents, Braddon didn't need a microphone. His voice radiated across the hangar deck, bouncing off immaculately restored war birds as if he was briefing his aircrew before a mission. His eyes sparkled; his voice reflected a pride in aviation history, and he was living proof from having flown several of the aircraft on display. He didn't need a script; he was history.

Between his tours Braddon and I sat down for a quick lunch. I played the portion of the tape where my father spoke about his crash-landing near Do Xa. While eating, I couldn't tell if Braddon had heard my father's cracked voice: "The U.S. Marines [later] had their own Cobra gunships. They didn't trust us, the South Vietnamese fighters. But we still went on an operation called Do Xa. D.O.X.A. We were on airborne alert. The helicopters didn't have enough firepower, so they requested support from us. I went in and got hit, and I crashed."

The museum was abuzz with announcements and more visitors. So I replayed my father's "Do Xa" comment.

I had come in person to ask Braddon only one question.

"Sir, why did you do it? You had to provide search and rescue for eighteen U.S. Marine helicopters. Why leave your flight and go after a Vietnamese pilot?"

Without a pause, Braddon interrupted me. "When I saw your father go down, I went after him . . . no hesitation . . . because he had supported us."

I shook Braddon's hands and thanked him—for his service, and for rescuing my father. I stopped thinking about what if he hadn't.

It was still early in the afternoon. As the museum shuttle driver weaved through traffic back to Washington, I could see the Marine War Memorial in Arlington, forever emblazoned in our nation's conscience and in my life. In the United States fallen soldiers will always be remembered. From the Tomb of the Unknown Soldier to the Korean War Memorial, I've visited them all.

The U.S. Capitol stood in the distance, far removed from military memorials, at the opposite end of the National Mall. The men and women inside that building retain the power to declare and end wars, past and present. I wish more of them could have experienced the effects of war and its lingering wounds. I wish I could someday meet those who voted for President Johnson's Tonkin Gulf Resolution in 1964 and those who torpedoed President Ford's plea in 1975 to help a collapsing South Vietnam.

The White House stood in the middle, its occupiers needing to be held accountable for their foreign forays.

I shake myself free of the bitterness. "The war had to end. We had been killing each other for so long." My father's voice echoes in my mind. *It's over! Let it go!*

Instead, I need to thank Congress for passing the Refugee Act and subsequent legislation that has enabled over a million Vietnamese to live here in freedom. Refugees are still coming, nearly thirty years after the war, from the last camps in the Philippines. A thirty-four-year-old Australian lawyer named Hoi Trinh is helping resettle the remaining 1,800 Vietnamese refugees. Some have been toiling in the camps for fifteen years.

I remember the images on the Internet of northwestern Vietnam where my father once wasted the prime of his life laboring in prison camps, trying to survive his incarceration. The fruits of his labor and those held in the camps of Son La and Hoang Lien Son (now called Lao Cai and Yen Bai) provinces were evident. Manioc plants had given way to rice fields and tea plantations. Ethnic minorities—Red Dzao, Nung, Zay, Black Thai, and various H'mong tribes—indigenous Vietnamese wearing colorful outfits—are able to live a meager and simple life.

The area where my father was imprisoned has become a hot destination for Western tourists, especially adventurers and photographers. Tall mountains guard endless fields split by the famed Red River, where, according to legend, the first Vietnamese (the "Lac") lived. The Hoang Lien Son Moun-

Accepting the Republic of Vietnam flag on behalf of my family at my father's funeral in California, 2000. (Author's Collection)

tains, the "Tonkinese Alps," look as beautiful as any destinations I've seen in person or on video. The entire area symbolizes peace and serenity. I doubt if any of the tour guides knew the grounds they were traversing had once been the soil upon which thousands perished. I wonder if visitors wonder why so many Vietnamese had to endure such revenge at the hands of their own people, the victors who had declared peace in April 1975.

A verse of the VNAF Hymn echoed in my head. *Ôi phi công danh tiếng, muôn đời. O pilot famous for life.*

I look up at the blue skies. Not a plane is in the air. I do not hear the afternoon traffic passing by. Life around me seems to have slowed down.

I imagine a VNAF A-1 Skyraider swooping low over the Mall then popping into a victory roll, but I force it out of my mind.

My head is clear, my breaths come free. I feel a sense of relief as I have never felt before.

GLOSSARY

AK-47: Assault rifle firing 7.62mm rounds. Standard issue for the North Vietnamese Army (NVA), the Viet Cong (VC), and Soviet-bloc countries

ARG: Amphibious ready group

ARVN: Army of the Republic of Vietnam

BOAT: Navy ship or "the boat"

BOQ: Bachelor officer quarters

CLASS "A" (MISHAP): A serious aircraft mishap typically involving loss of life or a major financial loss, defined as $1 million (U.S.) or greater

CO: Commanding officer

DMZ: Demilitarized Zone

FAC: Forward air controller (one who coordinates air strikes)

FNG: Fucking new guy

HAC: Helicopter aircraft commander

KIA: Killed in action

LZ: Landing zone (usually in reference to helicopters)

MEU: Marine expeditionary unit (comprising an infantry battalion, reinforced squadron with helicopters and Harriers, and a service support component embarked aboard amphibious ships)

MIA: Missing in action

NVA: North Vietnamese Army

NVGs: Night-vision goggles

OCS: Officer Candidate School

POW: Prisoner of war

PSP: Pierced-steel planking (for runways and taxiways)

RVN: Republic of Vietnam (South Vietnam)

SAM: Surface-to-air missile

SRV: Socialist Republic of Vietnam (since 1976)

TBS: The Basic School (six-month training course for new second lieutenants)

UN: United Nations

USAF: U.S. Air Force

VC: Viet Cong

VNAF: (South) Vietnamese Air Force

XO: Executive officer (or second in charge)

APPENDIX

Citation

The White House

By Virtue of the Authority Vested In Me as President of the United States and as Commander-In-Chief of the Armed Forces of the United States, I Have Today Awarded the Presidential Unit Citation to the 514th Tactical Fighter Squadron Republic of Vietnam Air Force for Extraordinary Heroism and Outstanding Performance of Duty

The 514th Tactical Fighter Squadron, a unit of the Republic of Vietnam Air Force, is cited for extraordinary heroism and outstanding performance of duty in combat against an armed enemy of the Republic of Vietnam throughout the period 1 January 1964 to 28 February 1965. Participating in daily actions in support of Republic of Vietnam ground operations, the courageous men of the 514th Tactical Fighter Squadron carried out their attacks on military targets with indomitable spirit and determination. The fierce determination to destroy the enemy displayed by the men of this unit was exemplified in the 6,000 sorties, and 13,000 flying hours compiled in support of ground operations during this period. Frequently, aircraft were landed just long enough to secure additional armament before continuing their attacks against Communist aggressors threatening their homeland. The determined and daring attacks launched by the valiant men of the 514th Tactical Fighter Squadron against the heavily armed and fanatical Communist insurgents, in the face of fierce ground fire, had a demoralizing effect upon the enemy, raised the morale and fighting spirit of the supported ground troops, resulted in inestimable damage to the Communist aggressors in the loss of men and materiel, and were instrumental in stemming the tide of Communist aggression against the Republic of Vietnam during this period. While a ground count of the many enemy killed and wounded was impossible, the heavy losses inflicted upon the enemy by this unit are known to have been significant, severely restricting his ability or desire to conduct sustained ground operations.

Despite being called upon to provide key personnel to cadre the organization of three additional fighter squadrons during this period, the 514th Tactical Fighter Squadron continued to carry out every assigned mission. The actions of the 514th Tactical Fighter Squadron reflect conspicuous gallantry and extraordinary heroism in keeping with the finest traditions of the military service and reflect great credit on the Republic of Vietnam.

—Lyndon B. Johnson

ABOUT THE TYPE

This book was set in Granjon, a modern recutting of a typeface produced under the direction of George W. Jones, who based Granjon's design upon the letter forms of Claude Garamond (1480–1561). The name was given to the typeface as a tribute to the typographic designer Robert Granjon.